MᶜCARTHY

M^cCARTHY

by
ROY COHN

THE NEW AMERICAN LIBRARY

To my mother and father, Dora Marcus Cohn and Albert Cohn; and to George E. Sokolsky, who often served *in loco parentis*.

ACKNOWLEDGMENTS

To Joan and Joseph Foley, who talked me into it. To Ed Kuhn, who helped so much after he gave up trying to convert me to liberalism; to Lester David, who put it into English; and to my friends Thomas A. Bolan, Louis B. Nichols, William F. Buckley, Jr., and S. I. Newhouse, Jr., for their guidance throughout.

CONTENTS

PROLOGUE

I AWOKE EARLY that Thursday. For an hour I talked on the telephone to three prominent friends in New York—a publisher, an attorney, and a political columnist. By eight, I was dressed. I stuffed papers into my briefcase and walked into a clear, bright morning.

In a matter of minutes, I had joined Frank Carr and Jim Juliana in Senator Joseph McCarthy's office. Francis Carr was staff director of Senator McCarthy's subcommittee and Juliana a staff investigator. Both had served with the FBI. For an hour and a half, we held one last conference to make certain all was in order. Just before ten, Senator McCarthy walked in, looking calm. He greeted us: "Okay, let's go down."

At five minutes past ten on this 22nd of April, 1954, we descended to 318, the ornate, high-ceilinged Senate caucus chamber. It was rapidly filling up with spectators, newsmen, television and motion picture people. A Senate policeman helped us shoulder our way to the conference table. White cards bearing our names showed us our places: my seat was third from the end and to the right of Senator McCarthy.

I sat blinking into the harsh glare of the television and movie lights, talking with the Senator, watching cameramen dart about, trying to answer reporters' questions across the table.

And then, as the babble grew more intense, Karl E. Mundt, Republican senator from South Dakota and committee chairman, picked up a glass ashtray and rapped for order. The great chamber grew quiet and one of the most remarkable and bizarre events of our time, an episode perhaps without parallel in the nation's history, got under way.

This event was the so-called Army-McCarthy hearing, in which I was destined to play a key role. It was the special Senate investigation into charges and countercharges involving Secretary of the Army Robert T. Stevens, Army Counselor John G. Adams, Assistant Secretary of Defense H. Struve Hensel, Senator McCarthy, Frank Carr, and myself.

Some twenty million persons all across the country watched the story unfold daily on their television screens, and other millions read the newspaper and magazine accounts. And yet, no matter how carefully these people watched and read, they could not know the complete story.

So much of the real drama of what was happening in the Senate caucus room through those frenetic weeks lay not in the scenes before the camera but in their unpublicized background.

I have been asked many times to relate the full story, including portions that were known only to Senator McCarthy and to me. Until now I have refused, because while I realized that many people were accepting half-truths and even lies as fact, I believed I needed the perspective of years to view the events of those days in their proper light.

Shortly after the hearings ended, I dictated into a tape recorder many details of those extraordinary days. This book is based partly upon that record and partly upon other recollections, official transcripts, and extensive conversations with countless friends, associates, and principal figures of those days. The conversations set down here are reproduced as closely as I can recall them, accurate in their meaning and substance if not in their every word.

As I proceeded with my task, I realized that the story of the hearings alone could not convey what needed to be said. And so I broadened the canvas to encompass the man McCarthy, the private as well as the public person whom I knew so well during the five years preceding his death.

I do not pretend, however, that this is a definitive, comprehensive evaluation of the man and his times, although I discuss what I know about McCarthy's beginnings, his work, problems, faults, and successes, and the final outcome. The full portrait of Joe McCarthy and the era in which he rose to such remarkable prominence and power must await the historian's special training, insight, and distance from the events.

I offer, then, a memoir mostly of my own years with McCarthy that is part autobiography, part biography, part analysis, part explanation, and part confession. Mainly, I am concerned with telling, as candidly as I can, the story of McCarthy, his work, and my own role with the subcommittee he headed.

Emerson said, "Whatever games are played with us, we must play no games with ourselves, but deal in our privacy with the last honesty and truth." To the best of my ability it is this I try to do in the pages that follow.

ROY M. COHN

M^cCARTHY

CHAPTER 1

WHEELING

I<small>T BEGAN</small> in the old McLure Hotel on the corner of Market and Twelfth streets in the city of Wheeling, West Virginia.

Late on a day in February, 1950, Joseph Raymond McCarthy, an obscure junior senator, flew into town from Washington to make a speech. No crowds greeted him, not even a delegation of respectable size. His welcoming committee consisted of a lone newspaper reporter, a congressman, and a local civic leader who had trouble recognizing the Senator as he walked down the ramp with the other passengers.

On the way to the hotel, Francis J. Love, Republican member of Congress from the area, pointed out the sights to the Senator. There wasn't time to see much. The dinner was to start in less than two hours. En route the reporter, Frank Desmond of the Wheeling *Intelligencer,* asked him: "Have you got a copy of your speech?" McCarthy replied, "No, but maybe you can make something out of this." He handed Desmond duplicates of a sheaf of notes and the reporter put them in his pocket.

There was just time after their arrival for a brief reception in the Senator's suite, where he met the local Republican leaders. He managed to squeeze in a private drink and chat with Desmond.

Shortly after seven, McCarthy came down to the Colonnade Room and received an enthusiastic greeting from three hundred guests, members of the Ohio County Women's Republican Club and their friends. Few in the audience knew much about him, practically none there had ever seen him before. However, he was a Republican senator and this was the traditional Lincoln Day dinner.

Speaking from notes he had placed on the lecturn, this is the way he began on that now historic ninth of February: "Five years after a world war has been won, men's hearts should anticipate a long peace and the minds of men should be free from the heavy weights which come with war . . ."

It was a dullish opening, but within a few moments he was talking about Communists and Communist sympathizers and it wasn't dull any longer. In a letter written by the then Secretary of State James F. Byrnes to Representative Adolph Sabath four years earlier, McCarthy said, Byrnes had reported that persons responsible for screening Government employees for loyalty had found 284 individuals unfit for Government service because of Communist activities and other reasons, but that only 79 had been discharged. By simple arithmetic, this meant that 205 persons were still employed in the State Department even though the President's own security officers had declared them unfit to serve. At his table, journalist Frank Desmond scribbled rapidly as he listened to McCarthy while trying to follow the notes the Senator had handed him in the car.

It has been widely reported that Willard Edwards, the correspondent for the Chicago *Tribune,* wrote the Wheeling speech, but this is untrue. A series of articles by Edwards on Communist infiltration was appearing in the *Tribune* at the time. George Waters, then McCarthy's press secretary, telephoned Edwards, saying: "Joe is interested in making a talk on the subject. Do you have any material that might be helpful?" Edwards then sent clippings of his articles.

Next day, the *Intelligencer* put Desmond's story on the front page. McCarthy was quoted as saying: "While I cannot take the time to name all the men in the State Department who have been named as members of the Communist party and members of a spy ring, I have here in my hand a list of 205 that were known to the Secretary of State as being members of the Communist party and who, nevertheless, are still working and shaping the policy of the State Department."

The Chicago *Tribune* printed only a few spare paragraphs on an inside page. No other newspaper reported McCarthy's Wheeling talk. This was understandable: the three-year record of the junior senator from Wisconsin in Washington was unspectacular. He had backed the constitutional amendment limiting the President's tenure to two terms; voted for passage of an income tax reduction bill over a presidential veto; refused to support Universal Military Training; and signed a letter requesting early hearings on a bill calling for aid to Nationalist China. He scarcely rated extensive coverage.

Next morning, McCarthy boarded a plane for Salt Lake City. By the time he reached Denver for a stopover, newspapers were waking up to the fact that a big story was breaking. He was met at the airport by journalists who demanded the names of the security risks. McCarthy told them that if Secretary of State Acheson wanted to call him, he would read the names over the telephone. McCarthy added that he intended to tell his story "over and over until the public gets so tired of it the Administration will have to clean up the mess."

McCarthy's sensational charges began appearing in newspapers across the country. In Salt Lake City, he withdrew the offer to give Acheson the names. A presidential order was then in effect, prohibiting the Government from turning over loyalty records of U.S. employees to anyone outside the Executive Department, including, of course, congressional investigating committees. What would be the use of giving Acheson the names of Communists and their sympathizers, McCarthy argued, unless their actual records could be obtained and proof shown to the people? What would prevent the Secretary of State from simply accepting the list, announcing that nobody on it was either a Communist or a security risk, and thus ending the matter?

On February 11, McCarthy sent a wire to President Truman, calling upon him to furnish Congress with a list of all State Department employees considered bad security risks, and asking him to revoke the presidential order. On February 14, in Los Angeles, he renewed his appeal to Acheson—the names would be given if the order was withdrawn. He made further speeches in Reno, Nevada, and Huron, South Dakota. The State Department's press officer, Lincoln White, issued a heated denial. "We know of no Communist members in this department and if we find any they will be summarily dismissed."

The incredible years had begun.

By the middle 1930's, Communist intrusion into American life was an established fact. Party recruiting proceeded rapidly, and many thousands of Americans joined Communist cells. Thousands more joined "front" organizations, which multiplied and flourished during the Depression years, exploiting the fears of those who were convinced that capitalism was now rattling loudly before expiring. When World War II began, Communists everywhere waged a peace offensive which was suddenly reversed when Hitler invaded the Soviet Union. Five months later, when Pearl Harbor was attacked, the United States entered the war with the Soviet Union as an ally.

The 103,000 votes the Communist party attracted in the 1932 elections was its highest reach, but the importance of the party was not in its voting strength. J. Edgar Hoover stated that according to the Communists themselves, for every party member there were ten others ready and eager to do the party's work. Its influence, particularly among the intellectuals and idealists who were in thought-molding positions, was profound. Amusing yet disturbing was columnist Leonard Lyons' story of the Moscow trip during which his guide injected comparisons unfavorable to the United States as he showed the sights. When they stopped at a library, the guide said proudly: "We have more books in here than you have in any of your colleges." At Moscow University auditorium, the guide boasted, "There are more seats here than in any auditorium in America."

After a time Lyons said, "Tell me, what percentage of your faculty are members of the Communist party?"

The guide thought for a moment.

"About sixteen percent."

"Well," Lyons said, "when I went to City College, about seventy-three percent of our faculty were members of the Communist party!"

Despite my respect for City College as an academic institution and despite the fact that my own father is a graduate of the school, I must admit that Lyons' story has an edge (though the statistics are of course figurative).

Since the early thirties, a subversive activities department within the FBI had operated by presidential directive, studying espionage, sabotage, and subversion. Its staff maintained up-to-date files on personnel and organizations in the Communist movement, the information coming from two main sources—an intensive analysis of events from the outside, and men and women planted on the inside. The people inside the party were volunteers who underwent a year of intensive training: housewives, teachers, auto mechanics, insurance salesmen, writers, editors, people specially chosen as acceptable to the Communists but who were in fact keen observers reporting back to the FBI what they saw, heard, and experienced. I came to know many of these undercover agents. More than one told me that probably their most sobering experience came early in their indoctrination when they were handed a tract called *The Communist Party: A Manual on Organization* by one J. Peters, known by several other aliases. Every party member had to study it and live by its precepts.

I do not think the reader can properly understand Joe McCarthy unless he realizes what the party in America was seeking to do. In my view, this manual offers an excellent introduction to the party's intentions. Today it is a collector's item, as the party has attempted to destroy all copies. Let me quote some passages.

The Role and Aim of the Communist Party

As the leader and organizer of the proletariat, the Communist Party of the U.S.A. leads the working class in the fight for the revolutionary overthrow of capitalism, for the establishment of a Socialist Soviet Republic in the United States, for the complete abolition of classes, for the establishment of socialism, the first stage of the classless Communist society . . .

Who Are the Professional Revolutionists?

A professional revolutionist is a highly developed comrade, trained in revolutionary theory and practice, tested in struggles, who gives his whole life to the fight for the interests of his own class. A professional revolutionist is ready to go whenever and wherever the Party sends him. Today he may be working in a mine, organizing the Party, the trade unions, leading struggles; tomorrow, if the Party so decides, he may be in a steel mill; the day after tomorrow, he may be a leader and organizer of the un-employed. Naturally, these professional revolutionists are sup-ported by the Party organization if their assignment doesn't send them to work in shops or mines. . . .

Every Communist must know that the Party has a historical mission to fulfill, that it has the mission of liberating the oppressed exploited masses from the yoke of capitalism, that it has the mission of organizing and leading the masses for the rev-olutionary overthrow of capitalism, and for the establishment of the new world, a Soviet America.

During World War II, the FBI was faced with a dilemma. The Soviet Union was our ally, but at the same time it was committed to an ideology no less alien to ours than that of Hitler's Germany. J. Edgar Hoover made a major decision—to continue secretly to build up the agency's dossiers on Communist infiltrators despite our alliance with the U.S.S.R. It was a delicate, dangerous task. Had someone in authority on either side made public this FBI activity—even though President Roosevelt had authorized it—the agency would have been accused of attempting to harm our relations with a major ally. But Hoover took the risk and quietly built his files while the war was on, files that were to play a crucial role in the exposure of Communists.

In 1945 Elizabeth T. Bentley, a former Communist spy, told the FBI that two extensive Soviet intelligence networks, involving American employees and controlled by local Communist organizations, had been established within the United States. One network was headed by Nathan Gregory Silvermaster, a Treasury Department economist, the other by Victor Perlo, an official of the War Production Board. Both were supplying information to Soviet couriers from a variety of Government agencies, including the Foreign Economic Administration, the War Production Board, the Justice Department, and the Board of Economic Warfare.

On a higher level were Alger Hiss, a State Department official, and Harry Dexter White, an assistant secretary of the Treasury and later an official of the International Monetary Fund. White, a key aide to Secretary Morgenthau, was delivering classified documents to the Communists for microfilming. Hiss, an adviser to President Roosevelt at Yalta and later chief aide to Secretary of State Edward Stettinius at the initial UN conference in San Francisco, was sent to the penitentiary following his conviction on perjury charges growing out of Whittaker Chambers' allegations that Hiss gave him official documents for transmission to Russia.

In 1945, agents of the FBI and the Office of Strategic Services raided the offices of *Amerasia,* a publication that followed the Communist line, and discovered some 1700 documents that had been stolen from the State Department, the Army, Navy, OSS, and OWI. Of the seized documents, 540 were classified.

These emerging patterns caused a deep unease. News appeared in the press about subversion; important voices were raised in alarm; legislation was placed on the books; a loyalty program was begun; prosecutions were undertaken. But against these steps there was monumental resistance. President Truman characterized as "red herrings" the proceedings of the House Committee on Un-American Activities before which Elizabeth Bentley and Whittaker Chambers testified. Liberals warned against a postwar hysteria that would make us see Communists under our beds and kept up a relentless attack on the loyalty program. When the FBI sent documents to agencies concerning Communists in Government posts it was never certain if any action would be taken. In March, 1942, for instance, the FBI informed the Federal Security Agency that Professor Doxey Wilkerson, who occupied an important post, was probably a Communist. The agency buried the report, and about a year later Wilkerson left the Government for another job. He became a Communist party organizer!

The obvious need was to convince the public that the threat was real, especially since treason in the fifties was unlike the crude and obvious variety of Benedict Arnold's day. In the age of the bomb, a few persons, strategically placed, could deliver information capable of destroying a nation. It was imperative that the public grasp this fact of life.

But how could this message be put across over the objections of powerful people in the communications field? Many opinion-molders, information specialists, and journalists were violently opposed to anti-Communist "witch-hunts." Many of these liberals were still bathed in the afterglow of the Soviet-American alliance, which had called for mutual cooperation against a despicable enemy. Moreover, a number of people in the communications field had themselves joined Communist and Communist-front organizations in the 1930's and 40's. These front or "cover" organizations were—and are still—a vital part of the Soviet propaganda framework. Organizations such as the World Peace Council, International Institute for Peace, World Federation of Trade Unions, World Federation of Democratic Youth, and the International Union of Students were among the many formed to conduct pressure campaigns, distribute literature, raise funds, and form public opinion. Nonsubversive organizations were infiltrated by the Communists and their activities warped to fit the party's need. Members of the communications industry, educators, scientists, clergymen, and assorted intellectuals joined these front organizations, some knowing they were in truth Communist-run, but many, perhaps most, unknowingly. They were drawn to them because of a similarity of interests, and persuaded to stay because of the nobly expressed aims: to fight for peace, seek equality of opportunity, end racial discrimination, foster Soviet-American cultural activities, and help refugees from fascism.

When the aims and methods of the Soviet conspiracy began to be revealed, the liberals faced a painful choice. They could either admit they had made a grievous and potentially tragic mistake, which was distasteful, or they could resist. Some made the admission, but the vast majority resisted. They brought enormous pressure to bear in their professional fields to fight against the exposures, and they were, by and large, successful. Opponents of Communism were ridiculed in large segments of the press, painted as witch-hunters, red-baiters, demagogues.

This, then, was the picture as 1949 drew to a close: the American public had heard Winston Churchill's ringing denunciation of the "Iron Curtain" and understood that the Cold War was beginning— but it was not accepting the extent of the Communist menace at home. The basic problem, as seen by a small but informed group in and out of Government, was the need to reach the public. No serious effort was being made by the Administration to discover how far the Communists had penetrated into the State Department and elsewhere. Over the intense opposition of so many powerful people in the communications field somebody was needed to alert the public.

Nobody, so far, had been able to make America listen.

How did the junior senator from Wisconsin come to the struggle that was to dominate his final seven years and cause such a convulsion in our national life?

Joe McCarthy bought Communism in much the same way as other people purchase a new automobile. The salesman showed him the model; he looked at it with interest, examined it more closely, kicked at the tires, sat at the wheel, squiggled in the seat, asked some questions, and bought. It was just as cold as that.

McCarthy told me that he had had no special interest in Communism prior to the late fall of 1949. He also had no special knowledge of the subject. He reacted in quite the same reflexive manner as most Americans to foreign "isms." He deplored them but saw no reason to become excited.

One day just before Thanksgiving, 1949, three men came to Joe McCarthy, and literally overnight the Senator decided to make the battle against Communism his issue. What brought them to Mc-

Carthy's Senate office? Events that led to this confrontation were set in motion by an intelligence officer in the Pentagon, a career man in his late thirties.

A report prepared by the FBI and circulated among certain key Government agencies had come to his attention. This one-hundred-page document gathered together the story of subversion as it was then known to the Bureau: not only the disclosures of Bentley and Chambers, but also the manner in which the spy networks operated; the methods and accomplishments of Communist cells in this country; the names of individuals known to be active in the party. The importance of the document lay not so much in its specific revelations, since many of the facts had been recounted, but because it was the first time the entire story had been pulled together with detailed evidence.

The G-2 officer realized that no special action was planned on the report; it had lain in the files for more than two years. Worried, he sought advice. He took the report from the files and gave it to individuals outside the Pentagon to read. They too were shocked. Conferences were held in several homes in New York and Washington. Ultimately a small group was formed, taking upon itself the responsibility of getting the story across to America.

This was not a mysterious, unknown document. The State Department had received a copy. A confidential memorandum dated June 10, 1947, sent to Secretary of State George C. Marshall by the Senate Committee on Appropriations stated: "On file in the Department is a copy of a preliminary report of the FBI on Soviet espionage activities in the United States, which involves a large number of State Department employees, some in high official positions. This report has been challenged and ignored by those charged with the responsibility of administering the Department, with the apparent tacit approval of Mr. Acheson. Should this case break before the State Department acts, it will be a national disgrace."

These men decided that the only way of awakening the public was from the halls of Congress—through the Senate rather than the House. Meeting in Washington one evening in November, 1949, the group sifted carefully through the roster of United States senators for one who might successfully undertake the task of educating his fellow Americans. They narrowed the list down to four possibilities, all Republicans.

Then they peddled the package around the Senate Office Building, producing the document, urging action. But for one reason or another, the first three senators refused. It is not difficult to guess a reason: the Communist issue was hot and one could get seriously burned.

Finally, the group reached the fourth name. The junior senator from Wisconsin had been placed on the list because he was young and vigorous and had already acquired a reputation for courage in tackling formidable foes. He was the man who had dethroned the powerful La Follette in the 1946 Wisconsin Republican primaries and gone on to win the election.

The three men talked to McCarthy for several hours in his office and then left the document with him. At the end of a weary day he slipped the document into his briefcase and took it home. After dinner, once he started reading, he could not stop until he finished the last page.

He told me later, "After a couple of hours' sleep, I got dressed and went to the office. I had made up my mind—I was going to take it on. It was fantastic, unbelievable. Take any spy story you ever read, any movie about international intrigue, and this was more startling."

The first telephone call McCarthy made that morning was to one of the group. "I got him out of bed," McCarthy recalled, "and told him I was buying the package."

Why, quite specifically, did Joe McCarthy "buy the package"? I believe he did so for two reasons:

The first was patriotic. He was worried about the threat to the country posed by the Communist conspiracy, and he decided to do what he could to expose it.

Secondly, I am sure he saw the dramatic political opportunities connected with a fight on Communism. McCarthy was gifted with a sense of political timing. Sometimes he misjudged, but on balance his sense of what made drama and headlines was uncommonly good. He had been told that three senators had rejected "the package," and he was convinced they had erred—that the time was now right, as perhaps it had not been before, to mount an offensive. He believed that the evidence had accumulated to the extent that the next man who flung himself into the fight would be successful. He had found, he thought, a politically attractive issue he could sink his teeth into.

There have been many accounts of how McCarthy was launched on the Communist issue. According to one oft-told version, Mc-Carthy telephoned William A. Roberts, a well-known Washington attorney, early in January, 1950, and said he stood in need of a strong basic issue. Roberts thereupon arranged a dinner at the Colony Restaurant with the late Father Edmund A. Walsh, regent of the School of Foreign Service at Georgetown University, and Professor Charles H. Kraus, who taught political science at Georgetown. After dinner, the four went to Roberts' office and talked. A number of ideas were offered, none of which appealed to the Senator. He rejected Roberts' idea of pressing for the St. Lawrence Seaway project; suggestions of his own were not fancied by the others. At length, Father Walsh, a student of international Communism who had written extensively about its aims, suggested the subject of Soviet imperialism's threat to the United States through widespread subversion.

Mr. Roberts confirms that the dinner and the subsequent conversation did take place, although a contradiction exists as to who wanted it and why. According to published reports, Professor Kraus wanted McCarthy to meet the three, all of them Roman Catholics, in order to "encourage in a young Catholic senator a serious approach to serious matters." Roberts, on the other hand, insists that McCarthy asked for the meeting "because he needed an issue and he got one there." Conceivably, the Senator may have wanted further information on Communism from the political-science experts that night. But the fact is that McCarthy had already bought the package a month or two earlier.

CHAPTER 2

COUNTRY BOY—
CITY BOY

JOSEPH RAYMOND McCARTHY was born on November 14, 1908, in a white clapboard house of eight rooms on a 142-acre farm in Grand Chute township, a remote rural area near Appleton, Wisconsin. He was the fifth of seven children born to Timothy and Bridget McCarthy in the heart of a section known as the "Irish Settlement," a small enclave in an area dominated by settlers of German, Dutch, and Scandinavian extraction.

The McCarthys were hard-working, pious Roman Catholics who lived the hard, lonely life of the back-country farm family. Bridget Tierney had been born in Ireland, but Joe's father was native-born, the son of an Irish father and a German mother. Joe grew up in an austere, no-nonsense household, learning to pitch hay long before he tried his hand at pitching baseball.

His father was a stern disciplinarian. Joe was his mother's special pride, and she sought to instill in her son a determination to rise above his beginnings. His sister Olive recalled long afterward that their mother did not pamper Joe but prodded him to "get ahead," to "be somebody."

This prodding got quicker results than expected. At fourteen, he decided to quit school and work full time in his father's potato and cabbage fields. The decision to abandon his education at so early an age grieved his mother, Olive recalled, particularly because Joe was a natural student with a phenomenal memory.

Working under the watchful eye of his father turned out not to be to Joe's taste, and he struck out on his own. With sixty-five dollars saved from doing part-time chores for an uncle, he rented an acre from his father and bought a flock of chickens. In two years he owned 2,000 hens, 10,000 broilers, a home-made chicken house, and a dilapidated truck to haul his poultry to market. The boy was the talk of Outagamie County and was ready to branch out further when influenza felled him. He hired a couple of neighborhood boys to care for his livestock but the boys were negligent, and while Joe was convalescing, a cold snap killed off most of his flock. His plans for a poultry empire destroyed overnight, Joe piled his personal effects into the truck, bade his family good-bye, and drove thirty miles off to a new world—the town of Manawa, a community of fewer than a thousand inhabitants but the big time compared with a back-country farm. Now a husky and brash nineteen, he quickly got a job as manager of a chain-store branch, but spent less time tending store than arguing local issues of the day with customers. He relished this give and take and soon was keeping open evenings so that his customers could relax over their pop bottles and give vent to the small-town gripes and enthusiasms.

It was these discussions that underlined for the young McCarthy the handicap of his lack of schooling. At the age of twenty, when local youths were well started on their lifework, he decided to get a high school education even though it meant sitting in classes with youngsters at least six years his junior. Joe persuaded the principal of the Little Wolf High School to enroll him as a first-year student, although he could hardly squeeze behind the desks.

He went through high school in record time and entered Marquette University, the Jesuit school in Milwaukee. For two years he worked hard at engineering school courses by day and earned a living by night as a short-order cook, dishwasher, truck driver, and construction-gang worker. He tried out for boxing. Impatient of technique, his style was to come charging out at the bell and stay on the offensive, no matter how powerful his opponent, until he won or dropped. When he encountered an experienced boxer he would take a severe beating. Several who remembered him at Marquette told me of his blind courage in the ring. Once Joe was so bruised and bloodied in a fight that his opponent wanted to stop. But McCarthy cried, "Come on! Come on!" grinning as though he relished it all.

After two dreary years of engineering studies, Joe decided that this was no career for him. It was exacting and there was no drama in it. What interested him more was the law students with their love of oratory and interest in politics. This, he decided, was for him. He switched to law. I know little about Joe at law school. He talked very rarely about the past; the present was usually too exciting. I do know that he went through fast and never doubted that he was on the right path.

In his first year as practicing attorney in nearby Waupaca, he was retained for only four cases—and two of these were dismissed. But he joined the Lions and the Junior Chamber of Commerce, made speeches for local causes, sold tickets for charity bazaars, and performed various civic duties he felt would bring him closer to the goal he realized he wanted to achieve above all else—a political career.

In the beginning, he cared little what political office he ran for so long as it would make use of his legal talents. Nor had he attached himself to any political party. In 1936, at the age of twenty-eight, he made his first bid for public office—the district attorneyship of Shawano County—on the Democratic ticket. I don't know why the Democratic ticket—I never asked him—but I do know that his political ideas were undeveloped then and party labels meant little to him.

He had little chance in that first contest and knew it, but he conducted an aggressive campaign that impressed the political professionals and paved the way for his next try. This came three years later when he announced his candidacy for the post of circuit judge, this time under the Republican standard he was to follow for the rest of his days.

Determined, the young lawyer drove from farm to farm, sampling housewives' pies and drawing on his country background to advise farmers on how to treat ailing livestock. His opponent was a highly respected jurist named Edgar V. Werner, who had served on the bench for more than three decades and had a large, devoted following. Playing upon the sixty-six-year-old incumbent's age, McCarthy spoke with concern in his voice about the strain such a post made on a man past his prime. Werner ineptly countered by accepting McCarthy's pre-selected battleground, justifying himself as a man old only in years. He went down to defeat by a wide margin in the state's political upset of the year.

McCarthy appears to have been a conscientious judge. Inheriting a backlog of some two hundred and fifty cases, he kept court in session past midnight for weeks, driving court reporter Pat Howlett to exhaustion. When he learned that it was the judicial practice to swap benches occasionally to get acquainted with different parts of the state, he embraced the custom with enthusiasm for its obvious political advantages. He crammed his notebook with the names of county and town leaders and data about them, their wives, and their children. The connections he made by playing so energetically this game of judicial musical chairs came in handy years later when he challenged the state's most powerful political dynasty for the Senate seat.

Pearl Harbor and the entry of the United States into World War II erased political thoughts from McCarthy's mind. At thirty-three, and though a judge exempt from military service, he volunteered for combat duty with the Marine Corps. On June 4, 1942, he was sworn in as a first lieutenant, and left for the base at Quantico, Virginia. For thirty months he served with the leathernecks, hopping islands in the Pacific war zone.

He spent most of his time as an intelligence officer with the Marine air arm, but served also as volunteer gunner on a number of combat missions. Stories have been told me about his noncombat adventures in the South Seas, but one of the most amusing occurred in December of 1943 when he was stationed at Munda in the Solomons. With Christmas approaching, McCarthy decided to throw a party. He collected quantities of native artifacts that he knew were valued as souvenirs, loaded them in a truck, and drove to the airstrip captured a few months before from the Japanese. There he borrowed a torpedo bomber—because it could hold more of what he had in mind—and a pilot, and took off for Guadalcanal.

He spent a busy day there, trading his souvenirs for supplies of food and liquor which he and the pilot loaded aboard the bomber and took back to base. On Christmas Eve, McCarthy threw his party. Penn T. Kimball, a journalist and professor at the Columbia School of Journalism, who was stationed at Munda with McCarthy, says that it was probably the biggest "blast" ever staged there.

"McCarthy was the Perle Mesta of Munda that day," Kimball recalled. "He invited everybody, and everybody came." Past midnight, some of the revelers fired off signaling flares which arched prettily into the night. Ten minutes later, a field telephone rang. A

British officer whose unit was stationed a short distance away asked, "Would you chaps mind raising your trajectory? We appear to be catching your fire."

"Come over and join the party," was the counteroffer. They did.

It was in the Solomon Islands that McCarthy first met John F. Kennedy. Lieutenant Kennedy had returned to active duty after his heroic adventure following the sinking of his PT-boat 109. He was given command of another PT, the 59, operating out of Vela Lavella Island, northwest of New Georgia Island where McCarthy was stationed. Marines on Munda would occasionally find their way northward and pass the time with the patrolling PT boat crews. On a hot, damp Sunday, Captain McCarthy got into conversation with young Lieutenant Kennedy, who took him for a PT ride. The following day, McCarthy told Penn Kimball about it. "I met this fellow Kennedy—a hell of a nice guy. His old man's the ambassador to Britain." Later, McCarthy accompanied Kennedy and his crew, unofficially, on two night-patrol missions up the Japanese-held Bougainville coast. Though he went as a passenger, he recalled with pleasure that he "got to shoot the machine guns." Despite their dissimilar backgrounds, McCarthy and Kennedy got along well. After the war they renewed their friendship and McCarthy became a frequent guest at the Kennedy home in Hyannis Port.

In mid-1944, although the two-hemisphere war was still to be won, Captain McCarthy's Republican followers in Wisconsin were able to persuade him to take a thirty-day leave and return home to run for the Senate against the powerful GOP incumbent, Alexander Wiley. Hurriedly, he prepared for the campaign. He decorated the backs of two trucks and a jeep with huge signs reading: "McCARTHY FOR U.S. SENATOR," and he had a similar inscription emblazoned across his tent.

He failed to unseat Wiley in the GOP primary, but by running up a respectable vote he established the beginnings of a state-wide political reputation.

A year after he had been mustered out of the Marines and returned to the bench, McCarthy announced his intention to run in the primaries against Senator Robert "Young Bob" La Follette. The news that this relatively obscure young judge intended to challenge the state's most powerful political figure, the offspring and namesake of old "Fighting Bob" La Follette, amused and astonished the sophisticated. This time, experienced politicians predicted, young McCarthy was going to fall hard.

He opened with a saturation mail-campaign, door to door canvassing, and flamboyant oratory. La Follette, feeling sure of his following after twenty-one years in the U.S. Senate, made the serious error of shrugging him off. He stayed in Washington, doing his work and returning home only two weeks before balloting time to put on a perfunctory campaign, so sure was he of winning.

McCarthy campaigned lustily and talked loudly. He attacked La Follette's domestic program but found that it was not vulnerable. Among the many excellent measures he had sponsored or backed was the recently enacted congressional reform bill for which the Senator deserved most of the credit. McCarthy then found a safer theme and hammered away at it: La Follette, he charged, was too much concerned with raising salaries for members of Congress. In the area of foreign affairs he hit hard at La Follette's isolationism. There he was on solider ground. By opposing world cooperation, McCarthy claimed, the Senator was playing squarely into the hands of the Communists.

Perhaps McCarthy's most controversial campaign tactic was his assault on La Follette as a "war profiteer." La Follette had purchased a 25 percent share of radio station WEMP in Milwaukee and had drawn a profit of $47,339 in the war years 1944 and 1945. He subsequently had voted for a Federal Communications Commission appropriation. It was, of course, the FCC that had licensed station WEMP. McCarthy implied that there was a conflict of interest involved in La Follette's vote.

When Primary Day—tantamount to election in GOP Wisconsin—arrived on August 13, 1946, the only confident person at headquarters was the candidate himself. And even he harbored doubts as returns came in from the back-country areas on which he counted for his main support. County after county voted for La Follette.

It soon became apparent that Milwaukee would prove the decisive factor, and in 1942 La Follette had carried Milwaukee by 55,000 votes. But then the teletypes began to tell a story that brought party workers crowding around the machines. One after another these labor precincts no McCarthy supporter had expected to win were turning against La Follette. When it was all over, the brash challenger had beaten La Follette by 207,935 to 202,539. After this, the election itself was an anticlimax. McCarthy defeated his Democratic opponent, Howard MacMurray, by a 2-to-1 margin.

The question has often been debated: What made it possible for McCarthy, the ex-farm boy, to defeat the most powerful political force in Wisconsin?

Ironically, one factor was the bitter opposition La Follette encountered from the Communist party, which at the time had infiltrated the Congress of Industrial Organizations in Wisconsin and was able to exert strong influence upon the membership, especially in Milwaukee. The Communists hated La Follette, who had attacked the Kremlin and its philosophies repeatedly. But it does not follow that hatred of La Follette made them favor McCarthy. Richard Rovere, in his biography of McCarthy, cites a doctoral dissertation by Karl Ernest Meyer at Princeton which examines the subject ("The Politics of Loyalty: From La Follette to McCarthy in Wisconsin, 1918–1952"). Even Rovere, hardly a McCarthy admirer, concluded that "the known facts will not sustain the theory that McCarthy owed his nomination to the votes controlled by Communists in Milwaukee. There is no evidence that the Communists instructed their following to enter the Republican primaries or gave McCarthy any assistance beyond their generalized attacks on La Follette."

Many have pointed out that Wisconsin is not an easy state to analyze politically. Complex factors entered into the defeat of La Follette, not excluding his loss of Catholic votes for his stand against Franco in Spain. But to my mind, what played the most direct and decisive role in the outcome of that memorable primary was the fact that McCarthy reached the people and made them feel they would have a representative in Washington, instead of a "great name" that had become faceless.

In December of 1946, wearing a new dark-blue suit, Senator-elect Joseph McCarthy arrived in the nation's capital. After checking in at his hotel, he went to the Senate Office Building, where he wandered alone down the unfamiliar corridors until he found his future headquarters on the fifth floor.

* * *

On a windy evening in 1936 a panel truck with huge posters on its sides cruised slowly along upper Broadway on Manhattan's West Side, the twin loudspeakers on the roof blaring "Happy Days Are Here Again." It stopped at the Eighty-sixth Street intersection in front of the Tip Toe Inn and a small crowd gathered. Moments before, a decorated Republican sound truck had passed, howling the cause of Alf Landon.

From the Democratic truck, plastered with the portraits of Roosevelt and Garner, there emerged, not a seasoned campaign haranguer but a small boy with a round solemn face. He wore a heavy lumberman's cap and a dark-blue overcoat buttoned to the neck against the chill. He mounted an improvised platform, and in a reedy voice told the audience that Mr. Roosevelt had taken the country out of its worst depression, had put through the Social Security Act, established the Good Neighbor Policy, and was on the side of "the people" and against "Wall Street." And that "I would certainly cast my ballot for FDR except that I am only nine years old."

He thanked his audience and ducked back into the truck. The knot of listeners applauded, and Roy Cohn, boy campaigner, moved on to his next pitch a mile south.

Law and politics fascinated me from the beginning. I came by this naturally, for my father was a judge of the Bronx County Court, and later of the State Supreme Court, elevated to that bench by Roosevelt when he was governor of the state. At the age of eight I would sit entranced in the courtroom, and in the evening at home my father would listen with a straight face to my impressions and the advice I had for the lawyers.

I met the President shortly after I had contributed so much to his reelection, for during the Easter vacation, my father took me to Washington. A high point was a visit with Supreme Court Justice Cardozo. At the White House the President asked if I were interested in public affairs. I responded enthusiastically. President Roosevelt asked, "What particularly interests you?"

"Your Supreme Court policy," I answered. FDR, angered because the Court had been striking down his New Deal measures, had sent Congress a message proposing that as each justice reached the age of seventy-two a younger man be named to sit with him, to a maximum of fifteen judges. Critics charged that this was an attempt to pack the high bench with pro-New Deal justices.

"What do you think of the plan?" the President asked, and I am sure he had to fight to keep a straight face.

I hate to admit it, but I told him I approved, and for a minute and a half gave my reasons. When I stopped, he thanked me solemnly for my support and told me the conflict was basically between the older generation's moss-covered ideas and the progressivism of youth. We shook hands and my father and I left.

I tell the anecdote because it suggests I was serious even as a kid. I did not lack self-confidence nor hesitate to speak up. This trait stayed with me.

My father came from a poor family and worked nights and weekends to support himself while he attended the College of the City of New York. He taught in the public schools, studied law at night, and at the same time managed to meet, court, and marry my mother, whose father, Joseph S. Marcus, was a successful businessman and noted philanthropist.

Father had always been a Democrat and was active in the party in the Bronx until elevated to the judiciary. He was closely associated with Edward J. Flynn, Bronx Democratic leader and friend of FDR. His first political appointment was as an assistant district attorney. He became chief assistant and prosecuted many of the famous murder cases of that day. One of his successes was won against the redoubtable Clarence Darrow.

First elected in 1930, he was thereafter designated by governors Herbert Lehman and Thomas E. Dewey for four terms on the Appellate Division of the Supreme Court. Shortly before his retirement, he was selected by the judges of the Court of Appeals, the state's highest court, to sit as one of them to break a deadlock. He was an active civic leader, President of District No. 1 of B'nai B'rith, and a man of integrity, humanity, and wisdom. While I possess a volatile temper, he rarely lost his. Some of my critics who knew my father mourn in me the lack of his good qualities, and I think they are right.

Some, however, make the mistake of suggesting that my father did not support me in the McCarthy years. As a matter of fact, he was a warm admirer of Senator McCarthy, a strong antagonist of Communism, and constantly concerned that Americans—particularly those of the Jewish faith—could lend aid and comfort to an ideology that would destroy the system under which he and so many other American Jews had been given the opportunity to succeed.

I don't suppose I need point out to the reader that I am proud of my father, of his rise from nowhere, of his career as a judge, and of what it all says about America.

At the suggestion of President Frederick G. Robinson of City College, a family friend, I was enrolled in the Community School for gifted students on Manhattan's Upper West Side. Either I wasn't all that gifted or the routine and I failed to mesh, because within two years I was well on my way to becoming a nervous wreck. Neurologist Dr. S. Philip Goodhart, observing my jumpiness, urged my parents to take me out. I was next deposited in the Fieldston Lower School in Riverdale, where the atmosphere was as relaxed as the Community School's was active. There I spent four pleasant years, until one day my father came and found me in a sewing and knitting class. He pulled me out and installed me in the Horace Mann School for Boys, a private high school in Riverdale with an awesome reputation for serious-minded education.

At Horace Mann I was studying more but enjoying it less. Already I had law and politics on the brain. One summer, my father took me to Albany to attend the Constitutional Convention. I gaped at the men in the hotel rooms, watched with awe the shrewd behind-the-scenes steering by Assembly Speaker Irwin Steingut, the father of the dynamic Brooklyn Democratic leader, Stanley Steingut, and I was entranced by the bustle on the convention floor. I wanted with all my heart to be part of the planning, the color, the action, the cloakroom conversations, the verbal clashes, the maneuvering. One evening, I went to my father and complained that I was bored with school life. His response was simple and practical: get done with it faster. I spent the summer being tutored, and was able to skip my final year at Horace Mann.

In 1944 I began my studies at Columbia College, continued them in Kent Hall, the law school, and by June, 1947, three and a half years later, had become bachelor of arts and of laws. Ordinarily it should have taken seven years, but in those postwar years a no-nonsense atmosphere prevailed; students studied, and vacations were canceled for the duration. Also the university offered students a "professional option" under which the last year of undergraduate work could be combined with the first year of professional school.

The case-book method bored me, and during campaign time I dodged classes and hung around Democratic headquarters. Ironically, my best mark at Columbia law was from Professor Philip Jessup, who became a target of congressional committees during my later service with them.

Although I had my law diploma neatly framed and hung in our apartment, I was not yet twenty-one and thus ineligible for a license. During the six months' wait I served as a clerk in the Federal attorney's office on Foley Square in Manhattan. But at last I was sworn in as a full-fledged lawyer and an assistant Federal prosecutor on the staff of U.S. Attorney John F. X. McGohey. Almost from the beginning I specialized in a controversial branch of the law—uncovering subversives and fighting Communism in the law courts and before congressional committees.

Why did I choose this line?

I was once told by a retired university professor who considered my views and Senator McCarthy's about the international Communist conspiracy far-fetched (he used stronger language) that had I been born twelve or fifteen years earlier my world-view and therefore my character would have been very different. "You would have attained maturity in the Depression; instead you reached it in the Cold War, in a period of reaction which always follows a major war, as right after Napoleon, after the Civil War, after both World Wars. You would not then have started your career preoccupied with subversion but rather with trying to set the tottering free-enterprise system on its feet. Franklin Roosevelt shook your hand, but you jelled in the very different world of Harry Truman. So don't think," he cautioned me, "that your beliefs are founded on Eternities. They are the accidents of your time, place, and et ceteras."

I turned this over in my mind. Maybe so. Anyway the theory helped me answer the question how I chose this particular kind of legal work. I did not choose it. It chose me.

At Columbia I was a typical college liberal, active in young Democratic organizations, founder of the Columbia Law School Democratic Club, and firmly on the liberal side of every public issue. From my reading of the newspapers, I was dismayed by the disclosures of subversive activity in the late 1940's, but did not fully grasp their significance. Who could believe that a vast underground network of spies existed? In 1947, when the House Committee on Un-American Activities began digging into alleged subversion in Hollywood, I was not conscious of anything overly important taking place.

Even after I joined the U.S. Attorney's staff, I was confused about the idea that an international conspiracy was afoot which reached even into public offices.

I believed at first that Alger Hiss was innocent. I felt that a sensational press was stampeding our judicial processes, and that given his day in court, Hiss would prove himself the victim of a conspiracy headed by Whittaker Chambers. I applauded Secretary of State Dean Acheson's announcement that he could "not turn my back on Alger Hiss." But my position crumbled before the facts.

My education came slowly. During the years I helped prosecute conspirators while in the U.S. Attorney's office, I learned that Communists in government presented a far greater threat to the national security than I had realized, or than any of my professors at Columbia had told me. I interrogated hundreds of witnesses and as part of my duties was required to read Communist literature from Karl Marx to William Foster. No American can devote himself full time to this subject without becoming fearful of his country's future.

Many underestimate this movement because they do not know its nature and its operations. They emphasize how small the Communist party appears to be on the surface. They do not grasp what I learned early—that this movement in every country is a religious force to which its votaries devote themselves fanatically.

It is here, thus early in this book, that I must underscore a point many Americans had difficulty grasping in those years and still do not understand easily. I was astonished when I first became aware of its truth and power.

For the first time in our history, we had to deal with a new brand of traitor. Not often before had men who betrayed their country been moved by considerations other than power, greed, rancor, or adventure. Beginning in the 1930's, a cause had overwhelmed many American minds and given them a mystical belief. Thus was created the ideological traitor.

To the ideological Communist, betrayal is not betrayal at all, but a justifiable act performed in behalf of his faith. Julius and Ethel Rosenberg and Dr. Klaus Fuchs, who transmitted our atomic secrets to Russia, were ideological Communists. So was Hiss. In my many interrogations of Communists over the years, I was struck time and again by their absolute conviction that they were serving a noble ideal.

The Rosenbergs, Fuchs, and other Communists cared little about pay and even less about thrills. Indeed, the Communist whose case history I will describe in full in the next chapter was such a timid man that the detective stories with which he read himself to sleep frightened him so that when he went downstairs to lock up for the night, his wife had to follow with a flashlight!

I did not learn all this at once. My education in the Communist conspiracy was slow but thorough.

Early in my job as a prosecutor, I gave some small legal assistance to U.S. Attorney (now Federal Judge) McGohey in the case against the Communist Top-Eleven charged under the Smith Act with engaging in a conspiracy to overthrow the Government by force and violence. The Top-Eleven (originally twelve, but William Z. Foster was separated because of age and illness) constituted the Politburo of the Communist party, U.S.A., the counterpart of the Kremlin Politburo, and was directly under its orders.

Day after day I sat in the prosecutors' offices with people who were about to testify, a number of them confidential Government informants who had infiltrated the Communist party, and listened to them spell out what they had learned—that the Communists were taught, and believed with an absolute faith, that the dream of a great revolution in this country could never come to pass "without the violent destruction of the machinery of the bourgeois state." Day after day, I heard incredible facts that linked the eleven defendants to plans that would implement that awesome ambition.

The details of that nine-month trial in 1949 and 1950 are beyond the scope of this book. Enough to say that all eleven were found guilty of conspiring to overthrow our government by force and violence. The display of bad manners and improper conduct by lawyers and witnesses for the defense was the worst this country has ever seen. The Communists did not fear conviction. Following instructions, they sought to turn the courtroom into a forum for their cause. The party had instructed them that they were expendable and they accepted it. They were also instructed to make the trial a burlesque. In the courtroom they laughed at us, at our judicial methods, at our judges. Judge Medina endured an ordeal to which no judge should be subjected.

Four of the eleven became fugitives from justice, forfeiting their $20,000 bail. Eventually two were recaptured. I conceived the legal theory under which these two were prosecuted and convicted for this act, as there was no applicable Federal fugitive statute at that time.

For a young man barely twenty-one, this firsthand experience with Communist leaders was enormously revealing in many ways. But one of my most important discoveries during that lengthy trial came when the Communists produced an impressive, learned gentleman as expert witness for their contention that our jury system excluded certain races and classes. He was Professor Doxey Wilkerson, a Government official who had held an important post with the Office of Price Administration and had been a member of the President's Advisory Council on Negro Problems. His reports to the President were part of the official Government record and were issued to the American people through the Government Printing Office.

While preparing material in rebuttal, I remarked to an FBI agent that it surprised me that a man with such an impressive record in government would agree to testify as he did for the Communist leaders.

The agent looked at me and laughed: "Wilkerson," he said, "is not only a Communist himself, but he's one of the top leaders of the party. He's been on their National Committee."

"But not while he was holding Government office?" I asked, shocked.

"You've got a lot to learn, young fellow, if it surprises you to find a Communist in a key Government spot," he replied.

Years later, when I became Chief Counsel for the McCarthy Subcommittee, I found that Wilkerson's books were being used in the State Department's overseas anti-Communist program. But what amazed me most was to learn that as early as March 26, 1947, in testimony before the House Committee on Un-American Activities, J. Edgar Hoover stated that *five years before,* a fifty-seven-page report spelling out Wilkerson's Communist activities had been sent to the Federal Security Agency, where Wilkerson was then employed. The FSA, however, took no action and Wilkerson went on to another, higher post in Government, with the OPA.

In the spring and summer of 1950, I found myself on a team handling the American end of the extraordinary confession of Dr. Klaus Fuchs, a German Communist scientist, employed by the British government and sent by them to the United States to work in the highly secret Manhattan Project at Los Alamos in New Mexico. Few Americans knew that such a project, which cost the American taxpayer $2,000,000,000 in its initial stages, existed. It was probably the best-kept secret of the war—that is, best-kept from the American people. Yet Fuchs, who had a Communist record in Germany and Great Britain, got into it without clearance from any American agency because he was then a British subject and the American government had agreed not to make British scientists undergo American screening. In 1950 Klaus Fuchs confessed that as a Soviet spy he had stolen the secrets of the atomic bomb production and had transmitted them to Soviet Russia.

Dr. Fuchs, in his confession, pointed to Americans who were associated with him in this espionage. The American through whom he funneled atomic secrets to the Kremlin was Harry Gold, a quiet, seemingly inoffensive young man who had no particular Marxist point of view but who had become a Soviet courier to please a friend who had been good to him. When Harry Gold was told by FBI operatives that Fuchs had confessed and had involved him, he in turn broke down and confessed. He had no intellectual or spiritual resistance to telling. He did not consider himself an informer. While he was sympathetic to Soviet Russia, he had never joined the Communist party but had accepted the party's discipline as part of a job. Harry Gold was a strange case.

How does a Communist courier go about his work? The essential facts have not changed since I first learned them as a young prosecutor of espionage agents. He transmits espionage data from the spy to the appointed official of the Soviet government. The spy rarely has direct contact with anyone but the courier. Often they know each other only by first names or an assumed first name. The courier may deal directly or through an intermediate courier with his boss.

The direct contact with Moscow is customarily carried out through officials and employees of the Soviet Embassy, Consulates, and the UN delegations, not only of Soviet Russia but of some of the satellite countries. In addition to these official persons, whose passports are in order, special representatives—like master-spy Jacob Golos—are smuggled into this country to handle espionage. Sometimes these special agents are more important than those who have official status. The international Communist movement—the Comintern—would have a spokesman such as Gerhart Eisler here to transmit instructions to the American Communist party and to direct espionage. We learned that several cells or teams operated simultaneously in the same area but were independent of each other and even unknown to each other.

The customary pattern was for the Secret Police or Red Army

Intelligence to work through the Soviet Foreign Office, which would send a representative to this country to direct spying activities. (The name of this organization has changed several times: Cheka, GPU, NKVD, MVD. To these must be added the Fourth Section of the Russian Army, which engages in all forms of espionage.) Generally, he would be a Soviet national or a high Comintern official. Once here, he would usually take an important behind-the-scenes post in the Communist party of the United States. This post would in most instances involve the Control Commission of the party—the group that spied on its own members to make sure that they stayed in line. (This body is currently known as the Review Commission.) It is in charge of disciplinary action against party members and conducts "purges" within the American Communist party. A top Communist agent would operate from party headquarters on Twelfth Street in Manhattan by virtue of his position on the Control Commission. But he would also direct the organization and maintenance of the Soviet espionage apparatus in this nation. He would screen promising young Communist prospects. He would arrange for couriers to collect secret documents and information. He would transmit this information to the Soviet Union through "diplomatic channels." Often he would also run one of the Soviet business agencies which could be used on occasion as espionage points. Such were Amtorg and World Tourists.

An example of such a man was J. Peters, also known as Alexander Stevens and by other names. Peters, a Hungarian, arrived illegally in the 1930's. He soon became an important cog in the Communist Party Control Commission. He was the author of the famous "Peters *Manual.*"

I was shocked to learn during the McCarthy hearings, when we questioned the head of Army Intelligence and Counterintelligence about his role in combating Communist infiltration, that he had never heard of this key work. The "Peters *Manual*" is not, however, J. Peters' only claim to fame. He directed a spy ring at the same time. And the courier Peters assigned to collect the stolen papers was Whittaker Chambers. When the House Committee on Un-American Activities broke the Hiss-Chambers case in 1948, Peters fled to the Soviet Union.

Jacob Golos was another Soviet commissar who assumed a top post in the American Communist party as the chairman of the Control Commission. Golos was also the head of World Tourists, a Communist front that posed as a legitimate travel agency, but which actually handled secret missions to Russia and forged passports for Communist functionaries. And, of course, he ran his spy network of U.S. Government employees. We knew much about Golos through Elizabeth Bentley, who served as the courier for some of his favorite spies and was his common-law wife until his death in 1943.

I worked closely with the prosecution team in the trial of Julius and Ethel Rosenberg and Morton Sobell. Rosenberg, helped by cash supplied by Russia, engineered the theft of Los Alamos atomic bomb secrets—the proximity fuse and the sky-platform. The Rosenbergs recruited Ethel's brother, David Greenglass, to assist them in their espionage.

The details of the case, which until the assassination of President Kennedy had been called the crime of the century, are far too complex to relate here, but I must set down the impact it had upon me. It was, I am certain, one of the turning points of my life.

I say it without reservation: nothing in my life has been as frightening, as confusing, and as truly sobering as that dreadful crime. It revealed to me as nothing else that there was a grave and imminent danger to this country from a criminal conspiracy dedicated to the establishment of world Communism.

I learned that Communist spies were active, resourceful—and, tragically, successful in this country. They had actually stolen plans for our most important, most secret, weapon.

I also learned that our country's security against Communist espionage was woefully lax, partly because the FBI wasn't given the opportunities it should have had.

How, for example, was David Greenglass able to penetrate Los Alamos? As an Army private, he was stationed there from August, 1944, to February, 1946. During this period, he transmitted to the Rosenbergs, and through them to Soviet Russia, all the secret data he could lay his hands on.

Greenglass actually received the *Daily Worker,* official organ of the American Communist party, at Los Alamos. Didn't *somebody* see and ask a question? In addition, I have read the correspondence between Greenglass and his family while he was at Los Alamos. The letters were filled with Communist news of all kinds—meetings, rallies, party decisions, gossip, and always the high resolve to continue to work for the day when socialism will capture America. All this in the place where the most vital research on making the atomic bomb was under way. Why was no effort made to prevent a person such as Greenglass from working in the area?

Similarly, the extent to which Klaus Fuchs was entrusted with top-secret information was dramatically revealed when we were preparing for the Rosenbergs' trial. I had asked for a certain sketch to which Greenglass, who had admitted his espionage activities, wanted to refer when he appeared on the witness stand. It was flown in under guard by special courier from Los Alamos. The room where we were preparing the case for trial was cleared. I stood on one side of the table while the security officers stood on the other, clutching the memorandum containing the sketch—which Greenglass had transmitted some time before to Russia. I was not allowed to hold the memorandum. However, I have good vision and from where I stood I could see the very top of the first page. Written upon it were the words: "Copy to Dr. Klaus Fuchs."

Julius and Ethel Rosenberg were executed in 1953 for their crimes. Harry Gold, after entering a plea of guilty, was sentenced to thirty years in prison. David Greenglass pleaded guilty and was sentenced to fifteen years. Morton Sobell was sentenced to thirty years for his part in the plot. The convictions were upheld all the way through the highest court of the land. Particularly impressive was the opinion written affirming the Rosenbergs' conviction by Judge Jerome N. Frank of the United States Court of Appeals, one of the country's great New Deal liberals. Despite the overwhelming evidence of the Rosenbergs' guilt, despite Sobell's attempt to escape behind the Iron Curtain after he learned Fuchs and Gold were talking—we were still deluged with liberal protests seeking to cast doubt on the validity of the convictions. And some who refuse to examine the facts still fall for these emotional diatribes. A recent example is a propaganda job entitled "Invitation to an Inquest" by a couple named Schneir—which received a praising review in *Newsweek* magazine, and which is a patchwork of outright untruths, inaccuracies, and false conclusions. Though the authors claim it to be an "objective" research job, they failed to interview a single person who had been connected with the actual investigation and prosecution of the case. The book formed the basis of a motion for a new trial for Sobell which was totally rejected by one of our most eminent jurists, Federal Judge Edward Weinfeld, in a scholarly and detailed opinion.

Few knew better than I that a widespread belief existed that prosecution of Communists was a witch-hunt. Many persons still believe that the prosecutions were politically motivated; that there was little if any substance to the charges; that the evidence, such as it was, was phony; and that, in sum, many persons were unjustly accused.

It might be illuminating for me to relate in detail one of the Communist cases upon which I worked closely before I met Senator McCarthy. The operation of the Soviet apparatus, its effect on a promising young American Government official, and the details involved in planning such a prosecution should come into perspective.

CHAPTER 3

STORY OF A "WITCH-HUNT"

H E HELD DEGREES from two Ivy League colleges and was a member of Phi Beta Kappa. His father had been an executive in a large corporation, his mother an art teacher. He married the daughter of a banker. He was handsome, brilliant, and a Government economist. He accompanied and advised our top economic missions. He held high office in the Department of Commerce. Nobody would have suspected William Walter Remington of being a spy for the Communists.

And yet Remington, during the years that he held important positions with the United States Government, supplied valuable classified information to a Soviet courier for transmission to Moscow. He was finally convicted of perjury in denying certain incidents involving his Communist associations.

Remington was born in New York City in 1917 and spent his childhood in Ridgewood, New Jersey, an upper-middle-income community with neatly shrubbed homes and tree-shaded streets about twenty-five miles from Manhattan. At the age of sixteen he enrolled at Dartmouth College, where he immediately established himself as an outstanding student. In fact, he showed such unusual promise that he was one of only seven young scholars permitted to study independently in his senior year instead of having to follow a prescribed course.

It was also while at Dartmouth that William Remington joined the Young Communist League, which was the official youth movement of the Communist party and which in the thirties and forties had many active chapters in colleges throughout the nation. Each YCL cell was headed by a full party functionary and students were frequently recruited by a member of the faculty. The turnover in the organization was large—many young people joined and then left rather rapidly when the purpose of the organization became clear to them. However, a number went on to become full-fledged party members, and many important American Communists received their basic indoctrination in the YCL.

In 1936, when he was nineteen, Remington took a summer job with the Tennessee Valley Authority in Knoxville, Tennessee. There he met Kenneth McConnell, a Communist functionary on an inspection trip of the party's apparatus in the area. Remington became a full party member and during the summer of 1936 went with McConnell to recruitment centers where he helped win new members for the party. He even approached one of his superiors, Rudolph Bertram; the plea was not successful.

The summer over, Remington returned to Dartmouth and shortly afterward met a Radcliffe girl named Ann Moos. Ann was a Communist with a banker father who lived at Croton-on-Hudson in Westchester County, New York. Before she agreed to wed William Remington she exacted a promise from him that he would continue to support the cause. It was a case of "love me, love my party." They were married in 1939 and settled down shortly thereafter at the Moos home in Croton. Remington worked for a master's degree in economics at Columbia University and attended courses in Marxist economics at the Worker's School. He stayed in constant contact with Joseph North, editor of the Communist *New Masses* and the man who had recommended the field of economics to Remington.

Next Remington got a job in the Department of Commerce under Thomas C. Blaisdell, a New Deal economist, who held many high posts including that of Assistant Secretary of Commerce and chief of the Mission of Economic affairs. When Blaisdell became assistant to the director of the War Production Board, he asked Remington to join him at a higher salary. Remington accepted the offer and arranged to meet Joe North in Washington to discuss how the party could take advantage of his new position.

During Christmas week in 1942, three respectable-looking persons lunched at Schrafft's Restaurant on Thirty-third Street and Fourth

Avenue in New York. At the table were Mr. and Mrs. Remington and Joe North. Soon they were joined by a fourth man, introduced to the Remingtons as "John." It was an important lunch—"John" was actually Jacob Golos, the top Soviet espionage agent in the United States, and this was a test to screen Remington.

Apparently he passed, because the next day the Remingtons again met for lunch at the same restaurant, but this time Elizabeth Bentley appeared. Miss Bentley was then Golos' chief courier, dealing with high officials in Washington. At the restaurant, Miss Bentley was introduced simply as Helen, her courier name. Elaborate arrangements were made for the manner in which Remington was to pass along information.

Remington regularly handed Elizabeth Bentley documents and information from the War Production Board which she took to Golos in New York. He gave her material such as airplane production schedules. One item was unique. Remington had learned that the War Production Board was working on a secret process to produce synthetic rubber from garbage. The project was under careful and secret scrutiny by the Government and large sums of money were being expended on its research. Remington got hold of the formula of this secret process. He considered it one of his greatest achievements and emphasized its potential importance as he turned it over to "Helen."

Remington applied for a commission in the Navy in April, 1944, and got it quickly. Later, Blaisdell asked for him to come to London on a special economic mission, where he remained a short time. In 1947, Blaisdell went to the Department of Commerce as director of the Office of International Trade, and took Remington with him in a ten-thousand-dollar-a-year post. In the Department of Commerce in 1948, Remington had an ideal position for a Communist spy: presiding over a committee with final control over the issuance of licenses for the export of goods to Iron Curtain countries.

The FBI had Remington under watch and sent confidential reports to his superiors, warning that he had been named a Communist spy by a reliable informant. The FBI had questioned him and he had admitted acquaintance with Golos and Bentley. However, Blaisdell ignored the FBI reports. He did confide with one person about what the FBI knew concerning Remington's activities and that was Remington himself. Remington assured Blaisdell that he was not a Communist spy. There the matter was closed—and Remington kept his job, passing on export licenses to Russia's satellites. The FBI could do nothing further about Remington since its jurisdiction was limited to passing along reports to agency chiefs.

In the summer of 1948, three years after she had told her remarkable story to the FBI, Elizabeth Bentley exposed William Remington.

She had been summoned before the Senate Subcommittee on Investigations by Senator Homer Ferguson, Michigan Republican. Calmly, she testified under oath, disclosing the full details of her conspiratorial relationship with Remington. Ferguson thereupon summoned the handsome young Government official, who said he had met persons he knew as "John" and "Helen" but denied he knew of their roles as Soviet agents. He admitted giving Helen money but denied it was his Communist party dues, insisting it was intended as a contribution to the Joint Anti-Fascist Refugee Committee, a Communist-front organization. He said Miss Bentley had claimed she was a reporter for a New York newspaper and the information he gave her was for use in her articles.

The revelations produced by the Ferguson committee now interested the Civil Service Commission's Fourth Regional Loyalty Board, which opened hearings of its own in the case of William Remington. After sifting the evidence, the board, on September 22, 1948, issued orders relieving Remington of Government office. Remington filed an appeal to the President's Loyalty Review Board, the final authority on security and loyalty in Government jobs. On February 10, 1949, the board reversed the earlier decision and ordered Remington reinstated with back pay, which amounted to approximately five thousand dollars.

Remington's supporters loosed a defense of their man that was staggering in its volume and vigor. Editorials scornful in tone appeared in the newspapers. *The New Yorker* published a long "Reporter at Large" article which was a strong defense. A lengthy defense was published in *The New Republic* by James A. Wechsler, then Washington correspondent of the New York *Post,* who currently bores his long-suffering readers with a column in the *Post.* The column is so influential that I usually don't find out he's mentioned me until weeks later. He can be counted upon to get involved with the wrong side of the wrong issue at the wrong time. He was once editor of the *Post,* but its wise publisher, Mrs. Dorothy Schiff, confined him to a column, over which he can put his own name instead of the paper's to his double-standard journalism. He was once a member of the National Committee of the Young Communist League.

Wechsler's impassioned three-page article, called "The Remington Loyalty Case," bore the subheading: "The long-delayed vindication of a man wrongfully banished from his work throws new light on Washington's witch-hunt." And its opening line was: "The case of William Walter Remington is officially closed." He noted "dreary signs that Remington still lived under a cloud." After several senators had challenged the decision, he wrote, Commerce Department officials agreed that Remington should not return to his former job of handling export licenses for Russia and the satellite countries. "How many times must a man be cleared before he is readmitted to the society that ostracized him?"

After Elizabeth Bentley repeated her accusations against him without immunity on the National Broadcasting Company radio program "Meet the Press," Remington instituted a suit for $100,000. When Miss Bentley refused to retract her statements, NBC and the program's sponsor, General Foods Corporation, made an out-of-court settlement for $10,000. It appeared as though Remington's vindication was indeed complete.

But while his supporters were convinced of his innocence, Government investigators were not. In the spring of 1950, the House Committee on Un-American Activities reopened the case. Investigators sent investigators to Knoxville to look into hitherto unexplored areas of Remington's career. There they discovered Kenneth McConnell, the party organizer who, by this time, had broken with the Communists and was willing to testify. McConnell quickly identified Remington as an active Communist party member in Knoxville. The public hearings on the case were reopened.

When the extent of Remington's involvement with Communists began to emerge, a Federal grand jury in New York became interested. Had Remington committed perjury in denying he had ever been a member of the Communist party? Witnesses were summoned, evidence accumulated. Thomas Donegan, the special assistant to the Attorney General, who was presenting evidence to the grand jury, learned that Ann Remington had divorced her husband and had broken with the Communist movement. He subpoenaed her to appear before the grand jury.

So Ann Moos Remington, who would not marry Remington unless he promised to marry the cause she had already espoused, in the spring of 1949 told her story to a grand jury in New York.

On May 25, the jury summoned William Remington and asked him the crucial question: "At any time have you ever been a member of the Communist party?"

Remington replied categorically and emphatically: "I never have been."

And in June that year, an indictment charging perjury was brought in against him.

We made our plans for the trial. Irving H. Saypol, Judge Mc-Gohey's successor and a highly competent United States Attorney, asked me how long preparations might take. I conferred with my colleagues, a group of young prosecutors who came to be known as the "pony backfield"—John M. Foley, Albert A. Blinder, and James B. Kilsheimer, III. Jim at the age of twenty-nine, we called "the old man." I reported back to Mr. Saypol: "We'll be ready in three weeks."

We built our case rapidly but carefully. We knew that in Remington we had a defendant at least as bright as and probably more cunning than Alger Hiss. In many ways, the two men's stories bore remarkable similarities. Hiss at first denied knowing Whittaker Chambers. But when that line became untenable, he suddenly "recognized" him. (Chambers' teeth had been fixed, Hiss had explained, altering his appearance.) But Hiss said he had known Chambers as a writer, not as a Communist. And he worked out fascinating little explanations for every tangible piece of information Chambers furnished. Similarly, when he was first interviewed by the FBI, Remington had denied knowing Miss Bentley and Jacob Golos. When evidence multiplied refuting this, he suddenly recalled them, but not as Communists. Miss Bentley, for example, was a newspaper reporter.

The defense staff, we discovered, was attempting some interesting stratagems in behalf of its client. Several of our key witnesses came from the Knoxville area. They knew of Remington's Communist activities when he was associated with the TVA there, and we were relying to a considerable extent on their testimony. Remington's counsel, former New York corporation counsel William C. Chanler, knew this too, so he dispatched some of his Ivy League juniors to the Great Smokies to attempt to defuse any damaging witnesses they could find.

Their first target was Kenneth McConnell, the Communist organizer in the TVA area who had broken with the party. One young Chanler aide went to see Mr. McConnell at his North Carolina chicken farm. Before paying him a personal visit, he made inquiries in the neighborhood about Mr. McConnell and learned that the chicken farmer enjoyed an occasional bout with the bottle. In fact, Mr. McConnell had been arrested and fined a number of times on charges arising from his drinking habits.

The young Ivy League lawyer got an idea. He would invite McConnell to a local tavern for a chat, buy him a few drinks, and, hopefully, after a while, the liquor would loosen up McConnell and a few facts that might exonerate Remington would slip out. At the bar, he ordered a bottle of Scotch and two setups. He poured two thirds of a glass for McConnell and a little for himself. Later, McConnell told me: "It was obvious the poor kid never had taken a drink in his life. When he finished pouring mine, I told him to pour one for himself too." It was not Ken McConnell who had to be carried out of the bar that afternoon.

Before McConnell took the stand at the trial, I went over his past record with him. While a Communist he had used different names, and he had been arrested several times for intoxication. I decided not to wait for Chanler to bring all this out on cross-examination, to discredit our witness. So on direct examination I had McConnell speak frankly of his drinking habits, showing they had no relation to his knowledge of Remington's Communist activities in Knoxville. He was not discredited on cross-examination.

But McConnell gave us another type of headache. He insisted that the Government furnish him with a qualified, experienced, and responsible chicken-sitter to mind the 15,000 fowl on his Weaverville, North Carolina, farm while he was testifying in New York. He told us he wouldn't come up until proper arrangements had been made. His demand caused a minor crisis in the Department of Justice offices at Foley Square until somebody found a regulation that covered the expenditure of funds for such a purpose. After the trial, McConnell gave the department further woes—he demanded reimbursement for the loss of some 150 chickens that died, he said, because they had not been properly handled by the Government's chicken caretaker. I don't know what happened to this request.

Remington's trial opened early in January, 1951. Chanler's opening to the jury was, in effect, an attack on Elizabeth Bentley. Then, shortly before adjournment on the first day, Irving Saypol announced his first witness and a slender brunette stepped forward. She was not, as everyone expected, Elizabeth Bentley, but Remington's divorced wife, Ann. A look of acute puzzlement spread across the face of Defense Counsel Chanler, who had obviously built most of his defense on discrediting Miss Bentley.

Quietly, tersely, Ann Remington told of her early acquaintance with Remington, whom she said she had known since 1937 when she was a student at Radcliffe. She told of a conversation they had had one evening as they sat parked in her car near a Dartmouth dormitory. "He told me he was a member of the Communist party," she testified, "and abjured me to secrecy on that." In 1938, she said, Remington told her he was dropping out of the Young Communist League. "It was more expedient and he could do more good outside," she testified. About her marriage, she said, "One of the requirements I asked was that he would continue to be a Communist. He said I need not worry on that score." She testified that during the time they lived in New York, they distributed Communist literature door-to-door. On their move to Washington, she said, Remington felt "out of touch" with the party, so he had Joe North introduce him to "John" —Jacob Golos.

Elizabeth Bentley later supplied a wealth of detail about Remington's involvement with her and the espionage conspiracy. Remington's defense was that he had never handled any classified material, hence could not have given any to Miss Bentley. But she remembered all the facts about the rubber-from-garbage invention. We had searched through the archives and discovered the files on the process. We also found the aircraft schedules, which were set up exactly as she said, and interoffice memos and tables of personnel which proved Remington had access to both these items.

We also discovered Remington's application for a naval commission in which he specifically pointed out that he was, in his present position with the Commerce Department, entrusted with secret military information involving airplanes, armaments, radar, and the Manhattan Project (the atomic bomb).

While Paul Crouch, a former Communist functionary, was checking reports that Remington had subscribed to a newspaper called the *Southern Worker,* which was the southern edition of the *Daily Worker,* he came upon something a good deal more significant. The Knoxville post-office box at which he received the *Worker* was the official box of the Communist party, and only trusted Communist party members were allowed to use it.

Crouch was called to the stand as a surprise witness. It was a dramatic afternoon. His son was dying in Miami, and we obtained special permission to have him called out of order. Chanler, visibly shaken when Crouch produced the Remington subscription card and told about the post-office box, asked to examine all the other cards that Crouch had in the shoe box—with a view toward showing that non-Communists as well as Communists subscribed to the *Worker.* Chanler passed the box to his staff of assistants sitting alongside him at the counsel table.

An aide was left shuffling the cards in the box. Suddenly, his eyes lit up, and he excitedly motioned to Mr. Chanler. I was sure they were about to show that J. Edgar Hoover or George Sokolsky also were on the subscription list! Chanler walked forward triumphantly with the card. He showed it to Crouch, and asked, "Was this one of your subscribers, too?"

Crouch, who has been on the editorial board of the *Southern Worker,* studied the card, and replied, "Yes." Anxiously, I asked to see it. It read: "Businessmen's Lunch Club, Chattanooga, Tennessee." I now knew why Chanler was so pleased. If a group of businessmen subscribed and received the paper at their lunch club, Remington's subscription would not be damaging. I gave Crouch a sick look but he winked and smiled at me. I got up and said: "No objection"—leaving Chanler free to read the card aloud. The spectators burst into laughter. Then Chanler turned to Crouch and asked:

Q: This one, the subscriber's the Businessman's Lunch, 25 East Ninth Street, Chattanooga, Tennessee. Do you know what the organization was?
A: I do very well.
Q: What was that?

A: It was a restaurant operated by a very active member of the Communist party and was a favorite meeting place of the Communist leaders in Chattanooga, Tennessee.

Chanler was stunned. We had scored decisively.

All together, the prosecution produced eleven witnesses, most of them former Communists, who testified they had known Remington as a political collaborator. In addition to McConnell, Miss Bentley, and Mrs. Remington, the witnesses included Rudolph Bertram, former TVA personnel director, who swore Remington had tried to get him to join the party; and Professor Howard Bridgeman of Tufts University and Christine Benson, a former TVA employee, who testified they had attended party meetings with Remington in Knoxville.

Remington's defense was based upon the claim that although he had had a casual flirtation with left-wing causes in his youthful years, he had never taken the step of joining the Communist party nor had he ever passed any of his country's secrets to anybody. His parents and a number of character witnesses appeared in his behalf. Remington himself took the stand, testifying that his college reputation as a Communist stemmed from joking references he made to himself as a "bolshevik." He insisted that he had never gone to any Communist party meetings in Knoxville, that he had never paid any dues to the party, and that he had not known Elizabeth Bentley as a Communist spy but as a newspaper reporter.

The testimony was predictable and answerable. For me, the most exciting moment in the trial came toward its close during the defense presentation. We learned that the defense was planning to produce a witness next day whom we knew only by his last name, Martin. There were two possibilities, since there were two Martin brothers who were in Knoxville with Remington. One was David Stone Martin, the other Francis Martin. I asked the FBI and our own investigators to obtain all the official records they could get their hands on about the two Martins, including personnel files. It was and is my practice to know as much about the cast of players as is possible.

Late that night, the last file arrived from Washington. An FBI agent looked through it and came over to me to report. He said that David Martin had been questioned under the Civil Service loyalty program about his activities in Knoxville years before. I asked if there was anything significant in his answers. The agent, with a straight face, said there was one answer I might want to see. I picked up the file and read the page he cited. I stared almost unbelievingly.

In the course of an answer in his loyalty quiz, David Martin had sworn in 1943 that while in Knoxville he had not known many Communists—"except Bill Remington. He was one of the towns-people and everyone knew him as a character. He was a young fellow who was fanatical in his political beliefs. I won't deny that he was a Communist, as that was well known, because he approached every-one and asked them to join the Communist party . . ."

This from the lips of a defense witness called by Remington. It would be a hell of a cross-examination!

Next day, Attorney Chanler called David Stone Martin as his first witness. Apparently all that Chanler had wanted to establish through him was that there was a sort of hot-rod atmosphere in Knoxville at the time, and that Remington was part of it. Direct examination was soon complete.

We had Irving Saypol all primed for cross. He asked some routine questions. Then he had Martin say that he always told the truth. If he had made statements to the Civil Service Commission years before—which he did not now recall—of course they would be the truth. He was then shown his interrogatories of 1943, which he recognized. We then read certain inconsequential ones to him. As to each answer, he impatiently asserted it was the truth—all his answers were the truth.

At this point, Saypol, smiling, walked toward the witness chair. Those in the courtroom knew that something was up, for Irving was not known for his warm treatment of defense witnesses. As defense witness Martin's own words, naming the man for whom he was testifying as an active Communist, rang through the courtroom, I knew that we had scored a devastating point. Later, while deliberat-ing, the jury asked for a copy of this 1943 statement by Martin.

The jury was out a short time. It received the case in the late afternoon and by 10 P.M., Judge Noonan received a note that the jury had agreed upon a verdict. The foreman stood and said, "We find the defendant guilty as charged."

In August, the U.S. Circuit Court of Appeals reversed the perjury conviction on the ground that Judge Noonan's charge to the jury had been "too vague and indefinite" in defining exactly what constituted party "membership." The court, which did not touch upon the guilt or innocence of the defendant, ordered a new trial to be held.

It seemed likely to me that a conviction on this charge might never stand up because the Court of Appeals failed to say what it would accept as a definition of "membership." It was ironical that the very kind of democracy Remington sought to undermine had come to his aid. As *The New York Times* stated in an editorial following the reversal: "The judicial reasoning in the reversal may be difficult for the lay mind to follow. What is not difficult to follow is that in the case of Mr. Remington, who denies ever having been a Communist, as in the cases of the admitted leaders of the Communist party, the accused persons have been given every benefit of the law."

Night after night, I sat home, poring over Remington's testimony at the trial. There was no question in my mind that he had lied to the court.

—He had denied turning over secret information to Elizabeth Bentley—yet she had testified that he gave documents to her and we had produced copies of some of the documents.

—He had denied that he had attended Communist party meetings in Knoxville—yet witness after witness, all former Communists, had come forth to swear that Remington had attended the meetings.

—He had denied that he had paid dues to the Communist party— yet both Miss Bentley and his own former wife had said that he did.

—He had denied that he had asked anyone to join the party—yet his former boss at the TVA had testified Remington had asked him.

—He had denied even knowing about the existence of the Young Communist League at Dartmouth while he was an undergraduate— yet a classmate had said they had discussed the organization when they were students.

The list was long. Several mornings later, I asked Jack Foley and Al Blinder: "Can someone be indicted for perjury committed while testifying at his own trial, even though his conviction was reversed on appeal?"

They would check the precedents. Soon Al came back and said, "The answer is yes. There's a Supreme Court decision that hits it squarely on the nose."

Instead of retrying Remington on the original indictment, we decided to move against him for perjury committed at his own trial because the issues were simple and clear—the statements were true or they were false. There were no complicating factors, such as a definition of "membership."

Remington's lawyers hit the ceiling, calling the move "a vicious device" to avoid a Supreme Court review of the original conviction. (It was nothing of the sort—because within a short time, on March 24, 1952, the U.S. Supreme Court rejected an appeal by Remington for an outright acquittal.) Actually, the indictment we obtained was based on a new set of lies made by Remington at a different time.

Remington was tried once again.

The end of the long drama came in the early hours of a cold January morning in 1953. At 3:40 A.M., a jury of eleven men and one woman announced its verdict to a nearly empty courtroom. Remington, the jury found, lied when he denied giving secret Government information to Elizabeth Bentley. And he lied when he denied he had known of the Young Communist League at Dartmouth.

On February 4, 1953, he was sentenced to a three-year term. The Court of Appeals upheld the conviction, the Supreme Court denied Remington's application to be heard, and he disappeared behind the walls of the Federal penitentiary at Lewisburg, Pennsylvania.

Remington's supporters were finally silenced. There were no more emotional defenses, no more profiles describing the agony of a man "wrongly accused," no more charges of "witch-hunt." James Wechsler did not even mention the name of William Remington in the two books he wrote about the period.

Twenty-one months later, three fellow convicts crept into Remington's cell while he was asleep and bludgeoned him with a brick wrapped in a stocking. Remington staggered out and collapsed at the foot of a stairs. He died sixteen hours later in the prison hospital. At first there was suspicion that Remington had been murdered for his political views. Later it was disclosed that there had been other motives. It was a tragic end to what might have been a brilliant career.

Before the curtain descended, a revealing incident was enacted in my office when I signed Remington's bail bond. For a few tense minutes we were alone. A conversation started in the course of which I said as sympathetically as I could that sometimes people get in water over their heads. He said that sometimes one has no alternative. I said that in this predicament there is an alternative, the acknowledgment of past mistakes. Remington, after a long silence, answered that sometimes it was too late to tell the full truth, because to tell it would let down a lot of persons who had risked a great deal on their belief in a friend's innocence.

To end this discussion I said, "Well, of course, we've been talking hypothetically anyway." He said, "No, Mr. Cohn, we both know we've been talking about me." I was moved. I felt myself to be in the presence of tragedy.

CHAPTER 4

OUR PATHS CONVERGE

T HROUGH THE YEARS I have read and heard many different stories about how Senator McCarthy and I met and joined forces. Rovere, who has become a kind of one-man bureau of misinformation on the subject, insists that Walter Winchell brought us together. Other versions were equally fanciful, including one that I simply knocked on the Senator's door and asked for a job. It hardly ranks with Boswell's historic meeting with Johnson, but here is the truth of it.

I first met the Senator early in December, 1952, in a hotel suite so overcrowded that it reminded me of a scene from a Marx Brothers film. Among the dozens of men and women in formal dress the Senator had removed his jacket, shirt, and tie. He wore tuxedo trousers, patent leather shoes—and suspenders over a T-shirt.

He had just won reelection, and because the Republicans had captured the Senate, was slated to become chairman of the powerful Senate Subcommittee on Investigations of the Committee on Government Operations. He had asked Robert Morris, chief counsel for the Senate Subcommittee on Internal Security of the Senate Judiciary Committee, to arrange a meeting with me. Morris had called me a few days earlier, saying the Senator would be in New York to address a veterans' organization, and wanted to talk with me. Could I come to his suite at the Hotel Astor about 11 P.M.?

His suite was easily identifiable by the dozens of persons milling outside. I made my way through and walked into the bedroom where Bob Morris saw me and introduced me to the Senator. McCarthy greeted me warmly. He possessed a rare gift of personality: he could be talking to a roomful of people and yet, by riveting attention on one person for a few moments, could convey the feeling that only that person's conversation was of consequence.

I recall vividly his first words to me: "My God, I'm glad to meet you—but you can't possibly be one-tenth as good as everyone says you are. I just want to find out what's public relations and what's real." I would have been less than human had I not been pleased.

He took me aside and talked to me in what for him was privacy. (There were always people around McCarthy.) "You know, I'm going to be chairman of the investigating committee in the Senate. They're all trying to push me off the Communism issue. A lot of people down there are advising me that I'm now in a strong political position and should not jeopardize it by continuing this fight. They're pointing to all the others who tried and were shot down. The sensible thing for me to do, they say, is start investigating the agriculture program or find out how many books they've got bound upside down at the Library of Congress. They want me to play it safe.

"I fought this Red issue. I won the primary on it, I won the election on it, and I don't see anyone else around who intends to take it on. You can be sure that as chairman of this committee this is going to be my work. And I want you to help me. I'm not sure in what capacity, but keep in touch with me. And I'll be in touch with you." Although the entire conversation had lasted only about three minutes, the lasting impression on me of this first meeting was of the man's energy and contagious spirit. He was jovial, hearty, outgoing. He wanted to be liked and he was liked.

I consulted a number of friends. There was a division of opinion. To a young man of twenty-five, it was a challenge and an opportunity that was virtually irresistible. But before making my decision, I had serious thoughts about the advice given me earlier by Federal Judge Irving Kaufman when I was asked to become special assistant to United States Attorney General McGranery in Washington, a job I accepted in August, 1952, and was holding at the time I met McCarthy. Judge Kaufman had advised against my acceptance. He spoke at length about the jealousies and intrigues in Washington which often made it impossible for a man to get a job done. The words turned out to be prophetic.

But the more I thought about McCarthy's suggestion, the more I was tempted. The job, if it came, would be an extension of the work I had been doing. I was convinced also that because of the special powers enjoyed by committees of the Congress, the work could be pursued with great effectiveness.

A few days later, McCarthy communicated with me again through George Sokolsky, the columnist. He called me in Florida and told me that I was being considered for a chief counsel's post with one of the Senate committees. The feeling was that perhaps I was a little young for the McCarthy committee job, and that it might be better if Bob Morris transferred there from the Internal Security Subcommittee, while I took his job. I suggested that since both committees occasionally operated in a common area, it might be wise to arrange some kind of staff coordination in order to avoid duplicating work.

Two or three days later, Sokolsky called again, reporting that a complication had arisen: Joseph P. Kennedy, the former ambassador, had telephoned McCarthy, asking if Bobby Kennedy could be appointed chief counsel.

Joe McCarthy, George told me, was anxious to "do something" for Joe Kennedy because of their close friendship. The Senator told the elder Kennedy he would name Bobby to his staff but hesitated about making him chief counsel because of Bobby's limited legal experience.

Since Joe Kennedy had contributed to McCarthy's reelection campaign fund, the Senator was concerned lest the appointment of Bobby to his staff be construed as a quid pro quo. "Joe is going to try to talk Joe Kennedy into having Bobby take a lesser spot at the beginning," Sokolsky told me. "Then, after a while, he will be moved forward. This should satisfy him."

Next I learned that Bob Morris had decided to remain with the Internal Security Subcommittee and that Bobby Kennedy would become assistant to Francis D. Flanagan, then general counsel to the McCarthy committee. Kennedy would be broken in for a few weeks, after which Flanagan would leave and I would take over as chief counsel.

A call came directly from Senator McCarthy: Would I take the post? I brought up the question of my personal political affiliation. I was a Democrat. Wouldn't it be awkward for a committee under Republican control to have a Democrat as chief counsel? "I couldn't care less about your politics," the Senator said. "I'm interested only in your ability to do the job."

Early in January, 1953, I went to Washington. A party was given for me that will not be duplicated in my experience. Those present included Vice-President Nixon, J. Edgar Hoover, some twenty senators, White House representatives, etc. My father came down for it. It was heady wine, I don't mind admitting.

In Washington my first problem was Bobby Kennedy, a problem that has escaped solution to the present day. Through friends I learned that he was disappointed at his failure to obtain the chief counsel's post. Moreover, he did not intend to accept McCarthy's arrangement just yet. I had been told his plan called for Flanagan to be retained as chief counsel, with himself as assistant. Presumably, this would satisfy the Senator's doubts about his lack of experience. Then, when McCarthy felt he had acquired enough seasoning in the subordinate position, he could move Bobby into Flanagan's job.

McCarthy could rarely say no to anybody. He committed himself to letting Flanagan remain at least for a short time. But it also turned out that McCarthy had no intention of dispensing with me.

A press conference was held announcing the staff changes. Just before he left his office for a committee session, which was to be followed by a meeting with the newsmen, Joe mumbled something I couldn't catch about Flanagan. Later, after the conference, a reporter told me: "You've been named chief counsel."

I wasn't surprised. But when he said, "And Flanagan's been named general counsel—what does that mean?" I was astounded. I hadn't the faintest notion what it meant. By this time, the reporters had followed McCarthy into his office. One asked, "Senator, you stated that Mr. Cohn is becoming chief counsel for the committee and that Mr. Flanagan is to remain as general counsel. Who is superior to whom? What does each title mean?" There was a long pause. Then McCarthy broke into a wide grin, spread his hands and confessed: "I don't know." And he actually did not. He kept Flanagan to placate Joe Kennedy. He made me chief counsel because he wanted me to direct the Communist hearings. But he had not figured out who was going to do what. I had my first hint of the chaos that was to prevail.

The Investigations subcommittee on which I began serving as chief counsel was delegated by Congress to keep watch over the Executive branch of our government. Charged with investigating governmental activities at all levels, the subcommittee had wide jurisdiction. The extent of our responsibility may be gauged by the fact that as of January 1, 1953, the Executive branch encompassed 2,115 separate departments, agencies, and independent offices employing 2,564,111 persons in a civilian capacity alone. To keep this giant functioning, Congress had appropriated for the fiscal year commencing July 1, 1953, nearly three billion dollars.

As watchdog over the workings of the Executive arm, the subcommittee as we saw it had two principal functions:

1. To investigate instances of waste or inefficiency. Our efforts led to the saving of millions of dollars in the engineering programs of the International Information Administration alone.

2. To concentrate chiefly on evidence of subversion. This, as we soon discovered, was often frustrating. Confronted by forces powerful enough to rally wide support in blocking any investigation, we found that anyone who tried to assist the subcommittee risked verbal attack and sometimes even political ruin.

These investigations were prompted by many sources. Some were suggested by members of the Committee on Government Operations under which our subcommittee functioned. Others were proposed by individual members of Congress or by agencies of the Executive branch itself. Sometimes we checked on reports of subversion supplied by private citizens and organizations. If such information seemed reliable, we investigated.

It has been alleged that Senator McCarthy and I had a large organization of underground agents, a network of spies feeding us information from all over the globe. This is nonsense. Our "network" consisted of many random letters and telephone calls from individuals who felt they had information valuable to us. Often it was misinformation; often it came from cranks and crackpots; but sometimes it stemmed from authentic sources and proved valuable.

It was not our function or our aim to have a voice in the operation of the Executive or any of its agencies. Nor did we have the desire or authority to send anyone to prison. That was the job of the Department of Justice and the Court. But we knew how to investigate inefficiency and subversion and we intended to do just that. A number of the subcommittee staff were lawyers or former members of the FBI and experienced in investigating techniques.

What yardstick did we use to determine if an individual was a potential threat to national security? We adopted the standards set up and used by United States agencies, particularly the State Department.

There are two types of "risks"—loyalty and security, of which the loyalty risk is the more serious. Sometimes the two have been confused. As a practical matter, had we sought only "card-carrying members" of the party, we probably would not have found any—except perhaps sentimental ones who were carrying cards as souvenirs—for in the late 1940's the party had ordered all membership cards withdrawn.

In 1947, John Peurifoy, then Deputy Undersecretary of State for Administration, said the department felt that any reasonable doubt as to an individual's loyalty should be resolved in favor of the Government. We thought this was sensible and fair and adopted it as our guide. As McCarthy once told me: "The test is not whether a man or woman is guilty beyond a reasonable doubt of espionage or Communist party membership, but whether the circumstances are such that we cannot take a chance when we are dealing with a sensitive post in a sensitive area." Circumstances, he said, should include irrefutable evidence that the individual had associated voluntarily with Communists or Communist sympathizers. Nor did McCarthy invent this last standard either—he took it from the State Department's own yardstick by which loyalty risks were measured.

Then there were security risks. General Conrad E. Snow, chairman of the State Department's Loyalty Security Board, stated that a security risk might be "an employee who talks too much, or who drinks to excess, or who is careless in the kind of people with whom he associates." The fact is that the standards were not enforced with any regularity. The FBI would send confidential reports to agencies containing information establishing that certain individuals were loyalty or security risks. The agencies were not bound to act on these reports. They could—and often did—bury them. The FBI was then helpless. When agencies did take administrative action, they were often rebuffed by the Review Board. Only a congressional committee had the jurisdiction and forum to expose these private cover-ups. Edward Rothschild remained in the Government Printing Office despite dozens of FBI reports concerning his communist activities—until he was exposed by our committee. Remington was "cleared" by the Loyalty Review Board until exposure by the House Committee led to his ultimate conviction. And Harry Dexter White rose to even greater power until exposure and subsequent revelation by Attorney General Brownell demonstrated that even the President had been fooled.

As time and our investigations went on, more and more criticism was voiced about our "methods." The "methods" criticism was, I believe, totally unfair. Our opponents were clever enough to avoid fighting back on the main battleground of what we were trying to accomplish. The criticism was almost always diverted to the question of how we were doing it.

To the assertion: "I don't like the way you go about things," I would respond: "What don't you like about the 'methods'? What is wrong with them?" The answer was always the same: "Innocent people are accused, innocent people are smeared."

Circumstantial evidence and indirect evidence can point to an individual's possible involvement in any type of illegal activity, including espionage. And it is possible that after the individual has been summoned and has given a full explanation, and after other witnesses are heard, the accusation will turn out to be baseless. This has happened before congressional investigating committees as it has happened in courts of law and before grand juries.

Under our grand jury system, indictments that are handed down are duly published in the newspapers and broadcast over radio and television. If an important case or person is involved, the entire nation is informed that the individual has been accused of a cime. He has not been convicted of a crime, and at this stage he is presumed innocent. Nonetheless, he receives adverse publicity: his friends, neighbors, and business associates talk and wonder. The law has published a document charging him with certain offenses.

A trial follows. In 80 to 90 percent of the cases in most jurisdictions, the indicted individual is convicted. In the minority of cases, the accusation is not sustained and the indicted person goes free.

Our committee gave witnesses and "suspects" rights that they do not enjoy in a court of law. For example, every witness that came before us had the right to have beside him at all times, in closed or open session, an attorney of his choosing to advise him. A witness before a grand jury or while on the stand in court does not have that right. The use of executive sessions, from which the press and public were excluded, also helped protect the witness. Hundreds of persons were called by the McCarthy committee every year and were told of the evidence that had been collected against them. If they were able to offer satisfactory explanations—and most did—they were dismissed and nobody ever knew they had been summoned.

As a memorable example of the unfair criticisms of our "methods," President Eisenhower in his memoirs, *Mandate for Change,* condemns McCarthy for making "wild charges" against James Bryant Conant, Harvard president, when Eisenhower nominated him United

States High Commissioner of Germany. Eisenhower said that the charges were contained in a letter sent to the President by the Senator. The facts are as follows:

In early 1953 McCarthy asked Bill Buckley to prepare a speech specifying why Conant should not be named. Three points were made. "None of them remotely insinuated that Dr. Conant might be disloyal. None of them was in any way 'wild,' " Buckley says. The speech pointed out that Conant was a poor choice because: 1) he was one of the earliest endorsers of the Morgenthau Plan* for Germany; 2) he did not, as witness his then-recent call for the abolition of private schools and certain other cited articles and speeches, truly understand American life, and so was not in a good position to be our representative to a renascent Germany searching for free ideals; and 3) in the field of security, an important responsibility of a High Commissioner, he was naïve, as witness his then-recent statement about the presumptive immunity of Harvard from penetration by even a single Communist. (It is inconceivable, he had told a congressional committee, that any member of the Harvard faculty was a Communist. To which the obvious reply, of course, was that it was inconceivable that the Communist party, over the years, should think of Harvard as too unimportant a place to try to penetrate.)

Senator Robert Taft, learning of the speech, prevailed upon McCarthy not to deliver it mainly because it would remind Germans of Conant's now-forgotten endorsement of the Morgenthau Plan and quite possibly limit his effectiveness in Germany. So instead McCarthy put his thoughts into a personal letter to the President. Eisenhower responded with a cordial note thanking him for his action and acknowledging the seriousness of the points made, though stating once again that he felt Conant to be the proper choice for the post.

How then could Eisenhower say in his memoirs that McCarthy was guilty of "wild charges" against Conant? McCarthy sent Buckley the Eisenhower letter but Buckley is unable to find it. Eisenhower has the only copy. On January 9th, Buckley wrote to Eisenhower, enclosing a statement of all the facts and requesting a copy of the letter. In March, 1964, Buckley published a plea to Eisenhower "to clear the matter up, in fairness to a dead man, by releasing a copy of his letter

---

* This provided that Germany, following its defeat, be stripped of its heavy industries and be converted into a nation mainly agricultural.

to Senator McCarthy." The General has not responded either to the letter or the published plea.

In its role of watchdog over the agencies of the Executive branch, the subcommittee exposed a disturbing lack of security in the Government Printing Office. Along with a lot of other pamphlets and books, the GPO also prints top-secret documents. Aware of the need to keep such sensitive material out of the wrong hands, officials of the GPO separated classified portions of secret documents before they were set in type for printing. These segments were eventually pieced together in the Assembly Section. Our investigators discovered that several clerks with records of Communist activity were working in this sensitive spot.

The GPO had its loyalty board for uncovering security cases, but the panel seemed to follow a policy of hearing only testimony favorable to "risks." It adhered to the rule that "mere membership" in the Communist party was not in itself sufficient ground to bar anyone from working in the GPO.

Among the proved security risks working in the Assembly Section was Edward Rothschild, about whom the FBI had already submitted some forty reports citing evidence that he was an active party member who had recruited others for the party. At hearings of the subcommittee in 1953, Rothschild was confronted with evidence of his party membership and recruiting activities. Witnesses, including Mary Markward, an undercover agent for the FBI, identified Rothschild as an active member. The investigation bore fruit. The principal security risks we had uncovered were discharged from the GPO, and Rothschild was removed from government employ altogether.

The GPO's loyalty board was dismissed and replaced by a new panel. And, corrective legislation was introduced by Senator Dirksen of the subcommittee.

This investigation, particularly the exposure of Rothschild, demonstrated the need for congressional committees like ours, and refuted assumptions that the executive branch and the Justice Department were able to cope with all violations of law and all security problems arising inside Government agencies. The head of the agency congratulated us. Charles Ford, counsel for Rothschild, thanked us for the "fairest hearing." He had been permitted to advise his client and to have questions asked by the chair of witnesses hostile to his client.

Our investigation of the GPO produced an amusing sidelight that had nothing to do with security, but gave an idea of the haphazard way that office functioned at the time. By chance, we discovered that a group of GPO staff members were running a flourishing bookmaking operation right in the office.

Many witnesses invoked the First and Fifth Amendments. The First Amendment provides no valid excuse for not answering; freedom of speech is not involved. As to the Fifth Amendment, however, we recognized witnesses' right to invoke it. We are a government of laws, not men, and the constitutional privilege against self-incrimination was of course respected by us. I am glad of this, for subsequent experience has demonstrated to me the dangers of excessive powers when placed in the hands of unscrupulous and self-seeking prosecutors, particularly when engaged in personal vendettas.

This begs the subsidiary question of what if any inference can be drawn from one's invocation of the Fifth Amendment. Does it follow that anyone who invokes it is automatically conceding involvement? The answer to this question must be different today from what it was fifteen years ago. A series of recent Supreme Court decisions points up the perils of a witness who is not in fact guilty, but is placed in jeopardy nonetheless. The legal development as of today suggests that no inference may be drawn. The ancipital nature of the problem always confused me. I could see so much logic on both sides of the argument that I would say my inclination is to avoid an inference unless the invocation is accompanied by affirmative proof of involvement.

Two or more investigations were often carried on concurrently by our subcommittee. This put a considerable strain on members of our staff, but it gave us a clearer picture of what was going on in the various Executive branches.

During our probe of the GPO, for example, we launched an investigation of the security situation in the nation's defense plants. We soon found there was urgent need for a housecleaning in these vital factories. We focused our attention on thirteen plants whose contracts with the Government ran into hundreds of millions a year in supplies for the armed forces, including sophisticated weaponry. Our investigators were seasoned men, but in spite of considerable experience with subversion in Government agencies, they were stunned to find scores of outright security risks holding important positions of trust in strategic plants where with little difficulty they could, if they chose, paralyze important parts of our defense effort.

During the course of the probe, 101 witnesses appeared before the subcommittee. Two informants—William H. Teto, who had been employed by the General Electric Company at Fitchburg, Massachusetts, and Herman E. Thomas, who had observed Communists at work in the great Bethlehem Steel Company—provided information concerning the Red spy network.

Teto testified that in 1945 Richard Linsley, international representative of the United Electrical Workers Union, summoned Communist employees of General Electric's Fitchburg plant to a meeting in Boston. There, Teto stated, they received a pep talk from Fannie Hackman, organizational director of the party, who told them that their mission was to "colonize" G.E. plants and all other basic industries in America. Teto explained that "colonize" in the Communist lexicon meant to take control of the shops and that their goal at the moment was "three cell members working in any war plant."

The party displayed the same efficiency boring into the steel industry. Thomas testified that vital information about activities in certain steel plants was channeled by Communist workers to a district commission, where the data was evaluated and forwarded to the National Steel Commission of the Communist party. Finally the information was correlated, Thomas testified, and sent to the Soviet Union. This same procedure of gathering and digesting classified material and relaying it to the international Communist apparatus applied to all basic defense industries, he disclosed. The question immediately arose in the minds of subcommittee members, How do known Communists obtain employment in the defense plants of efficiently run corporations? In part the answer appeared to lie in the fact that two or three powerful unions involved in defense work were Communist-dominated.

As a result of the subcommittee's exposures, twenty-eight employees working in vital plants were discharged outright, and four were suspended and later dismissed.

The investigation had other far-reaching results. General Electric, for instance, drastically revised its security regulations. Its policy statement, signed by President Ralph J. Cordiner, read: "The company has noted with great concern the public hearings of congressional committees in which some General Electric employees, though few in number, have refused to answer questions concerning espionage, sabotage, or their Communist affiliations. . . . The company has grave doubts concerning the possible danger to the safety and security of company property and personnel whenever a General Electric employee admits he is a Communist or when he asserts before a competent investigating Government body that he might incriminate himself by giving truthful answers concerning his Communist affiliations or his possible espionage or sabotage activities. Such conduct by General Electric employees also undermines the confidence of the Government and the public that the vital productive facilities of General Electric will be fully and immediately available to the country in time of national crisis. . . ."

Communists operating directly inside the government played a major role in one of the most extraordinary transactions ever given official stamp: the unprecedented transfer of our currency plates to the Soviet Union. In April, 1944, an agreement was reached in Washington between Ambassador Andrei Gromyko and our top Treasury officials, and shortly afterward our equipment was handed over so that the Soviets could print Occupation money. Alvin W. Hall, director of the Bureau of Engraving and Printing, told us there was no other record in history of delivery from one sovereign government to another of plates for the printing of currency.

The transfer of plates had been the subject of a prior investigation by Senator Styles Bridges, who found that a few years later the United States had to redeem with its own funds at least $225,000,-000 in Allied military marks. The Soviet Union was not held accountable for a cent. Bridges' investigation did not disclose, however, how the Kremlin managed to bring about this bizarre transfer of American currency-making equipment, including the actual printing plates, paper specifications, formulas for the proper ink, and complete directions on how to run off the notes. In 1953 our subcommittee discovered that the transfer was engineered by a Communist spy cell operating within the U.S. Department of the Treasury. Its aim was to turn U.S. monetary plates over to the Red Army so that the Soviet occupation of Germany, and the pay for Red troops then

(April, 1944) driving westward in Europe, could be carried out without cost to the Soviet Union.

The central figure in this strange drama was Harry Dexter White, Assistant Secretary of the Treasury and U.S. Representative on the International Monetary Fund. The senators on the subcommittee reported that White "had risen to this position of responsibility and advantage at the policy-making level while a member of the Communist party and a member of an espionage ring." While wearing the cloak of confidant and adviser, he could "press for favorable consideration of policies, decisions, and dispositions designed to fulfill the desires of his foreign master." He "could and did betray the confidences of these inner-circle operations via the espionage group to a foreign government." Details supplied by Elizabeth Bentley and information given by Mr. Hall of the Bureau of Engraving and Daniel W. Bell, former Undersecretary of the Treasury, enabled us to piece together the story of this betrayal. Miss Bentley testified that in late 1943 or early 1944, her Russian espionage superior instructed her to obtain samples of U.S. occupation currency through White, who supplied them. Here is what happened, as disclosed by Miss Bentley:

MR. LA VENIA (of the subcommittee): Where were these samples of occupation currency delivered to you?

BENTLEY: In the Silvermaster home.

LA VENIA: Where had they been procured?

BENTLEY: They had been procured from the Treasury.

LA VENIA: Do you know from whom in the Treasury they had been procured?

BENTLEY: It was my understanding that they came from Mr. White's office.

LA VENIA: That is Harry Dexter White?

BENTLEY: Yes.

When La Venia asked her where she took the notes, she replied that she gave them to her Soviet contact in New York. "What was the next step?" she was asked.

BENTLEY: Well, either the next meeting or the one after that, which would make it either two weeks or a month, they were returned to me, with the comment that they were unable to photograph them so that they would be useful,

> *and that therefore we must ask the Silvermasters to put*
> *pressure on Mr. White to turn over the plates for making*
> *the marks to the Russians.* [my italics]

And this is precisely what the Soviet agents succeeded in doing. Hall disclosed that he received orders in April, 1944, from Secretary of the Treasury Morgenthau to turn the plates and all the needed equipment to print U.S. currency over to Soviet Ambassador Gromyko. Both Hall and Bell objected strenuously, but to no avail. Bell said White had urged that the transfer be made and personally supervised the negotiations.

The plates were taken in secrecy aboard an Army truck to the Soviet embassy. It was a classic example of the Soviet strategy of working at two levels when they wanted to get something from another government. While Soviet diplomats maneuvered openly through the State Department to obtain the plates, their spy network operated under cover in the right places to make sure the transfer went through.

To critics who may still wonder aloud what the McCarthy subcommittee accomplished, I commend this statement in our report of the case: "This particular operation clearly indicates the need for a tighter security in all the free capitals of the world if the cause of freedom and the peace of the world is not to be jeopardized by the infiltration of Communist agents into top-level positions in our Government and that of friendly nations where they directly influence decisions to the direct advantage of Soviet imperialistic communism." We hoped that the hearings would have the effect of preventing similar incidents.

We know that if the committee's warnings had been heeded, we would not in 1968 be reading about Harold Philby, who waltzed through British security into the key post on the Communist desk of British Intelligence itself, from which vantage point he spied for the Soviet Union until the day he went behind the Iron Curtain himself.

Soon after the subcommittee completed its investigation of the currency case, it was caught up in an unforeseen internal crisis that suddenly ballooned into a national sensation. McCarthy became the target of impassioned attacks by some of the nation's most prominent clergymen, as well as by his Democratic colleagues in Congress and finally by the White House itself.

The storm swirled around the figure of J. B. Matthews, Methodist minister who had served energetically as director of research for the House Un-American Activities Committee from 1938 to 1945. Matthews, who had not held a pastorate for some years, was embarking on a new assignment as staff director of our subcommittee.

The furor was touched off by an article by Matthews in the *American Mercury* for July, 1953, a few weeks after McCarthy had announced his appointment. The opening sentence read: "The largest group supporting the Communist apparatus in the United States today is composed of Protestant clergymen."

When I first saw this explosive statement quoted in a Washington newspaper, I must admit I was startled. I had always felt it was impossible to say what group had the heaviest infiltration of Communists. I talked to McCarthy about it, and he too was concerned. While realizing full well that the clergy had not escaped infiltration, he believed, as did the rest of our staff, that the vast majority of American clergymen had been effective fighters against Communism. "After all," he said to me, "they know better than anyone that Marxism, with its creed of atheistic materialism, could not be reconciled with religious faith."

But, like myself, McCarthy was inclined to shrug off the incident, especially since we found upon examination that the article as a whole hailed the record of Protestant churchmen in the anti-Red crusade. The article, about four thousand words long, pointed out that only a small minority—7,000 out of some 250,000 ministers, or 2.8 percent—were Red-tainted and most of these were innocent dupes of Communists. Matthews explicitly stated that "the vast majority of American Protestant clergymen are loyal to the free institutions of this country and to their solemn trust as ministers of the Gospel." Still, it must be acknowledged that the effect of the article was damaging.

The first sign of trouble came when the subcommittee's Democratic minority, some of whom had obviously been searching for such an opening, opened attacks on both Matthews and Senator McCarthy, citing the offending sentence. Anxious about the possible consequences, some of McCarthy's supporters urged him to dismiss Matthews at once, to take the pressure off himself. But that was not the Senator's make-up. He was conscious of the whipping-boy role in which his staff members might be placed, and his loyalty was not withdrawn even in the wake of errors of judgment on their part.

Something about the whole affair puzzled me, especially the provocative first sentence that did not reflect the intent of the article. When I asked Matthews about it, he confirmed what I had felt intuitively: *he said he had not written the words in the manner in which they appeared in print.* His original version—less inflammatory, more scholarly and precise—had been reworded by a member of the *American Mercury* staff to give the article greater impact. He certainly succeeded.

Editorial revision of this nature, though admittedly sharp practice, is not unknown in magazine journalism. I am told that the Society of Magazine Writers has long fought for the right to see galley proofs prior to publication—with only limited success. As soon as I learned what had happened I asked the magazine official involved to come to Washington to talk things over. Our meeting included Matthews, Senator McCarthy, several members of our staff, and the *Mercury* man. I put the matter squarely to the editor, proposing that since he had changed the lead paragraph he ought to issue a public statement releasing Matthews' original one, making it clear that the offending passage was not the author's. This, I felt, would satisfy the Democratic minority and the howling press.

But the *American Mercury* man was unwilling to come forward because the credibility of the publication would be damaged. "You don't have to say you did anything dishonest," I told him. "All you need tell is the truth—that the sentence as published was not written by the man himself." He still refused.

Matthews pointed out that any attempt on his part to disclaim authorship would hardly be believed. "Everyone would say I was trying to evade responsibility," he said. I became increasingly angry at the unfairness of the situation as the discussion proceeded, and in the growing argument the *American Mercury* man and I almost came to blows. The conference broke up on an angry note.

Mrs. Ruth Matthews, J. B.'s widow, now says that the first sentence of the article, as it was submitted to the magazine by her late husband, was substantially the same as it appeared in print. As documentation, she cites the existence of a memo bearing Matthews' signature which states that he has heard it said that his article was altered to make it more sensational, but that the changes made by the publication did not appreciably alter the sense of the statement he wrote. The memo bears no date.

I have no other comment on the memo, but merely state that my own recollection is clear and the events I have described took place at the meeting.

Matthews insisted on resigning, but before he could do so the affair took a new turn.

On July 9, President Eisenhower received a telegram from three leading clergymen urging him to speak out against "the sweeping attack on the loyalty of Protestant churchmen."

The message was signed by the Reverend John A. O'Brien of the University of Notre Dame, Rabbi Maurice N. Eisendrath, the president of the Union of American Hebrew Congregations, and the Reverend Dr. John Sutherland Bonnell, pastor of the Fifth Avenue Presbyterian Church. As national co-chairmen of the Commission on Religious Organization of the National Conference of Christians and Jews, they represented a combined force that could not be ignored.

A group of Eisenhower advisers, including Sherman Adams, James Hagerty, and Emmet John Hughes, drafted a presidential reply which gave full support to the churchmen's protest. In angry terms, the White House message charged that "generalized and irresponsible attacks that sweepingly condemn the whole of any group of citizens are alien to America. Such attacks betray contempt for the principle of freedom and decency and condemn such a vast portion of the churches or clergy as to create doubt in the loyalty of all. The damage to our nation is multiplied."

The press, viewing the statement as a direct presidential slap at McCarthy, made headlines of it. Thus, when McCarthy reluctantly accepted Matthews' resignation later that same day, it was generally regarded as a move forced on the Senator by White House censure.

But the clergymen's protest and the presidential reply turned out to be a prearranged affair, cynically stage-managed by the White House staff to injure McCarthy. The full story of the goings-on within the Executive Mansion was confirmed in 1963, when Hughes published *The Ordeal of Power,* a revealing chronicle of his years as one of Eisenhower's speech writers. Recalling the Matthews incident, Hughes said he and other aides watched with fascination as, "defying the instant public outcry" over the article, "McCarthy seemed to stand by Matthews' side."

"Suddenly," Hughes said, "the Wisconsin Senator was vulnerable to direct attack on an unclouded issue."

Hughes then recounted how he, Deputy Attorney General William Rogers, and other staff members working with colleagues in New York who were safely unconnected with the White House, "decided to encourage a telegram of protest to the President from the National Conference of Christians and Jews in New York."

"We also agreed on the need to move swiftly," said Hughes, "since McCarthy was too astute not to realize at almost any hour that Matthews had become a dangerous liability who would have to be dismissed.

"Accordingly, while our mutual friends outside government spurred the National Conference in New York, I hastened the same day to get the agreement of Sherman Adams to our plan *and to draft the President's reply to the message we still awaited.*" [my italics]

In other words, this presidential message that rang with indignation was actually worked up before receipt of the protest to which it was supposed to reply.

The stage was set, but the stage managers neglected to let the President in on their strategy. This omission almost wrecked the scheme. When they finally succeeded in provoking a protest from the church leaders, they were unable to reach Eisenhower to get him to sign the prepared reply.

"By the time the signals were at last cleared," Hughes recalled, "afternoon was upon us; the President, not yet even advised of what was afoot, was closeted with important visitors; and the rumor was raging across Capitol Hill that McCarthy was about to dismiss Matthews and publicly invite applause for his own fair-mindedness. Soon I began to get increasingly frantic phone calls from Rogers on the Hill: 'For God's sake, we have to get that message out fast, or McCarthy will beat us to the draw.' "

Adams suggested taking the reply to the President alone, Hughes said, adding somewhat sheepishly, "since the President tended by now to discount the heat of my own feelings about McCarthy."

At last they got the President to affix his signature—not a moment too soon, for while the stencil for the mimeographed press release was being recut for minor changes, word came from Rogers that Senators McCarthy and Mundt had just finished conferring and were on their way to the Hill, probably with Matthews' resignation.

At this point the Vice-President, according to Hughes, buttonholed

McCarthy in the Senate Office Building and kept him in conversation until Hughes could telephone the "all clear" signifying that the presidential statement was in the hands of the press.

Thus were the clergymen's protest and the presidential reply maneuvered by the group of Eisenhower aides who, as Hughes freely admits, had long been awaiting an opportunity to get Senator McCarthy over a barrel.

One desired investigation that never got started was that of the Central Intelligence Agency, headed by Allen W. Dulles. Our staff had been accumulating extensive data about its operations and McCarthy was convinced that an inquiry was overdue.

Our files contained allegations gathered from various sources indicating that the CIA had unwittingly hired a large number of double agents—individuals who, although working for the CIA, were actually Communist agents whose mission was to plant inaccurate data. Since the function of the CIA is to compile estimates of the military capabilities, defensive systems, and moral strengths of nations, and since top-level policies and decisions are based upon these estimates, false information accepted as true could be disastrous.

We also wanted to investigate charges:

——that the CIA had granted large subsidies to pro-Communist organizations.

——that persons who were remnants of the China mistake occupied high positions in the agency. These individuals had supported the Institute of Pacific Relations position that the Chinese Communists were harmless agrarian reformers.

——that although we spent far more for intelligence than other countries, the quality of the information we were receiving was so poor that at times the CIA found out what was happening only when it read the newspapers.

These were grave questions that urgently called for answers. When the subject of an investigation was discussed at a subcommittee executive session, only Senator Stuart Symington voiced strong objection. He wanted McCarthy to clear it with the White House. Recognizing that highly sensitive matters might be involved, McCarthy agreed.

When the news broke that McCarthy was contemplating an inquiry into the CIA, consternation reigned at 1600 Pennsylvania Avenue. Vice-President Nixon was assigned to the delicate job of blocking it. He arranged for a small private dinner to be held in a Washington hotel suite, to be attended by Senator McCarthy, the three Republican members of the subcommittee (Dirksen, Potter, and Mundt), and several top-level officials of the Government.

Nixon spoke at length, arguing that an open investigation would damage national security, harm our relations with our allies, and seriously affect CIA operations, which depended on total secrecy. The meeting lasted late. Finally, the three subcommittee members, not opposed to the inquiry before they went to dinner, yielded to Nixon's pressure. So, too, did McCarthy, and the investigation, which McCarthy told me interested him more than any other, was never launched.

The subject of a CIA investigation arose once again toward the close of the Army-McCarthy hearings. On June 2, 1954, during the morning session, McCarthy observed that "Communist infiltration of the CIA . . . disturbs me beyond words." Immediately speculation arose that he was planning an investigation. Interesting developments followed.

On July 4, former President Herbert Hoover announced that his Government commission had named General Mark W. Clark to head a task force to look into the "structure and administration" of the CIA. About the same time, President Eisenhower secretly named Lieutenant General James H. Doolittle to conduct a separate study. The existence of the Doolittle group was not revealed until its findings were announced.

In the fall, the Doolittle committee reported that it found little to damn but much to praise: some areas "could and should be improved," but generally a "creditable" job was being performed. In July of the following year, Clark's Task Force found no "valid ground" for McCarthy's assertion that Communists had infiltrated the CIA. It did note a number of administrative flaws and cited a "lack of adequate intelligence data from behind the Iron Curtain." Said the report: "There is still much to be done by our intelligence community to bring its achievements up to an acceptable level." The investigators also recommended creation of a congressional watchdog committee.

Senator Mike Mansfield, Montana Democrat, sponsored a resolution in the Senate to create a committee of twelve members, six from each House, to be named the Joint Committee on Central Intelligence. Without it, he said, "we will have no way of knowing whether we have a fine intelligence service or a very poor one." It took until 1956 to bring the resolution to the floor and then it was defeated, 59 to 27.

Thus it remained for a muckracking magazine published by young West Coast radicals to expose in sensational fashion the CIA's soiled linen to an astonished public—fourteen years after Joe McCarthy had been denied access to this holiest of holies.

CHAPTER 5

THE KENNEDYS

O_{NE} AFTERNOON I remember Joe McCarthy was on the telephone when I entered his office. He pointed to the receiver from which crackling sounds were emerging, shrugged helplessly, and mouthed, "Joe Kennedy." While he listened, he toyed with a pencil. Every ten or fifteen seconds he would nod and say, "Sure, Joe," "I see," "That's a good point." After a while he stood up and, still holding the phone to his ear, began pacing behind his desk. After a few more minutes, he put the instrument on his desk, the voice of Kennedy still crackling, and left it there for a bit. Then he picked it up, said "Sure, Joe," and sat down. He scribbled a note and passed it to me.

It read: "Remind me to check the size of his campaign contribution. I'm not sure it's worth it."

Joseph P. Kennedy telephoned Senator McCarthy often with advice on the conduct of our investigations as well as with copious comments on national issues. He would suggest in much detail moves to make and pitfalls to avoid.

Despite his impatience with the long telephone sessions, McCarthy was fond of the elder Kennedy. He was, in fact, on close terms with the Kennedy family. "In case there is any question in your mind," the former ambassador was quoted in *Life* magazine in 1961, "I liked Joe McCarthy. I always liked him. I would see him when I went down to Washington, and when he was visiting in Palm Beach he'd come around to my house for a drink. I invited him to Cape Cod." At the Cape, McCarthy sailed with the Kennedys, played touch football, and for a while dated Pat Kennedy in Washington and Hyannis Port. Once Bob Morris, then chief counsel for the Senate Subcommittee on

Internal Security and now president of the University of Plano in Dallas, went to dinner with Pat and Joe in Washington. "It was a wonderfully gay evening," he said. "They enjoyed each other's company; he liked her vivacity, and she apparently enjoyed his company." When Pat started going out with Peter Lawford, they were the Senator's guests at our Fort Monmouth hearings in New York.

The close relationship between McCarthy and the Kennedy clan became politically significant in 1952, when John F. Kennedy, then a hard-working young congressman from Massachusetts' 11th District, sought the Senate seat held by Republican Henry Cabot Lodge, Jr. Despite the intense preparations he and his family had been making for his campaign since 1950, despite his own popularity, Jack Kennedy was not given much chance of defeating Lodge, an able, experienced legislator, a handsome member of one of Boston's oldest families, and a good vote-getter. With war-hero Eisenhower running for the Presidency, with the growing discontent with President Truman's policies and personnel, and above all, with the issue of Communists in government gaining momentum, it did not look like a good year for Democrats.

By this time McCarthy had attracted considerable strength in the country, not the least in Massachusetts with its big Catholic population. The feeling all across the Bay State was that Kennedy, while making a good run, would not survive an Eisenhower victory, especially if Joe McCarthy campaigned there. The fear was not unfounded. McCarthy with his "issue" had beaten Millard Tydings in Maryland, Scott Lucas, the Senate Majority leader, in Illinois, and other Democrats in Connecticut.

Joe Kennedy realized that whatever chance son John had of defeating Lodge in the face of an Eisenhower landslide depended upon McCarthy's absence from Massachusetts. The Republican National Committee, as well as Lodge supporters, knew this too, and urged McCarthy to go in. But Kennedy had shown many acts of friendship toward McCarthy, including some financing for the Wisconsin campaign. Joe Kennedy knew it would be difficult for McCarthy to say no to a generous friend.

So Joe Kennedy pleaded with McCarthy to stay out of Massachusetts. McCarthy wavered. He liked the father and had admired the son since their wartime meeting in the Pacific. Moreover, he was not enchanted with Lodge-type Republicanism, which he considered as weak and as ineffectual as Eisenhower's was turning out to be.

McCarthy stayed out, and Jack Kennedy won by 70,000 votes while Eisenhower carried the state by 209,000. And the entente between the Kennedys and McCarthy was more firmly cemented.

We come now to another Kennedy—Bobby. I should like to say that it is not my purpose here to express my personal or political views about Bobby Kennedy, then or now, but simply to recount a couple of the instances when our paths crossed. Robert F. Kennedy resigned from the McCarthy subcommittee after serving as assistant counsel for under seven months in 1953. In his book, *The Enemy Within,* Kennedy says he left because he was dissatisfied with our investigative techniques.

"Most of the investigations," he wrote, "were instituted on the basis of some preconceived notion by the chief counsel or his staff members and not on the basis of any information that had been developed. Cohn and Schine claimed they knew from the outset what was wrong; and they were not going to allow the facts to interfere. Therefore no real spadework that might have destroyed some of their pet theories was ever undertaken. I thought Senator McCarthy made a mistake in allowing the committee to operate in such a fashion, told him so and resigned."

On July 29, 1953, Kennedy wrote McCarthy the following letter:

Please accept my resignation as assistant counsel and deputy staff director of the Senate Permanent Subcommittee on Investigations, effective as of the close of business July 31, 1953.

With the filing in the Senate of the subcommittee report on trade with the Soviet Bloc, the task to which I have devoted my time since coming with the subcommittee has been completed. I am submitting my resignation at this time as it is my intention to enter the private practice of law at an early date.

I have enjoyed my work and association on the subcommittee, and I wish to express to you my appreciation for the opportunity of having served with your group.

Please accept my sincere thanks for the many courtesies and kindnesses you have extended to me during these past seven months.

Two days later, Senator McCarthy replied:

Dear Bob:

This is to acknowledge receipt of your letter of resignation. I know it is needless to tell you that I very much regret seeing you leave the committee. In accordance with our conversation, I sincerely hope that you will consider coming back later on in the summer to complete the project with Mr. Flanagan and the full committee.

From discussing your work with the other members of the committee, I can tell you that it was the unanimous feeling on the part of the senators that you were a great credit to the committee and did a tremendous job.

With kindest regards, I am

Sincerely yours,
Joe

Kennedy himself was certainly a vigorous prosecutor. Take, for example, an episode during the hearings in 1953 on foreign ships that were trading with Communist nations.

In May of that year Bobby testified that "an absolute minimum" of 162 foreign cargo ships had been trading with Communist China in the first three and a half months. The year before, 193 ships had engaged in the same trading. He documented his statements with figures from naval intelligence which showed that one hundred of the vessels trading in 1953 were British-owned, while the rest flew the flags of Greece, Norway, Denmark, Sweden, Finland, Italy, France, the Netherlands, Pakistan, India, Portugal, and Japan. Two of the British-owned ships, he said, carried Red Chinese troops along the Chinese coast.

Later, the subcommittee issued a report disclosing that in the three years since the outbreak of the Korean war, Western Allied trade with Communist China and other Communist nations had exceeded two billion dollars. McCarthy was aghast, but at the same time he was well aware of the delicate diplomatic questions involved. McCarthy was no isolationist; he knew the importance of maintaining close relations with our allies. But some action had to be taken.

After the Kennedy disclosures, McCarthy checked into the Bethesda Naval Hospital for treatment of an old leg injury. While he was there a proposed letter was drafted by Kennedy and addressed to President Eisenhower, asking in strong words for an official position in the matter of Allied trading with Communist nations.

Such a letter from the chairman of the committee could hardly have been expected to bring aid and comfort to the White House.

McCarthy forwarded the letter to the White House, where it

aroused consternation. "If Eisenhower answered it with a statement of policy regarding trade with the Communists, as McCarthy was demanding," wrote Sherman Adams later, "he could avoid neither antagonizing the British nor stirring up criticism from anti-Communist groups at home." What to do? The solution finally came from Vice-President Nixon. He telephoned McCarthy at the hospital and persuaded him to withdraw the letter. The Senator did not need urging. The letter was returned, never having been received "officially."

Bobby Kennedy did not go into the private practice of law after he resigned from our subcommittee. He served until February of the following year as a counsel for the bipartisan Commission on Organization of the Executive Branch of the Government—the Hoover Commission—but apparently found the work unexciting, because he returned to the McCarthy subcommittee as minority counsel. His job: to aid and advise the Democratic senators on the subcommittee. It was while Bobby was functioning in this role that we had our celebrated encounter in the Senate Caucus Room.

My blowup with Bobby is difficult to analyze because there are few facts about it other than that it happened. Although an undercurrent existed, we never had an overt argument before that one incident at the hearings. We never had acrimonious discussions of any depth or duration. It was something that just happened.

The explosion came on Friday, June 11, 1954, during the famous Army-McCarthy hearings.

My testimony had ended. Joe McCarthy was on the stand. Near the close, the discussion turned to a plan for selling democracy globally that had been prepared by G. David Schine before he joined the McCarthy committee as a consultant. The plan listed fifteen channels through which democracy might be promoted in areas into which Communism was spreading. Its basic aim was to "inspire native leaders everywhere to express democracy in every field of social action and to develop democratic groups and parties." And to achieve this end, Schine had made some commonsense suggestions that embodied a grass-roots approach: encourage the formation of native democratic parties, help train the armed forces in the principles of democracy, establish within the nations social service and health agencies, and teach religious tolerance.

Now, Bobby Kennedy's job was to write out pertinent questions for the Democratic senators to ask at the hearing. In this Schine plan he saw an opportunity to gibe at us. He fed his questions to Senator Jackson, who used them to fire a barrage of ridicule. Schine, for example, had written: "We must create a 'Deminform' or association of democratic parties on the basis of mutual cooperation free of the charge of American imperialism." Jackson seized upon the word to inquire scoffingly: "Isn't the word 'Deminform' pretty close to 'Cominform'? Aren't some of the people going to get mixed up?" McCarthy caught him up short with: "Let's be fair, Mr. Jackson."

Schine had written that it was important to encourage the clergy to play a role in the support of democracy. Jackson, grinning, wanted to know: "Is he going to infiltrate the clergy?" Schine had mentioned the need for special appeals to leaders of community thought, including fraternal organizations such as the Elks and the Knights of Columbus. Jackson (himself an Elk) derisively questioned whether Pakistan had an Elks lodge. McCarthy explained that the intention was to make a special appeal to fraternal and veterans' groups. "What is wrong with that?" he asked. Schine's plan, McCarthy said, dug deeply, and was a much better way of getting anti-Communist ideas across than "putting out the thirty-thousand-odd books written by Communist authors which we found in our investigation."

But Bobby—and Jackson—would not give up. They picked at point after point in Dave's plan, finding something hilarious in each. And every time Kennedy handed him something, Senator Jackson would go into fits of laughter. I became angrier and angrier as the burlesque proceeded. Finally, Jackson's ten-minute question period terminated. Shortly thereafter the session was adjourned.

I gathered up my papers, and as I walked out came face to face with Bobby Kennedy. I told him angrily that what he had done was unfair. His voice rose as he criticized my actions and warned me that I wasn't going to get away with it and that I was going to be stopped.

People lingered to listen, but Bobby paid no heed. "Look," I said, "apparently there is only one way to settle this," and I started to swing at him. Two men grabbed me, Bobby moved away, and no blow was struck. Since touch football and mountain climbing are not my long suits, I probably was the gainer in the stopping of the fight.

Next day, newspapers headlined an alleged threat I had made during the argument with Kennedy to "get" Senator Jackson. I was supposed to have told Bobby that we would produce a letter of recommendation for a job written by Jackson on behalf of an individual who figured in an investigation of Communists. Jackson served formal public notice that he would not be intimidated by any "retaliatory action." The story of the so-called threat came from a couple of newsmen who belatedly decided that they had overheard the acrimonious discussion between Kennedy and me. (The only actual witness I recall was Walter Winchell, who had an uncanny skill for popping up in the middle of the big news-breaks.) I was used to this type of press treatment at certain hands, based upon any lead that could be discovered or, as in this case, invented. Next day I told Senator Mundt by telephone from New York: "I never made any such statement. I don't know of any such letter." Senator Mundt said to the press that he had known of the existence of the feud for a long time. "I don't know why and I don't care why," he said. "It is something that has no place in the hearings and it isn't going to have a place in the hearings. They are just popping off and they can stop it."

About two years later, I met John Kennedy at an April-in-Paris ball at the Waldorf in New York when we were both guests of Mrs. Winston Guest. We had an interesting conversation.

"I'm sorry you and Bobby are always at each other's throats," he said to me. "I think you've got a great deal of ability and I like the job you've done against Communism. The fight between Bobby and you hasn't carried over to us."

Jack Kennedy was without question deeply devoted to Bobby, and always worked closely with him. He knew that Bobby could be rough and that in a campaign there was need for his type of single-minded tough devotion. In the 1960 campaign it was Bobby who said to a group of reform leaders battling the regular Democratic organization in New York: "Gentlemen, I don't give a damn if the state and county organizations survive after November, and I don't give a damn if you survive. I want to elect John F. Kennedy."

An analysis of the John F. Kennedy-Joe McCarthy relationship is not easy.

It is nonsense to insist, as many now do, that the future President was strongly opposed to McCarthy but simply did not say so for one reason or another. There is no question in my mind but that John Kennedy liked Joe McCarthy, although he was not as close to him personally and ideologically as his father. Kennedy told James Mac-Gregor Burns: "I was rather in ill grace personally to be around hollering about what McCarthy had done in 1952 or 1951 when my brother had been on the staff in 1953. That is really the guts of the matter." Part of the guts perhaps, but not all. There was also his father's deep commitment, his wartime friendship renewed when McCarthy visited Cape Cod and dated his sister Pat, and the very real possibility that antagonizing McCarthy's friends might cost him votes in Massachusetts with its high percentage of Catholics and McCarthy backers.

John Kennedy was gravely ill following an operation on his spine on the December day in 1954 when the vote to censure Joe Mc-Carthy was taken in the Senate. Theodore C. Sorensen, then his legislative assistant, has stated that in view of the Senator's condition the responsibility for recording the Kennedy vote fell upon his shoulders. Sorensen believes that had Kennedy been there, he would have voted for censure.

Sorensen's loyalty to his chief is commendable. But the insistent question, even after the passage of years, remains: Why did JFK not speak up before, and why did he not speak up afterward? "Since I had never really been especially vigorous about McCarthy during his life," he answered this question once, "it would make me out to be a complete political prostitute to be champing and jumping to change, to denounce McCarthy when he was gone politically."

Five years after the censure, Kennedy did disclose that he had, after all, prepared a speech in July of 1954 in support of the censure during the debate. Sorensen stood at the rear of the Senate, mimeographed copies of the speech in his hand, ready to distribute them. However, the debate over censure ended when the Senate voted to let a select committee handle the question, and the speech was never given.

In a review of the Rovere book on McCarthy for the Washington *Post* in 1959, Kennedy mildly criticized the Wisconsin senator. A number of times, in interviews, he repeated that he thought the censure was a "reasonable action."

When Arthur M. Schlesinger, Jr., referring to the McCarthy matter, observed that "he had paid a heavy price" for titling his book *Profiles in Courage,* the President indirectly touched on the matter in his reply.

"Yes," he told Schlesinger, "but I didn't have a chapter in it on myself."

CHAPTER 6

THE BOOK BURNERS

In 1967 Theodore H. White, author of *The Making of the President, 1960,* and *The Making of the President, 1964,* and I appeared on noted columnist Irving Kupcinet's TV program in Chicago. White's greeting was, "I haven't seen you since you burned my book out of the libraries of Europe." He referred to his *Thunder out of China,* co-authored with the late Annalee Jacoby.

After fourteen years, such is the hypnotic power of the press that misconceptions still exist about the investigation G. David Schine and I made of the State Department's Information Program in Europe. We were derided as snoopers, Rover Boys, Innocents Abroad, and junketeering gumshoes. Author White was one of many who denounced us as "book burners" because we discovered that more than thirty thousand works by Communists, sympathizers, and unwitting promoters of the Communist cause were on the shelves of our overseas libraries.

The information program that caused such bitter controversy consisted of American libraries and reading rooms set up in foreign countries. They weren't intended to function as public or general libraries but to house reading matter about our country, its people, and their way of life. They were Cold War products whose purpose was to win friends.

My question was and is a simple one: Wasn't it self-defeating to stock the shelves with anti-American books? Why should we sponsor the propaganda of our socialist adversaries at this critical time?

"Free circulation of ideas, not censorship, is true Americanism," some would reply. I agree. We took no volumes off library shelves in the United States. My job on the McCarthy subcommittee was to see that the American taxpayer was not footing the bill for ideas only a small minority of Americans stood for. Not censorship but salesmanship was the issue.

To President Eisenhower this made sense. Following a cabinet meeting on the subject, a policy statement was issued by the International Information Administration's chief: the Government was under no obligation to place in these centers reading matter that directly or indirectly advocated the destruction of American freedom or institutions. Controversial books were acceptable, including those criticizing America. Books written by Communists or their followers might in special cases be included if the material "affirmatively serves the ends of democracy." So might fiction or humor by leftist authors.

Robert Donovan, in his *Eisenhower: The Inside Story,* thus sums up the President's attitude: "He was opposed to suppression of ideas. He believed, however, that the United States should not pay for books to be put on shelves abroad which advocated a system of government that would destroy the United States. Books advocating communism, he felt, should be excluded. . . ."

These presidential attitudes constituted the slide rule by which we measured the actual impact of the information libraries abroad. An additional guide was Public Law 402, which set up the libraries: "The objectives of the Act are to enable the Government of the United States to promote better understanding in other countries, and to increase mutual understanding between the people of the United States and the people of other countries."

The subcommittee hearings into the work of the overseas centers ended in July, 1953. The significance of what we had developed seems to be supported by the findings of the senators on the committee that:

1. "An inexcusably large number" of books written by Communists or individuals with "long and substantial records of aiding and supporting the Communist cause" were in these tax-supported libraries.

2. A considerable number of books in the libraries were "unequivocally pro-Communist, pro-Soviet, or anti-American in content or character."

3. "Although some anti-Communist books were stocked, the number and selection of them was wholly inadequate and disproportion-

ate to the heavy preponderance of pro-Soviet, pro-Communist literature . . ."

Fixing responsibility for the choice of the books and magazines
was like trying to catch a greased pig in a dense fog. We were never
able to discover who ordered the purchase of one single Communist
or pro-Communist book. Bureaucratic confusion—quite possibly
manufactured—prevailed. Consider this bizarre exchange from a
hearing of the Senate Appropriations Committee in June, 1953,
following our own subcommittee hearings:

MC CARTHY: Have you ever . . . run down the purchase orders
so you can come in today and say, "John Jones bought this
Communist book on the tenth of August, 1952," or whatever the date was? Is there any way of doing that?

RICHARD HUMPHREY (Acting Director of the Information
Center Service): There is not any way of actually doing that,
Senator. I have made every effort to see whether that could
be done.

FERGUSON (Senator Homer Ferguson, Michigan): You mean
you have a chain of command and you cannot tell who is
responsible for the purchase of books for overseas libraries?

HUMPHREY: May I expain that the judgments on the purchase of
any . . .

FERGUSON: We are not talking about judgment on the purchase.
Who purchased them?

HUMPHREY: We order the books in Washington.

FERGUSON: "We" does not mean a thing on this record. I think
there are 42,000 in the State Department.

HUMPHREY: The Information Center Service orders the books in
Washington.

FERGUSON: That means about 11,850. Let us get down to who is
responsible for ordering the books.

HUMPHREY: Ultimately, it is my responsibility at the present time
in the name of my people.

FERGUSON: How long ago were you asked to get the data as to
who was responsible for the purchase of alleged Communist
books?

HUMPHREY: I would have to say I think about April.

FERGUSON: Do you mean to say you have not the answer yet?

HUMPHREY: I do not think it is possible to give it in that form. I
did request a special security check of our whole Service in

the light of this question to determine whether or not any such person could be on the rolls.

FERGUSON: You mean since April you have not been able to get out of the Department an answer as to who was responsible for the purchasing of these alleged Communist books? . . . I want to know who bought the books.

HUMPHREY: I can give you the lists of our people who select books.

FERGUSON: No. Who did purchase these Communist books?

HUMPHREY: There is no record, purchase record, from Washington of the purchase of any of the books by known Communists.

FERGUSON: They were paid for by the United States Government.

HUMPHREY: Some of those were and some of them were not. Some of them were presumably given in the field and some of them may have been bought in the field, but we have been unable to determine who bought them.

Dead end!

Let me set forth just a few excerpts from books our State Department made available to foreign readers as an introduction to the American way of life and thought, designed "to advance American ideas on the struggle against Communism."

The seizure of political power by the working class is the first step in the revolution. The second step is to recast the social order and to crush the resistance of the capitalist class to the change. Leo Huberman, *The Truth about Socialism,* 1950, p. 228.

The Soviet Union plays the role of clearing the path, of facilitating world progress, of proving by its own example the superiority of the socialist system. James Stuart Allen, *World Monopoly and Peace,* 1946, p. 228.

The history of the Communist Party shows that the victory of the common people is impossible without a disciplined party working within it, a party free from opportunism and irreconcilable to compromise and capitulation; a party of the working class which has mastered the laws of social life and is able to find the right orientation in any given situation. . . . Hewlett Johnson, *The Secret of Soviet Strength,* 1948, p. 159.

The status quo in reactionary countries, such as Italy and France, Portugal and Greece, are merely held to the Right by American money and pressure, will go Leftward when these forces diminish or cease. Nothing is more important in history than this trend of the world (including Asia and Africa), and almost nothing is written about it because it is contrary to the American status quo policy. . . .
George Seldes, *The People Don't Know,* 1949, pp. 307–08.

And the one hopeful light on the horizon—the exciting and encouraging conditions in Soviet Russia, where for the first time in history our race problem has been squarely faced and solved; where for the first time the fine words of the poets, philosophers and well-meaning politicians have been made a living reality: Robert Burns' "A man's a man for a' that"; France's "Liberté, Egalité, Fraternité"; America's "All men are created equal" and "are entitled to life, liberty and the pursuit of happiness." All these grand ideas and statements have been hauled down from the dusty reference shelves at the backs of men's minds and have been put into active, vigorous, successful practice by the Russians, so that men and women and children of all races, colors and creeds walk the streets and work out their lives in dignity, safety and comradeship.
Eslanda Robeson, *African Journey,* 1945, p. 47

Soviet youth has not worked for Russia alone. It has been trained to believe that socialist construction gains in the Soviet Union are gains for mankind. Events have demonstrated the correctness of this view. Successes achieved in many branches of Soviet endeavor have made the Soviet Union a pioneer and leader in world cultural advance. The Soviet Union is pioneering on the social frontier and its achievements have already modified human society. Individually and collectively the Soviet people have a record of which they may be justly proud and look forward into a future which they are actively helping to shape.
Scott Nearing, *The Soviet Union as a World Power,* 1945, p. 18.

One answer commonly made by revolutionists is that force must be used, blood must flow, not because they want to use violence, but because the ruling class will not give up without it.
Leo Huberman, *Man's Worldly Goods,* 1945, p. 241.

The encouragement of popular participation in cultural, economic, and political programs, according to most observers, created a new psychological atmosphere or morale in those wartime areas where the Communist program became effective. Participants in the new order have been moved by a new creed, a humanitarian love of the peasant masses. This religion of the common man embraces the revolutionary ideal that modern technology and a new social organization may be used to remake and enrich the life of the peasant.

John K. Fairbank, *The United States and China,* 1948, p. 268.

(There were twenty-eight copies of this last Harvard University publication in information libraries.)

Two self-identifying titles were *Communism in the United States* by Earl Browder, and *Pages from a Worker's Life* by William Z. Foster—two party chiefs.

The last book I'll mention is Marguerite Ann Stewart's *Land of the Soviets,* 1942, from pages 70–71:

Perhaps the most striking section of the 1936 Constitution is that describing the rights and duties of Soviet citizens. Following are the basic rights as outlined in the Constitution:

"In accordance with the interests of the working people, and in order to strengthen the socialist system, the citizens of the U.S.S.R. are guaranteed by law:

"a. Freedom of speech;
"b. Freedom of press;
"c. Freedom of assemblies and meetings;
"d. Freedom of street processions and demonstrations."

Now, the Soviets have endowed their country with heavy industry, the atomic bomb, and numerous sputniks. They have sent satellites to the moon. But if they have gotten around to giving their citizens these guaranteed freedoms, it's one of the best-kept secrets in the world today.

Much hissing and booing accompanied our suggested removal of nonpolitical books written by Communists or fellow-travelers, such as Dashiell Hammett's thrillers. Eisenhower thought these should have been left undisturbed. I concede that an error in judgment is involved here. Hammett complicated matters for himself by going bail for Communist leaders charged with violating the Smith Act. When they jumped bail Hammett refused to tell where they went, and was himself imprisoned. But certainly no one would be wooed to Communism by *The Maltese Falcon.*

When David Schine and I went to Europe to look into charges of inefficiency and disloyalty in the information service, we considered the trip routine, a journey of the kind undertaken dozens of times yearly by members of Congress and their staffs. It turned out to be one of the most publicized trips of the decade. We soon realized, although neither of us could admit to this distressing fact, that it was a colossal mistake. We had to go through with it as best we could.

What we failed to foresee was the propaganda uses to which our critics would put the journey. David Schine and I unwittingly handed Joe McCarthy's enemies a perfect opportunity to spread the tale that a couple of young, inexperienced clowns were bustling about Europe, ordering State Department officials around, burning books, creating chaos wherever they went, and disrupting foreign relations.

Why did the European press react so violently to the trip? The papers were virtually unanimous in equating McCarthy's investigations with a resurgent American isolationism. In those Cold War years, Europe worried about the growth of a right-wing, anti-European movement in this country. It was thought that there had gathered under McCarthy's banner many of the groups that had opposed American involvement in World War II—which was true enough—and that a new isolationist force, like that following the First World War, was gaining strength. But McCarthy was no isolationist: his preoccupation was to keep Western Europe (and Asia) from falling to Communist control.

And, in addition, there was the groundless belief that we were the advance elements of a "crusade" McCarthy was planning in Europe. The Bonn correspondent of the Manchester *Guardian* warned ominously: "There is a strong possibility that Senator McCarthy is going to extend his apparent control of propaganda from America to other Western countries. Britain may even be included . . . American observers in Germany believe that this is only the beginning of a McCarthy crusade in Europe. The Senator is known to have his private agents in Bonn and elsewhere who are keeping him supplied with information on the subject of 'deviationist Democrats.' "

The European press had a definite interest in discrediting McCarthy. The arrival of his two emissaries offered a golden chance.

Reports flew that Cohn and Schine were on a "book-burning" spree. Next, we were attacked for the hurry with which we conducted our inquiries. The hours we spent in each capital were added up: forty in Paris, sixteen in Bonn, nineteen in Frankfurt, sixty in Munich, forty-one in Vienna, and so on. Had we come as presidential emissaries to survey economic conditions, then the time we spent would have been far too limited. But for the narrow scope of our inquiry the hours we spent were ample. We needed only to look in each place at an area consisting of some three rooms, and ask a few individuals specific questions. It doesn't take long to do that.

Hordes of journalists followed us everywhere. Their stories were more noteworthy for invention than for accuracy. The critical barrage was relentless. An occasional touch of humor lightened the mood, such as the exchanges among State Department employees: "See you tomorrow, come Cohn or Schine." In Germany, the official in charge of the information program, Theodore Kaghan, called us "junketeering gumshoes." In England, we were "quiz kids." Years later, Arthur Schlesinger, Jr., with the trip in mind, called us "a pair of juvenile comedians." This was critical acclaim from the man who displayed his own mature comic genius by plunging fully clothed into a swimming pool at a party given by the Robert Kennedys.

So discouraged was I at one point that I thought of curtailing the trip and flying home. In Athens, I confided my feelings to Ambassador John Peurifoy. "What good would it do to stop?" he argued. "They would say you ran away. Go through with it!"

From Germany, I spoke by telephone to Senators McCarthy and Mundt.

"Are you having a good time?" McCarthy asked me.

"Not very," I answered.

"Don't let it bother you," he counseled. "You're in a rough spot. All you and Dave can do is finish the job and come home."

Those who read the newspapers and heard the broadcasts that April were given no notion of what The Trip was really about. Let me attempt to reveal what actually happened.

We arrived in Paris on April 4. Representatives of the State Department escorted us to the Hotel Crillon. Frank Dennis, one of the top figures in the information program in Paris, briefed us.

Dennis, part-owner of the Washington *Post* before he went into the

State Department, told us there was duplication, even triplication, and consequent waste of taxpayers' money in the program's administration. In addition to the State Department's regular Paris setup, including a Public Affairs office with a large staff, the information branch of the Mutual Security Agency duplicated the State Department's work. A third information program was run by the President's Special Representative to France.

We went next to Frankfurt. We were met at the airport by William Montecone, an aide representing Acting Deputy Director Theodore Kaghan of the Office of Public Affairs of our High Commissioner in Germany (HICOG). One of Kaghan's responsibilities was supervision of the information program in Germany, including the America House libraries.

Bill Montecone, a pleasant fellow, rode with us from Frankfurt to Bonn. We dined with him and Mr. Hoopnagle, another Office of Public Affairs man, and the check for the four of us came to twenty or twenty-five dollars, which I paid out of my own pocket. Subsequently, our "lavish spending" was played up in the German press.

Hoopnagle asked us whether we would like to visit HICOG the next morning. I wanted to talk first to several people in Bonn who could give us some background. Nevertheless, early the next morning Montecone appeared at our door. It took all my tact (which isn't, I admit, a great deal) to get rid of him, for I was expecting some people who worked at HICOG, and I knew they would not want their visits reported to Kaghan.

One of these HICOG personnel told us that the people who worked there had no understanding of the anti-Communist movement and disliked congressional committees. But, he said, most of HICOG's blunders were due not to subversion but to stupidity. He cited as an example a film about a girl's college made for the information program at the cost of several thousand dollars. Someone decided that the sight of college girls in shorts might offend the German sense of propriety, so the film was junked—and taxpayers' money went down the drain. Our informant also alleged that HICOG was grossly overstaffed and that many of its employees had never had a security check.

Later that day, April 6, we went over to HICOG headquarters and talked, first, to Glenn Wolfe, Executive Director. Wolfe was hostile; he refused to discuss Kaghan.

On the advice of a public relations man from the State Department, we submitted to a press interview. The air was thick with hostility—natural, perhaps, for the newsmen were dependent on HICOG for information the whole year round. They asked us why we had not seen Kaghan, who had professed himself eager to talk to us. We wanted to talk to him too—for one thing, to arrange for his appearance before the committee—but we had hoped to gather more information about him first. However, we decided to see him at once.

We met Kaghan in Wolfe's office. I came right to the point and asked him whether he was the same Theodore Kaghan who had signed the nominating petition for a Communist party candidate. To my astonishment, he would not discuss this and other related matters, although he had insisted on seeing us. Wolfe advised him to answer.

He then said that he had in fact signed the petition but that he would not give us any further information. He specifically refused our request for the names of people known by him to be Communists who were still in the Government or working for the information program. He then claimed that he had been denied an opportunity to testify before our committee. This was not true. We had never been advised that he wished to testify; on the contrary, he had failed to answer a public invitation to do so. However, I now saw to it that immediate arrangements were made for him to go before the committee.

In talking with other people about HICOG, we discovered that it had authorized and paid for the publication of a book entitled *Synchronoptische Weltgeschichte.* This was a world history written by two Germans, dealing with modern times and intended for wide use in German schools and for distribution by our State Department as a part of its information program to fight Communism. It turned out to be sheer Communist propaganda. Subsequent uncontradicted testimony of witnesses before our committee revealed a Communist line from first page to last. Religious bodies were maligned, particularly the Catholic Church. Stalin and the Soviet Union were glorified. The United States and its form of government were defamed. Here is Stalin:

Soviet statesman bound up the solution of national questions with the international class war. Created the first Socialist constitution; realized planned economy with the First Five Year Plan, and built up the Red Army as a people's army, thereby succeeding in saving the Soviet Union when attacked by the Fascist powers, and supporting the revolution in Europe and Asia. As the accepted leader of world Communism he gave the teachings of Marx, Engels, and Lenin their present valid form.

Winston Churchill was portrayed as follows:

Son of an aristocratic English father and an American mother. After service as a colonial officer in the Boer War, prepared England by propaganda for war against Germany. After the defeat of Germany he sought to overthrow the Soviet state by intervention and also fought in England against the rising Socialist movement . . . In the Second World War he led England on the side of the Soviet Union and the United States to victory over Germany. Since then, he has tried to unite the states of Western Europe against the Soviet Union in dependence on the United States.

This "synchronized world history" described Mao Tse-tung in these words:

Chinese statesman; son of poor peasants . . . When the Kuomintang under Chiang Kai-shek abandoned its Socialist aims, he founded a Red Army and continued the revolutionary fight against great odds. Under his leadership, the revolution was fully victorious against the armies of Chiang Kai-shek supported by the United States. Since then he has labored, in close alliance with the Soviet Union, to construct a Communist economy and culture.

Our intervention caused HICOG to stop this book's distribution.

Another disturbing situation called for attention. When the United States took over in Germany under the Occupation Treaty, all the existing newspapers were closed down, and commissions set up to make sure new periodicals would not be under Nazi domination. One would expect equal care to be taken to see that they did not fall into Communist hands. But it wasn't. A clue as to why so many of the newspapers in our sector of Germany adopted the Communist line, or at least a strong anti-American policy, lies in the sympathies of some of those put in charge of licensing newspapers in the Occupation's early days.

German newspapers in most cases existed only by virtue of American loans. But we found that in addition to subsidizing these newspapers, HICOG ran one of its own. There was, hence, no need for subsidizing the Frankfurt edition of the German newspaper *Neue Zeitung*. When we brought this fact to light, this duplication was eliminated at a saving of some millions of dollars a year.

It also developed that HICOG had installed as editor of this newspaper one Hans Wallenberg, who had supported the Communist line during the Hitler-Stalin pact, and who, while editor of the *Neue Zeitung,* had used the services of five writers who were active Communists. Another Communist writing for this American-subsidized newspaper was novelist Stefan Heym, who has since fled to the Soviet zone and proclaimed openly his Communist membership and his allegiance to the Soviet Union.

After talking with a number of other people at HICOG, Schine and I prepared to leave for Berlin. While we were in Wolfe's office, Bill Montecone came in. He was very talkative, and when it was time to leave for the airport he said he would ride along with us. Annoyed by his constant attentions, I told him this wasn't necessary. "Well," said he, "give me a lift home—it's on your way."

Arrived at the destination, he said, "Will you wait here just a moment?" and dashed into the house, emerging minutes later with a suitcase. I asked, "What's that for?" He said, "I have to go to Berlin too. I'm supposed to meet two incoming congressmen, and I just received instructions to take the plane with you fellows."

It began to be obvious that Montecone was spying on us. Dave Schine so charged him, but he indignantly denied it. In Berlin he accompanied us to our hotel: "I'm supposed to wait for the congressmen here." He asked to join us for dinner. Dave was about to tell him to get lost or at least get a table of his own, but I did not want to be discourteous.

Later, Kaghan admitted to our subcommittee that an "escort officer" had been assigned to us despite our request for privacy, and that the escort had duly reported our activities to headquarters. Thus HICOG knew where we went, whom we interviewed, and even the questions we asked and the answers we received. Parts of our schedule were subsequently leaked to the newspapers in such a form as to make us appear in a bad light.

The next day, April 7, the Director of the office of HICOG, Cecil Lyon, at my request drove us into the (as yet unwalled) Soviet sector. It looked deserted, except for Soviet police and military units.

On the walls of the Soviet Information Center hung the usual pictures of Stalin, Lenin, and other Communist heroes, and posters requesting readers to write to the American President to commute the death sentences of Julius and Ethel Rosenberg.

Leaving, we were stopped at the door by two Soviet employees peddling a book to all who came through. It had a cover picture of Stalin and related the achievements of Communism. From his brief-case Dave Schine pulled a copy of *McCarthyism—the Fight for America,* with a picture of Senator Joseph McCarthy on its cover. Dave held out the book to the Russians, indicating that he would exchange it for the one they were selling. They whispered together, then accepted the trade. American Joe for Soviet Joe! As we walked down the steps, we saw them puzzling over it. I wrote to Senator McCarthy that he could no longer claim in speeches that the Soviet Information Center failed to carry his book.

On April 9, we went to Munich. People from the embassy took us to a hotel, but our uneasiness over the antics of Montecone made us decide to check out and to go to a guest house on the outskirts of Munich, where "Monte" would not be breathing down our necks and where our rooms wouldn't be wired.

There we had the opportunity of speaking to Hede Massing, the former wife of Gerhart Eisler, a top Communist leader and repre-sentative of the Comintern in the United States. Convicted, he jumped bail and became an official in the Soviet zone of Germany. Hede, although a strong anti-Communist, was unable to get a job with our State Department in Germany. She had considerable knowl-edge of the Communist movement, was intelligent and articulate, and could have done valuable work in the information service. And yet she was not employed.

At that time, the State Department Information Service was spon-soring a series of lectures in Munich. Their purpose was to demon-strate the objectives and ideals of the United States and its way of life, particularly in the struggle against Communism. But just a few weeks before our visit, we were told, a lecturer had shocked his audi-ence by informing them that the Soviet system of education was much better than the American. He also asserted that he knew Premier Georgi Malenkov personally, and that Malenkov wanted peace. If there were war, said our lecturer, it would not be the fault of the Soviet Union.

The man in charge of the Information Center confirmed this astonishing story. Schine thereupon sat down at a typewriter and wrote out our witness' statement just as he dictated it; the man signed it.

In Munich we also visited the branch of the Voice of America that broadcasts to areas behind the Iron Curtain close to Germany. This division was under the direction of Charles Malamuth, a dedicated and able executive. We spoke to the personnel of his unit and found among them many whose work for the Voice of America meant much more than a living. Having had personal experience of Communist tyranny, they were dedicating themselves to warning former friends and neighbors of the nature of Communist slavery. It was particularly disheartening to these people to encounter roadblocks and discouragements in instituting a vigorous anti-Communist campaign.

From Munich we went to Vienna. At the hotel, a delegation called from the office of the High Commissioner, headed by a Public Affairs officer in Vienna. He seemed hostile. "Well," I thought, "no one loves to hear the investigator's knock." One of the officials in the Security Department called me aside and explained, "Don't mind this fellow. He has been around stirring the newspapers up against you."

We had the usual problem with the press. The information people we were investigating kept the press informed of our movements and supplied it with a line of questioning that might embarrass us. Finally we refused to talk to any more newsmen. Then the State Department protested our "rudeness" as reflecting upon it. We gave in. Looking back, I am sorry we yielded.

In Vienna we went through the U.S. Information Library, then to the Soviet sector and went through theirs. We discovered that some of the same books—for example, the works of Howard Fast—were stocked by both. One of us—the United States or the Soviet Union— had to be wrong.

In Vienna a high official of the Austrian government met us in secret. He told us many distressing things about conditions in Austria, with particular reference to our State Department.

"Is it true," I asked him, "that a Communist shop has the job of printing U.S. information circulars?"

He laughed. "Quite true. That has been going on for some time."

"Can you prove it?"

"Very simply."

He gave us the name and address of the shop and the dates and numbers of the contracts. We found his information to be correct. The practice was then stopped.

British journals must be read to be believed. For slanting of news, callous distortion of facts, and outright inaccuracy, I have never known their equal. Witness, for example, how the British newsmen treated the visit David Schine and I planned to make to the BBC, where we hoped, if time permitted, to study the outstanding job the official British network had done in broadcasting behind the Iron Curtain. In headlines, in the emphasis and tone of the stories and pseudo-"facts" reported, they plainly sought to convey that Schine and I intended to "investigate" the BBC—something we had neither the right nor the wish to do. They raised such a furor that the subject was brought up in Parliament. On April 15 a Laborite, G. Wigg, rose in the Commons and asked the Assistant Postmaster General, whose department controls the BBC: "Would the Honorable Gentleman extend to these gentlemen [i.e., to us] the customary British welcome, but would he also assure them that we should regard it as thoroughly reprehensible that any visit to this country should be used as an occasion to gather evidence to prosecute and deliberately smear liberal-minded persons in America?"

The Assistant Postmaster General replied, "No application whatever has been made to the BBC or to the Post Office for any facilities for these two gentlemen."

This should have ended the matter, but no. The same day the *Daily Mail* had us canceling the investigation we never intended to make: "McCARTHY'S BOYS 'PUT OFF' BBC PROBE." The *Daily Mirror* that morning said: "WITCH-HUNT BOYS GET COLD FEET." Its story, a marvel of invention, stated that Schine and I "have thought better of coming to London to give the BBC 'the works.' " The Manchester *Guardian* reported upon our departure from London: "Mr. Cohn and Mr. Schine have arrived, investigated and departed. They landed at Northolt shortly after two o'clock and left punctually at eight, protesting to the last that they had never intended to investigate the BBC . . ."

British press distortions had come to our attention while we were still in Greece. Ambassador Peurifoy told me not to be disturbed— the British establishment was notoriously soft toward Communism. This wasn't exactly news—in the Dr. Klaus Fuchs case, the Dr. Allen Nunn May case, and others, the British establishment had refused to grapple effectively with the Communist problem. But Peurifoy explained that the British went beyond this: they not only did nothing about their Communist problem, but ridiculed anyone who took it seriously.

My impression remains that many in England to this day refuse to regard Communism as anything but a political movement and the Communist party as just another political party. Therefore, anybody who interferes with it or challenges it in any way is thought to be meddling with the freedom of speech and liberty of political action. The British are unconvinced that Communism presents a deadly threat to those very free institutions they prize so highly and did so much to develop. While it is true that the Communist vote is tiny and therefore the party has no political role in Great Britain, Red influence is powerful in a number of important trade unions, especially the electrical and engineering ones. (John Gunther found that some conservative industries actually prefer Communists in their plants because the Communist shop-stewards are efficient and hard-working!) In 1962, a report disclosed the alarming extent to which Communists were penetrating the British Civil Service. With its sagging economy, its "brain drain" or siphoning off of top talent, and its astonishing lack of awareness of the perils, Great Britain is a prime target for continuing Communist penetration of its democratic institutions. It took over a decade—until late 1967—for the shocking Burgess-McLean-Philby story to sink into the British consciousness. The way the British promoted Harold Philby, a dedicated Communist spy, from one key security post to another is simply not to be believed even if read in a Helen MacInnes or Ian Fleming spy novel.

One final comment on the British press: American newspapers certainly have not been sparing in their criticisms of me, but no American reporter has ever stooped to so low a level of personal abuse as did some British journalists. For example, no American paper ever alluded to a scar I bear on my nose, the result of a boyhood accident. I am not an especially vain man: I could have had the scar removed by plastic surgery but never saw fit to have it done. One Alan Fairclough wrote in the *Daily Mirror* on April 20 about ". . . scar-nosed Roy Cohn . . ." I simply note that to my knowledge he was the only journalist who ever made mention of it as a significant factor.

I did get a laugh from "Peterborough's" column, "London Day by Day," in the *Daily Telegraph*. He wrote that pending our arrival, he had been carrying out his own investigation of the American Library in Grosvenor Square, adding: "In the library—on the right-hand side of the entrance—there is a book called *The A.B.C. of American Wines*. It contains a long section on red wines. While I do not believe that there is a strong enough case for removing this book, I suggest that everyone who reads it should be carefully watched."

In New York we were greeted at the airport by a gaggle of reporters, including the usual agit-prop squad from the New York *Post*. The latter concentrated on Dave Schine, reading him a list of business enterprises his father is supposed to have been involved in. I could not see the relevance of this to our work with the McCarthy committee—particularly since it came from the *Post,* which has repeatedly declared itself against guilt by association.

In Washington, Dave and I reviewed the trip with Senator McCarthy. He said it had been most productive and that we had established a number of points bound to be of great help to the committee in ridding the information program of pro-Communist influence and in saving money. He particularly liked the case we had developed against the subsidization of German newspapers in competition with the newspaper we ourselves published in Germany at the cost of $3,000,000 a year. He called hearings to explore these and other matters we had uncovered.

Unfavorable publicity in the American press, particularly in the New York *Post* and the Washington *Post,* reached a crescendo. I was painted as an ungifted clown, without ability or knowledge for the job I was supposed to do, who had made a fool of himself and his country in Europe.

It is hard to laugh off such unfairness. I had done some six years of investigative work, with over two hundred successful prosecutions and investigations in the Department of Justice, plus years of work with the Secret Service and the FBI, satisfactory enough to win me commendatory letters from J. Edgar Hoover, from U. E. Baughman, the Chief of the Secret Service, and from Commissioner Harry Anslinger of the Bureau of Narcotics.

As for our conduct, we worked hard day and night. We talked to hundreds of witnesses, examined many documents, and wrote daily reports. Dave kept a detailed log of everyone we saw, every witness interviewed, and how every hour was spent. We did not "live it up." We had had no time for tomfoolery.

Hostile critics charged that the trip's cost was excessive. Actually it was one of the least expensive, insofar as public funds are concerned, ever made. We paid most of our own expenses. When Philip Potter of the Baltimore *Sun* reported that the trip had cost the taxpayer $74 a day, I gave him the facts and he published a retraction with the correct figure—$28.

Concerning the effectiveness of the trip, I think the best proof is the interim report, unanimously submitted by the United States Senate Permanent Subcommittee on Investigations, listing the facts we uncovered. These resulted in eliminating much duplication and in correcting abuses such as those involving the Communist printing shop and the slanted textbook. The State Department received the resignation of Kaghan and several others, and ordered the removal of all books "of any Communists, fellow travelers, et cetera," from the information centers. Finally, it led to the entire information program's being redefined and clarified by order of President Eisenhower.

All this does not alter the fact that the trip itself was not successful at all in terms of public relations and the impression we made, owing to our inability to cope with the propaganda onslaught against us in hostile territory—a counterattack we hadn't foreseen.

Lawrence Spivak, the television moderator, invited me to tell our side of the story on "Meet the Press," and I succeeded there because I had a bad case of mike-fright. Anyone that rattled must be telling the truth, people concluded. I was able to get across a lot of facts, and fortunately my ego got buried out of sight—and to the viewers, apparently I seemed a far different person from the callous Rover Boy depicted by the press.

My father, in Washington for a B'nai B'rith convention, had come to the studio with me. It was worth the klieg-light ordeal to see the pleasure the telecast gave him. As soon as the program was over, telegrams and phone calls poured in. For the first time in weeks I felt alive again. Louis B. Mayer phoned the studio; Senator Symington conveyed a congratulatory message from Bob Hope—they had watched together. And my mother, who was watching on television in New York, called the studio to say that my necktie wasn't straight.

CHAPTER 7

WHO PROMOTED

PERESS?

In SEPTEMBER OF 1953, Joe McCarthy and I had a long conference in his Palm Beach hotel suite. While we talked of subversion and other sordid matters, a beautiful young woman would enter the room, listen, interpose an idea, and wander off to resume her reading or puttering about. She was the newly wedded Mrs. McCarthy, as intelligent as she was handsome.

From time to time his enemies had insinuated that the Senator tried to hire for his staff every pretty girl he ran across in another senator's office. To my observation, only one young lady was so tagged with any accuracy. She was a cute little brunette. He was fond of her, and without question a clandestine romance progressed for a couple of years. It would become active whenever the Senator was on the windward side of his stormy courtship of the beautiful, brilliant Jean Kerr of Washington. Jeannie and Joe were as close and devoted to each other as any couple I have known. But they were both strong-willed, and Joe was difficult to domesticate. The obstacle that delayed their marriage was known to Joe alone—he did not want to inflict on Jeannie the heartache and agony that resulted from the attacks on him. What finally changed his mind was the realization that her concern for him was just as great without a wedding ring. He told me one evening driving in Florida that he had finally come to that conclusion and had decided to marry her. When we got back to Washington, however, they had another blowup over some petty thing. I remember talking to Jean from a phone booth at the airport. She said everything was all over—period. I said, "You'll be married by summer." She cried, "Small hope!" and we ended betting a quarter. That spring I was an usher at their wedding—and Jean sent me a plastic-encased quarter. I still have it on my desk.

My interruption of the McCarthys' honeymoon could be called the beginning of the Peress case. If the bride resented the intrusion of business into her wedding trip she gave no sign. Actually, Jean Kerr, Washington-born and -bred, who had worked as Joe's secretary, was accustomed to business at any hour of the day or night. The two had hoped for a peaceful holiday and had kept their plans secret. They had managed to spend a quiet first night in Washington after telling everyone that they were off for the South. They went on to an island off the coast of Florida where communication with the mainland was only by radio. I had the call number with instructions to use it only in an urgent matter.

Such a matter had suddenly come up. After radioing McCarthy I joined him in Palm Beach. From that evening the Peress case, the General Zwicker affair, and the whole Fort Monmouth investigation escalated rapidly.

It had started slowly, with a trickle of reports from informants. Civilian employees, Army officers, and enlisted personnel came in person or wrote or telephoned about conditions they thought alarming at the Signal Corps installation at Fort Monmouth, New Jersey. When the reports had accumulated to the point where they could not be ignored, we launched the investigations of Communist infiltration of the military which was to culminate in a head-on collision with the Army itself.

Between August, 1953, and October, 1954, we heard 71 witnesses at executive sessions and 41 at open hearings. Criticism of our Monmouth hearings has been sharp and bitter: it was, we were told, a waste, a farce, a fruitless exercise, because we uncovered no active espionage ring, we produced no Rosenberg protégés, no masterminds at work funneling our secrets to the Kremlin. It is true that McCarthy, with his penchant for the dramatic, invited much of the critical storm by making statements that could be construed as promising too much. In October, he told the press that the Monmouth investigation "has all the earmarks of extremely dangerous espionage." Ominously he added that the committee had in its possession some evidence that

Julius Rosenberg himself had created a spy operation at Monmouth that "may still be in operation."

While we did not produce another Rosenberg, we uncovered a system so dangerously lax that a security risk had been commissioned in the Army, that the civilian personnel employed by the Army had been infiltrated by subversives, that this infiltration extended particularly to the Army secret radar laboratories at Fort Monmouth, and that the FBI for a period of years had been warning Army officials of persons with Communist affiliations at work in the secret installation.

The Army's cooperation with our subcommittee was less than wholehearted. We had difficulty obtaining personnel records on possible security risks. Obstacles were placed in our path when we sought to question Army personnel about how security risks had managed to get their assignments—and how they were permitted to remain after their records had become known.

Some Government agencies resented and resisted our investigation, others cooperated. McCarthy believed that if an agency was being run in the best interests of the nation, it had nothing to hide. "If there were mistakes and inefficiencies, they should want to cooperate in every way to correct the abuses," he said once. "But those who have vested interests in covering up mistakes and who, in general, dislike congressional committees and fear them as an encroachment upon their freedom of action, won't cooperate."

The Army's lack of cooperation was demonstrated forcibly in their treatment of Major General Kirke B. Lawton, the competent Fort Monmouth commanding officer. General Lawton, a sturdily built man in his middle fifties, was just as disturbed as we were about evidence of Communist infiltration. Within the bounds of military regulations, he cooperated with the subcommittee, helping us obtain interviews and information. But the Pentagon, learning of the General's helpfulness, ordered him to report to Walter Reed Hospital for a medical examination. He was found to have a physical disability and was confined to quarters there for weeks. I understand he was given an elaborate suite and was quite comfortable. Lawton, unfortunately, never returned to the post where he could cooperate with the Congress. He was given a "disability" discharge.

It was during the Monmouth hearings that Dave Schine involuntarily began playing a major role. Dave was an able young businessman with a keen interest in the fight against Communism. I had persuaded him to work for the subcommittee, and he had worked hard. Association with the McCarthy committee was not the best way to avoid making powerful enemies, and naturally enough a fair number of persons was soon after Dave. He had at the time a 4-F draft classification because of a slipped disc, a fact soon seized upon by columnist Drew Pearson, that old McCarthy foe. Pearson's office telephoned Schine's draft board in California and demanded that the case be reopened.

Dave was reexamined, reclassified, and in November of 1953, ordered back into service. He wanted to go; in fact, he felt strongly that he should be separated quietly from the committee and fulfill his military obligation. I thought it was logical for him to apply for a commission and be permitted to complete his pending work with us. Schine was a Harvard graduate and had served in the U.S. Merchant Marine for two years, had run a large business, and had worked effectively for a congressional committee. Far less qualified candidates had received commissions.

An application for a commission for Schine was thereupon channeled in routine manner by Senator McCarthy through the liaison office the Department of Defense maintains in Washington with Capitol Hill. A staff is on duty for the sole purpose of processing applications submitted by legislators, administration officials, and others on behalf of individuals they believe to be qualified. I followed up the application with calls and visits to certain persons, again normal procedure. Meanwhile, Dave was taken into the army and assigned to Fort Dix as a private. He was to become the most talked-about private soldier in many years, giving rise to an apochryphal tale of the time—that Mrs. Schine, Sr., ran into a friend on the avenue and inquired, "Have you heard that my David is in the Army?"

Now another person joined the cast of characters of the developing Fort Monmouth drama. His name was Irving M. Peress.

One of the most frequently asked questions about those days still is: How did we find out about Peress? Who told us about the case that within a few months was to involve us in deep and angry controversy with the Pentagon and the President of the United States and to set off the historic Army-McCarthy hearings?

We learned about it from one of the high-ranking generals in the country. In December, 1953, a call came to Senator McCarthy at his subcommittee offices. He was given a telephone number and was asked to call at a certain time. He did. It was a pay station and the General answered the ring himself. The General spoke urgently for a few minutes, telling the Senator about an explosive situation then existing. When he hung up the phone, McCarthy called me into his office and told me to leave the very next afternoon for New York, where I had an appointment with a young lieutenant, aide to the General, at the bar of the Sherry-Netherland Hotel. There, he said, I would learn the full details of a remarkable case.

In the spring of 1952, a round-faced, slightly balding young dentist had applied for a commission in the United States Army. His name was Irving Peress, and for the past dozen years he had practiced his profession in Elmhurst, a crowded business and residential section of Queens lying about five miles eastward of Manhattan.

The year before, Dr. Peress had registered with Draft Board No. 59 in Forest Hills, a neighboring community, as required by the Doctors Draft Act of 1950. The act also provided that doctors summoned for military duty may apply for a Reserve commission. This he did. As part of his application, he filled out and signed Department of Defense Form No. 390, in which he certified that "I am not now and have not been a member of any foreign or domestic organization, association, movement, group, or a combination of persons advocating a subversive policy or seeking to alter the form of Government of the United States by unconstitutional means." Peress was appointed a captain in the Army Dental Corps, took his oath, and completed Department of Defense Form 98, a loyalty certification. But he claimed the Fifth Amendment in three separate places in refusing to answer questions concerning membership in certain subversive organizations. He was ordered to active duty effective January 1, 1953, and assigned to Brooke Army Medical Center at Fort Sam Houston, Texas. After four weeks of basic training he was ordered to proceed to Fort Lewis, Washington, for further assignment to the Far East Command at Yokohama, Japan.

While at Fort Lewis, Washington, and awaiting transportation overseas, Peress received emergency leave to return home to New York because of the illness of his wife and six-year-old daughter. While on leave he applied for and received reassignment to Camp Kilmer, New Jersey, some thirty miles from New York City, and his orders assigning him to the Far East command were rescinded.

Meanwhile, First Army's G-2 (Intelligence) had received the loyalty forms executed by Dr. Peress, taken note that he claimed constitutional privilege, and, wondering why, ordered an investigation. This investigative file was forwarded to the Pentagon with a report that sufficient evidence of subversive tendencies existed to warrant removal of Peress from the service as a security risk. The file then went on a remarkable journey—across the country to Army jurisdictions where it was thought Peress was stationed. It took nine months and seven separate requests for dismissal by high Army officials, who affixed their own recommendations to the file when it came to them, before Peress was honorably discharged from the service.

While these recommendations for his dismissal were moving around the country, Peress wrote a letter (dated September 9, 1953) requesting a promotion from captain to major. A law had been passed by Congress in June of that year stipulating that any Reserve corps doctor or dentist ordered into active duty should be "promoted to such grade or rank as may be commensurate with his professional education, experience, and ability." Thus on the basis of his age and experience, Peress was entitled to an automatic promotion. His request was forwarded through channels for action. On September 23, First Army recommended the reappointment of Captain Peress in the grade of major, and exactly one month afterward, the Department of the Army, office of the Adjutant General, duly promoted Peress. The order was signed by Major General William E. Bergin, U.S. Army, "By Order of the Secretary of the Army." Two days before, on October 21, the Kilmer CO, Brigadier General Ralph W. Zwicker, outlined the case against Peress in a letter to the First Army which bore the notation: "Subject: Elimination of Security Risk." Zwicker recommended in the letter that Peress be relieved from duty without delay.

Picture, now, the situation that existed: an officer in the United States Army, who had invoked the Fifth Amendment three times in answering Army loyalty questionnaires, had been investigated by the Army's own intelligence unit. Dismissal from the service had been recommended on the ground that unfavorable security information had been found against him. The officer's own commanding general had also recommended his dismissal. Nevertheless, the officer's request for a promotion to field grade was processed and approved.

But the unbelievable laxity—or frightening stupidity—of Army bureaucratic procedures was made clear. Obviously, the Army was operating on different levels, the officers who promoted unaware of the officers who investigated. At the White House, Sherman Adams tried to find out what was happening, but, he admits, "sorry answers" were received from the Army. Major General Wilton B. ("Jerry") Persons, an Eisenhower friend and aide, discovered, according to Adams, that "the blunders were caused by red tape and inefficiency; the promotion and the honorable discharge had simply gone through channels faster than the security information could catch up with the record."

In November, the Pentagon finally decided something had to be done about Peress. By letter dated January 18, 1954, the "Department of the Army, Office of the Adjutant General" directed the commanding general of the First Army to relieve Major Peress from active duty and honorably discharge him from the Army at the earliest practicable date, depending upon the officer's desires but not later than ninety days from the day the letter was received. Peress was advised of this directive by General Zwicker and chose March 31 as his discharge date.

We learned about the Peress matter in early December, when the General who finally called us became increasingly alarmed at the inefficiency of the Army's security program. He had watched the Peress case develop and had become convinced that the Army was planning to cover up the entire scandalous situation without taking corrective action. Thus the door would be left agape for a recurrence.

Immediately after I learned the story, I spoke to Army counselor John G. Adams, giving him Peress' name. A few days later, Adams told me he had checked and was taking action. I reported this to McCarthy, who suggested we leave the matter in the Army's hands, at least for a while. Throughout December and January, McCarthy asked me almost daily if anything had been done about the Peress case. It was no longer Peress we were interested in, of course, but those in the Army who had ignored his Communist background and had permitted his commissioning and then his promotion. I checked often with Adams; nothing was being done.

Finally McCarthy said to me: "I don't believe the Army is planning to do a damned thing. The committee has to move on it now. Have a subpoena served on Peress."

On January 30 we summoned Major Peress to appear before our subcommittee in executive session. The proceedings were subsequently made public.

THE CHAIRMAN: Did anyone in the Army ever ask you whether you were a member of the Communist party or a Communist party organizer?

MAJOR PERESS: I decline to answer that question under the protection of the Fifth Amendment on the ground that it might tend to incriminate me.

THE CHAIRMAN: You decline to answer whether or not they asked you? Are you a member of the Communist party today?

MAJOR PERESS: I again decline, claiming the privilege for the reason previously stated.

THE CHAIRMAN: Were you a member of the Communist party at the time you were indicted?

MAJOR PERESS: I again claim the privilege.

THE CHAIRMAN: Did any Communists intervene to have your orders changed so you would not have to leave the country?

MAJOR PERESS: I again claim the privilege.

THE CHAIRMAN: You are entitled to the privilege. Is your wife a member of the Communist party?

MAJOR PERESS: I again claim the privilege.

*   *   *

MR. COHN: Now, Major, you are a graduate of the leadership training course of the Inwood Victory Club of the Communist party, are you not?

MAJOR PERESS: I decline to answer that question under the Fifth Amendment.

MR. COHN: Did you attend courses in leadership of the Inwood Victory Club of the Communist party at 139 Dyckman Street?

MAJOR PERESS: I claim the privilege.

*   *   *

MR. COHN: Did you yourself deliver talks at Communist discussion groups at which you discussed the doctrine of Marxism and Leninism urging the overthrow of the Government of the United States by force and violence?

MAJOR PERESS: I again claim the privilege.

MR. COHN: When you went down to Camp Kilmer, specifically, when at Camp Kilmer, did you attempt to recruit any of the military personnel there into the Communist party?

MAJOR PERESS: I again claim the privilege for the same reason.
MR. COHN: While stationed at Camp Kilmer did you have Communist party meetings at your home, attended by one or more military personnel from Camp Kilmer?
MAJOR PERESS: I again claim the privilege.

*   *   *

MR. COHN: While you were at Camp Kilmer, were you taking orders from any functionaries of the Communist party?
MAJOR PERESS: I again claim the privilege.

*   *   *

MR. COHN: While at Camp Kilmer, did you, in fact, recruit military personnel into the Communist party?
MAJOR PERESS: I again claim the privilege.

*   *   *

THE CHAIRMAN: How much of your salary, if any, do you contribute to the Communist party?
MAJOR PERESS: I again claim the privilege for the same reason.
THE CHAIRMAN: Did you attend a Communist party meeting within the last week?
MAJOR PERESS: I again claim the privilege.
THE CHAIRMAN: Is there a Communist cell at Camp Kilmer of which you are a member?
MAJOR PERESS: I again claim the privilege.
THE CHAIRMAN: Did you not organize a Communist cell at Camp Kilmer?
MAJOR PERESS: I again claim the privilege.

Matters now moved rapidly.

Two days after his appearance before our subcommittee, Major Peress had a meeting with General Zwicker during which he requested an immediate release from the Army instead of waiting until March 31. On the same day, Senator McCarthy sent a letter by messenger to Secretary of the Army Robert Stevens in which he pointed out that a thorough investigation was now indicated. This, he said, "would disclose the names of those responsible officers who had full knowledge of his [Peress'] Communist activities and either took no steps to have him removed or were responsible for his promotion thereafter. They also, of course, took an oath to protect this country against all enemies, foreign and domestic. Aiding in the promotion of, or the failure to expose the Communist activities of a fellow officer is a violation of that oath and without question should subject them to a court martial."

Stevens was in the Far East but was expected back in a day or two. In his absence, the letter was handled by Army counselor Adams in Stevens' behalf. Frank Carr telephoned Adams several times on February 1 and 2, urging him not to permit the honorable discharge, or at least to hold it up until Stevens returned. Adams declined to do so. On February 2, Major Peress was whisked out of the Army at Camp Kilmer with his honorable discharge.

McCarthy was furious. He telephoned Adams that evening at the latter's home and told him, frankly, fully, and acidly, what he thought of the manner in which the Peress case had been handled. McCarthy felt the Army was attempting, in the clumsiest way imaginable, to cover up a scandal. "When they want to move fast," he said to me bitterly, "they can shuffle those papers faster than you can see them."

A year later, when Senator John McClellan became chairman of the subcommittee, an exhaustive investigation was conducted into the entire Peress case. In its report, the committee stated that Adams "showed disrespect for this subcommittee when he chose to disregard Senator McCarthy's letter of February 1, 1954, and allowed Peress to be honorably discharged on February 2, 1954." The Washington *Star*—certainly not a McCarthy supporter—observed editorially: "It is hard to believe that this [discharge] was a routine move, made in routine fashion. It is hard not to believe that someone at a high level made the decision to get rid of Major Peress before the McCarthy group could complete its investigation. If the inference here is justified, the Army ought to reveal the identity of that official."

The Senator, seeking answers, ordered hearings for February 18 in New York. Testifying at the public session in the morning was Miss Ruth Eagle, a New York City policewoman for eleven years who, for the past two and a half years, had been on a special undercover assignment as a member of the Communist party. She submitted written reports regularly on Peress and his wife and their activities at party functions. She testified that Peress had acted as a liaison between a Communist cell and the American Labor party; that he submitted to her lists of American Labor party members who were Communists and other American Labor party members whom he was organizing; and that he attended the Leadership Training Course of the Communist party.

When we met for an executive session that afternoon none of us realized that in the next ninety minutes the fuse would be ignited which would cause that historic detonation—the Army-McCarthy hearings.

General Zwicker had been called to testify because we were eager to fix responsibility for the promotion of Peress and for the disregard of Peress' testimony before our subcommittee as well as the letter McCarthy had sent to Secretary Stevens by special messenger. In that letter, McCarthy had reviewed Peress' testimony and made several suggestions, including a recommendation that court martial proceedings be instituted against the major. Stevens had gone to see President Eisenhower, who advised him to admit promptly whatever error had been committed and to give the subcommittee all pertinent facts upon request. Accordingly, two days before the executive session, a reply had come from Stevens admitting "defects" in Army procedure and stating that corrective charges had been instituted and an investigation begun. But nothing could change the fact that Peress had been hurriedly handed his honorable discharge a day after McCarthy had sent his letter and that he was now safely out of the Army's hands.

Five days before the session, Jim Juliana interviewed General Zwicker at Camp Kilmer and found him cooperative. Zwicker told Juliana that he was opposed to giving Peress an honorable discharge and that he had been in communication with the Pentagon on the case. We had ample reason to believe that Zwicker would tell us who was responsible for the mishandling of the case. But later we found out that Zwicker conferred with Army counselor John G. Adams after he (Zwicker) talked with Juliana.

Zwicker and Senator McCarthy met for the first time that day at lunch and chatted amiably. At 4:30 in the afternoon, the General took the stand at the executive session. I began the questioning, then McCarthy took over. He hadn't gone far when he realized that Zwicker's attitude had undergone a transformation. The friendliness he had shown McCarthy and Juliana privately was gone. He was hostile and uncooperative. McCarthy took him carefully over the facts, but Zwicker was evasive, split hairs, contradicted himself. At first he said that on the day Peress got his honorable discharge, he was not aware the major had specifically refused to answer any questions before the committee. Then he stated he did know Peress refused to answer questions but was not aware they referred to his alleged Communist activities. Finally, he admitted he knew Peress had refused to answer questions about these activities. On a number of occasions, Zwicker declined to answer because he was forbidden to do so under the Truman 1948 directive providing that information relative to the loyalty of Federal employees "shall be maintained in complete confidence." (This was justifiable, but as McCarthy later stated: "He could refuse to answer a question on the grounds of a presidential directive but he was not entitled to give an evasive answer or an answer that was not the truth.")

At this point it is instructive to leap forward three years and one month and listen to General Zwicker describe his own performance that day. The occasion was a hearing before the Senate Armed Services Committee on March 21, 1957; the subject was Zwicker's nomination to the rank of major general. Discussing his testimony, the General stated: "I think there are some circumstances . . . that would certainly tend to give a person the idea that perhaps I was recalcitrant, perhaps I was holding back, and perhaps I wasn't too cooperative. . . . And I am afraid that I permitted unconsciously, really, myself an attitude to be built up where I felt I was kind of on the defensive rather, and I was perhaps also afraid that, and built up in my mind, 'You have got to be awfully darn careful. Anything that you may say that really you could say of an unclassified nature, perhaps they are using that to lead into something of a classified nature that you might slip and give them.' And I am afraid I was perhaps overcautious and perhaps on the defensive, and that this feeling . . . may have inclined me to be not as forthright, perhaps, in answering the questions put to me as I might have been otherwise."

Zwicker's own description of his performance makes it easier to understand McCarthy's growing impatience and frustration. His tone and his questions became edged. He fought to control his temper, and lost.

MC CARTHY: General, let's try and be truthful. I am going to keep
    you here as long as you keep hedging and hemming.
ZWICKER: I am not hedging.
MC CARTHY: Or hawing.

The General also denied he was hawing. "I don't like to have anyone impugn my honesty, which you just about did."

Now McCarthy flared up. "Either your honesty or your intelligence," he snapped. "I can't help impugning one or the other, when you tell us that a major in your command who was known to you to have been before a Senate committee, and of whom you read the press releases very carefully—to now have you sit here and tell us that you did not know whether he refused to answer questions about Communist activities. I had seen all the press releases, and they all dealt with that. So, when you do that, General, if you will pardon me, I cannot help but question either your honesty or your intelligence. One or the other. I want to be very frank with you on that."

Later, the Senator asked this hypothetical question:

MC CARTHY: Let us assume that John Jones is a major in the United States Army. Let us assume that there is sworn testimony to the effect that he is part of the Communist conspiracy, has attended Communist leadership schools. Let us assume that Major John Jones is under oath before a committee and says, "I cannot tell you the truth about these charges because, if I did, I fear that might tend to incriminate me." Then let us say that General Smith was responsible for this man receiving an honorable discharge, knowing these facts. Do you think that General Smith should be removed from the military, or do you think he should be kept on in it?

GENERAL ZWICKER: He should be by all means kept if he were acting under competent orders to separate that man.

MC CARTHY: Let us say he is the man who signed the orders. Let us say General Smith is the man who originated the order.

ZWICKER: Originated the order directing his separation?

MC CARTHY: Directing his honorable discharge.

ZWICKER: Well, that is pretty hypothetical.

MC CARTHY: It is pretty real, General.

Zwicker sparred with the central question, had it repeated by the reporter, finally felt it was not a question for him to decide. McCarthy pressed him. "I want to know how you feel about getting rid of Communists," he insisted. When Zwicker replied he was "all for it" McCarthy demanded he answer the hypothetical question about the general who gave the honorable discharge "unless you take the Fifth Amendment. I do not care how long we stay here, you are going to answer it."

"Do you mean how I feel toward Communists?" Zwicker asked.

Now McCarthy's temper snapped again. "I mean exactly what I asked you, General, nothing else. Anyone with the brains of a five-year-old child can understand the question."

The question was once again read by the reporter, and finally Zwicker answered it.

"I do not think he should be removed from the military," he said.

At this point, McCarthy's patience ended completely and his temper exploded. His face flushed and his voice rose. He leaned toward Zwicker and snapped out the words that were to plague him for the rest of his life:

MC CARTHY: Then, General, you should be removed from any command. Any man who has been given the honor of being promoted to general and who says "I will protect another general who protected Communists" is not fit to wear that uniform, General. I think it is a tremendous disgrace to the Army to have this sort of thing given to the public. I intend to give it to them. I have a duty to do that. I intend to repeat to the press exactly what you said. So you know that. You will be back here, General.

There can be no denial. McCarthy's control over himself had broken. He should never have uttered those words.

Nevertheless the Senator's position in the matter was unassailable. The committee had every right to fix responsibility. In the national interest, the Army should have extended itself to the utmost to be cooperative and to allow us to probe the situation to the very bottom. Instead, the General who could have given us the information chose to offer us silence, hostility, and indifference. Thus McCarthy's impatience at his refusal to help was, in my view, understandable.

Weren't we somewhat foolish to raise all that fuss about an obscure Army dentist? How much harm could he do, actually? Wasn't it true that the only sensitive area in which Dr. Irving Peress worked in the military was the exposed nerve of a diseased tooth?

The questions are relevant. Perhaps there was too much stress upon the possible damage our country might suffer from the presence of Peress in the officer corps. We did not intend to give the impression we felt Stalin himself had planted Peress in the armed forces to steal our most vital secrets.

Perhaps we should have emphasized more the alarming implications of the Peress case: Peress was promoted by a woefully lax security system supervised by people untrained in the detection of subversion. (The McClellan Committee found that a total of forty-eight errors "of more than minor importance were committed by the Army in connection with the commissioning, transfer, promotion, and honorable discharge of Irving Peress.")

This same type of laxity made it possible for David Greenglass to be taken into the Army and assigned to the A-bomb project at Los Alamos. Greenglass, an outright Communist, remained completely undetected in his job and went on to steal atom bomb secrets and turn them over to Julius Rosenberg and Harry Gold. This one example made the persistence of this condition, as evidenced by the Peress case ten years later, a matter of utmost importance for the subcommittee and for the nation. Buckley and Bozell have written, in *McCarthy and His Enemies:* "The great traitors of the past have swung battles, not wars. An Alger Hiss, critically situated, can, conceivably, determine the destiny of the West. A Klaus Fuchs can deliver . . . what may well be the key to world conquest."

There was another lesson we learned from the Peress case, phrased by Lionel Lokos in his documented study, *"Who Promoted Peress?"* "It proved," he wrote, "that serious mistakes affecting the nation's security could be hidden from Congress and the public indefinitely, perhaps even permanently, by an administration armed with the unbridled power to slap a secrecy stamp on anything it chose, and seal the lips of every employee in the Federal Government. . . ."

As a direct result of the Peress case, Army security regulations were thoroughly overhauled. On March 4, President Eisenhower stated:

"1. The Department of the Army made serious errors in handling the Peress case and the Secretary of the Army so stated publicly, almost a month ago.

"2. The Army is correcting its procedures to avoid such mistakes in the future. I am completely confident that Secretary Stevens will be successful in this effort. . . ."

Secretary of Defense Charles E. Wilson, in a letter dated March 31, disagreed with the decision of the Department of the Army concerning the honorable discharge granted to Irving Peress. Secretary Wilson wrote that the case of Peress stemmed from improper administrative handling; that Peress should not have been commissioned and would not be commissioned under present regulations; that since he should never have been commissioned in the first place he should not have been promoted while he was being investigated. In connection with the honorable discharge of Peress, Wilson stated, "My review of all the available facts in this case makes it apparent that this judgment was faulty."

The Department of Defense subsequently issued corrective regulations.

On April 8, a new directive was issued by the department: "Personnel records and all investigative records in regard to the security of personnel not now effectively correlated should be correlated without delay in each of the military departments to insure that full facts are available for prompt and fair administration of all personnel matters." The Army also adopted a new system of correlating intelligence and personnel files by establishing "flagging" procedures. All personnel files would henceforth be flagged to show that action was being taken by Army Intelligence, which would preclude favorable personnel action. Upon receipt of a final determination favorable to an individual, the notification is removed, and upon receipt of final determination unfavorable to an individual the notification becomes a permanent part of the file.

Secretary Stevens told the Armed Services Committee on July 15 that under the new procedure:

". . . First, any person known to be disloyal or subversive will not knowingly be taken into the service either in a commissioned or enlisted grade.

"Second, a person in the service found to be disloyal or subversive will be discharged.

"Third, if any person while in the service commits subversive acts, he will be brought to trial by court-martial. . . ."

Finally, Congress made much-needed amendments to the Doctor Draft Act, which until then had made it mandatory for the Army to give commissions to all doctors and dentists. To prevent the presence of another Peress in the commissioned ranks, this mandatory provision was stricken out. The act was amended to read that "any person heretofore or hereafter inducted or ordered to active duty under the authority of this Act who fails to qualify for, or to accept, a commission or whose commission is terminated may be utilized in his professional capacity in an enlisted grade or rank."

These results show that we had not been shadow-boxing. The bureaucratic system responsible for Peress' promotion had been exposed and revised.

The hostility between the Army and the subcommittee was now at its peak. From the Commander in Chief down, the military establishment was seething with resentment. The Army felt its prestige had been severely damaged.

Counterattack was inevitable.

CHAPTER 8

"CROSSFIRE!"

ALTHOUGH NO OUTWARD SIGNS were visible that fall and winter, events were moving toward a political explosion.

Strange happenings were taking place behind closed doors in Washington and New York. Deeply involved were the White House, a number of key congressmen of both parties, and top-level Pentagon officials. The sole objective: to stop McCarthy. The senator from Wisconsin was charging ahead too fast to suit many of the nation's leaders.

In the White House, the Eisenhower wing of the Republican party, after years of agonizing indecision which included acceptance of McCarthy support in 1952, finally realized that something had to be done about the rambunctious Senator. It was now evident that McCarthy's power was growing, both in the Congress and in the party's own right or anti-Eisenhower wing. McCarthy would doubtless play an important role in the off-year 1954 elections, which would be fought—not over the Eisenhower program as the General's forces wished—but over the Senator's Communists-in-Government charge. And, as everyone in the Eisenhower group knew only too well, this had become a "gut issue" that could sweep the nation and return to Congress a powerful Republican right-wing bloc that would challenge the leadership of the Eisenhower faction. Clearly, then, a move of some kind against McCarthy had become essential.

On Capitol Hill, the Democratic leadership also peered into the future, at least as far as the following November, and glimpsed with a shudder the shape of things to come. The memory of McCarthy's role in the defeats of Millard Tydings in Maryland and William Benton in Connecticut was still fresh and painful. Democrats knew that McCarthy fought his political battles in rugged style, and those who were up for reelection did not look forward to a tangle with him. Finally, McCarthy's unfortunate castigation of the Democrats as the "party of treason" still rankled.

Certainly at the Pentagon nothing would please the Department of the Army more than to find some way of curbing the cause of so many headaches under brass hats.

Thus the following events came to pass as 1953 waned.

One day in the fall, a distinguished-looking gentleman who remarkably resembled the President of the United States journeyed to New York City for a lunch with George E. Sokolsky, the syndicated columnist. He had a wide smile, like the President's, and was, in point of fact, the President's scholarly younger brother, Dr. Milton S. Eisenhower, then president of Pennsylvania State University and one of his President-brother's closest advisers.

Now, this particular noontime, Dr. Eisenhower was performing another important task for his brother in the White House—exploring accommodation with Senator McCarthy.

He had sought out Sokolsky because the columnist was close to the Senator and was my long-time friend and adviser. As Sokolsky related the incident to me afterward, Milton put the question squarely to him: "What can be done to work things out?" The President's brother, sent to conciliate, was told that McCarthy was in an unconciliatory mood and undoubtedly returned with a message of small comfort to the White House.

In the same month, the White House made a second attempt to seek an accommodation. White House aide I. Jack Martin was sent to see the Senator. Martin, formerly administrative aide to Senator Taft, was a trusted White House liaison man and troubleshooter. After Taft's death, he had moved over to the White House to "handle" the conservative Republicans on the Hill.

Martin sent word to McCarthy, requesting a private talk somewhere away from Capitol Hill. A meeting was arranged at the home of Mrs. Ruth McCormick Tankersley, publisher of the Washington *Times-Herald*. "Bazy" Tankersley, niece of Colonel Robert McCormick, the late publisher of the Chicago *Tribune,* knew Senator McCarthy well. The story of this meeting is here recounted for the first time.

I accompanied the Senator to Bazy's suburban home. Martin, a jovial Cincinnatian with a famous sense of humor, greeted us, and he and the Senator went downstairs to a basement den for a private conversation. After some twenty minutes, McCarthy rejoined the party, followed by a crestfallen Martin. McCarthy took me aside and said, "This one really takes the cake. Poor Jack has to give blood to Ike or he'll be out of a job. Listen to the deal they offered me: stop all public hearings and hold only executive sessions. The minutes of the executive sessions will be taken to Ike personally. He will read them closely and take what they call appropriate action on an administrative level against the people named in the testimony."

McCarthy had rejected the proposal flatly. He was, in fact, amazed at Martin's suggestion because it violated one of the fundamental principles upon which this government rests. The Government Operations Committee of the Senate, through its investigations subcommittee, was designed to keep an independent eye on the Executive branch as part of the system of checks and balances devised by the Fathers of the Republic. How could such a committee shut the public off and submit its findings only to the Executive branch that it was supposed to be investigating? Indeed, why was a United States senator even asked to do this? McCarthy asserted that it was unthinkable that he yield the authority of the Legislative branch. And besides, he told Martin, the minutes of the hearings probably would wind up in Eisenhower's wastebasket. When Martin suggested that the Senator might perhaps think about the proposal, McCarthy said he thought for almost one second before replying "No!"

Riding home that evening, Senator McCarthy predicted that his "No!" would infuriate the President and widen the split between them. "I guess," the Senator said, "I will just have to lead a life deprived of tea and watercress sandwiches on the White House lawn!"

One of the questions most frequently asked me is: "What did McCarthy really think of Eisenhower?" The President's own feelings toward the Senator are on the record: "I will not get into the gutter with that guy," he told C. D. Jackson, a special assistant who had drafted a sharp statement for Eisenhower attacking McCarthy. That about sums it up from the President's side. For his part, McCarthy thought Eisenhower a lightweight. He was contemptuous of what he saw as the President's weakness in allowing himself to be swayed and many of his policies dictated by the extreme liberals with whom he had surrounded himself. In fact, he was contemptuous of what he regarded as Eisenhower's weakness, *per se,* as a President.

He was convinced that the Eisenhower group was not interested in aggressively exposing and combating Communism. He was convinced —and this he told me many times—that if he turned over our findings to the "boys in Ike's camp," they would find a way to cover up the evidence. He was so angered by Eisenhower's inaction on the Communist issue that in a typical McCarthy phrase, he tacked the first year of Eisenhower's Administration on to those of Roosevelt and Truman, charging they had together been responsible for "twenty-one years of treason."

McCarthy rejected conciliation with Eisenhower because it would have meant abdicating the basic position he had taken. Besides, he was not tempted by anything the President had to offer him—not patronage for his friends, which was *never of prime importance* to the Senator, and certainly not the social prestige that comes of basking in presidential favor. He cared nothing about a place on the White House dinner list. He hated formal dining and receptions, and went only when he couldn't find an excuse.

There can be little doubt that McCarthy's blunt rejection of Jack Martin's proposal triggered a high-level decision to destroy the Senator. What could not be accomplished by diplomacy was to be attempted by political force.

At the time, however, I knew nothing of the stratagems that were being devised, and frankly I had few suspicions. Still new to the ways of official Washington, I possessed a marked degree of political naïveté. Had I been wiser as to politics and politicians, I might have foreseen what was coming.

My first inkling that something was being hatched came during a meeting I had on a January afternoon with Senator Stuart Symington, the Missouri Democrat who sat on the McCarthy subcommittee. It was in his office and it can only be described as incredible.

I will never forget that scene.

The Senator, a tall, imposing figure, greeted me warmly as I entered his office, and motioned me to a chair beside his desk. He rose, walked to the door, closed it carefully, returned to his chair. He leaned forward slightly, looked at me steadily, paused for several seconds. Then he murmured, ever so softly: "Crossfire."

I looked at him, faintly puzzled, but said nothing. The Senator waited a full quarter of a minute, then once again he spoke in that mysterious manner the same single word: "Crossfire."

"Senator," I said, "I gather this is supposed to mean something to me, but it doesn't register. Could you tell me—I mean—what is this all about?"

And a third time, the handsome Senator leaned toward me and, his voice raised only slightly, repeated: "You have to worry about a crossfire."

I laughed nervously. "I'm afraid, Senator," I said, "that I just haven't a clue."

"Now, you're a bright young man," replied Symington. "Soon you're going to know what I mean." And once again, as if to make certain that the word registered indelibly upon my mind, he repeated: "Crossfire."

Symington rarely came directly to the point in discussions of political matters, preferring to be circuitous and enigmatic. This is a contradiction in the character of the man, for indeed the Missouri senator has taken some forceful positions on key issues. For example, the race he ran in 1952 for the U.S. Senate over President Truman's opposition certainly marked him as a man of courage and decision. As the nation's first Secretary of the Air Force, serving from 1947 to 1950, Symington firmly supported the 70-group Air Force, again over strenuous White House opposition.

Now he walked me to the door and his good-bye was: "Be careful, because you may be caught in the crossfire."

Who would fire at me? From what direction? When I asked, "Is there anything I can do?" He replied: "If I can, I will let you know."

He did. A few days later, the phone rang in my New York apartment. It was Senator Symington and again he was cryptic.

"Resign," he said.

"Resign, Senator?" I exclaimed. "Why should I resign?"

"Crossfire. Resign." The telephone went dead.

I hung up the phone and stared at it for long seconds. Then I rose and went to the window and looked out at the rooftops. I cannot recall a moment in my life when I was more thoroughly bewildered and uneasy.

Next, Senator McClellan, the ranking Democrat on the subcommittee, entered the picture. Visiting McCarthy in his office, the Arkansan said that he was deeply disturbed at the turn the Army probe was taking.

McClellan began talking vaguely about Dave Schine, broke off, then said the Army felt it was being pressured. Finally he came to the point and suggested we drop the Army investigation altogether. McCarthy said he would talk to me but that he didn't agree with McClellan's idea.

Mounting hostility toward McCarthy and toward me began to color the sessions of the subcommittee. The members kept harping on the Schine situation. They needled McCarthy about the Army investigation in general. And through it all they kept up a drumfire of attacks on me.

By this time, I realized that the Dave Schine affair was intended to be the fuse to set off the blast. The initial line of attack was to be a claim that I had exerted undue influence on the Army—which was under investigation by the committee—to gain preferential treatment for Dave. The forces arrayed against us would try to persuade the public that I was part of a plot to attack the Army on many fronts because it refused to help "a pal" of mine. Victory would include my discharge and the collapse of the investigation into Communist infiltration of the Armed Forces.

Were my calls in Dave's behalf more frequent and insistent than was usual in these cases? Probably. And the reason is obvious. I had received word that the Army planned to block a commission for Schine, that it had no intention of handling his case in the normal way, but had decided to retaliate against him for being associated with our committee. I liked Dave. He was a friend. I respected his ability and common sense. He was a valuable trained member of the staff and one of its hardest workers. I was angry that a man, one serving without pay, was being subjected to the same politically motivated attacks that were the lot of any investigator who disturbed the status quo, particularly where security was concerned.

Although by the end of January, the campaign to stop McCarthy was escalating, another conciliatory gesture was made, this time with a more specific *quid pro quo* than the Jack Martin proposal. And with more of a threat as well.

I had gone to Florida for a few days' rest and sunshine. There Senator McCarthy telephoned me a lengthy report about a visitor to his Washington residence late one evening. The caller was John Adams, the Army's counsel. Adams attempted to persuade the Senator to call off the investigation of Peress and of infiltration of the Army. His particular concern was to cancel the subpoenas we had served on the members of the Army's Loyalty and Security Screening Board to learn how risks had managed to get through the barriers supposedly erected by the Administration to keep them out. The Eisenhower people opposed producing the Board members; they feared their executive authority would be weakened if a congressional committee was allowed to ask searching questions. In fact, the charge was made that our committee was really after control of the Board's decisions. As it turned out, the Army did not produce for questioning even one member of the Board.

This visit disturbed McCarthy, for from the way Adams talked, the Senator divined that he had backing higher up.

He had, indeed.

Actually, Adams had been sent to see McCarthy following a secret high-level conference on January 21 at the Justice Department, attended by Sherman Adams, White House Assistant Gerald Morgan, Henry Cabot Lodge, who was both UN Ambassador and a special White House assistant, and John Adams himself. (Subsequent revelations about Sherman Adams and what went on behind his holier-than-thou front explain not only his "withdrawal" from Government but his underhanded tactics concerning Senator McCarthy.) Months later, the nation was to learn about this famous January meeting, at which Sherman Adams told John Adams to prepare a white paper in the form of a chronology detailing my "pressures" upon the Army in Schine's behalf.

This document was not meant to be made public at the time, nor was it foreseen that any answers would be made to the charges it contained. Instead, it was to be used as a club, to force my resignation and thereby, in their opinion, weaken the McCarthy threat to the Administration.

Anyone who hopes to have a clear understanding of the events of those strange months must be aware of these facts:

The men who met in the Justice Department that day were among the masterminds behind the movement to stop Senator McCarthy. It was this group that tried conciliation at first and, when that failed, successive degrees of coercion which did not stop at outright blackmail.

The day after this meeting at the Justice Department, John Adams paid his above-mentioned three-hour call on Senator McCarthy. According to the Army's later version of the visit, Senator McCarthy sought a commitment from Adams for a New York assignment for Dave. McCarthy, the Army stated, warned that I was planning to battle the Army even if I were separated from the committee, and that I had important press allies to help me.

But in his telephone call to me after Adams' departure, the Senator gave me an entirely different version of the visit. Adams, he said, had made these proposals:

———I was to get out and the investigation of the Army was to cease.

———If we refused, we would be destroyed by a report on my "improprieties" in the Schine matter.

———If we agreed, he indicated there would be no problem in giving Dave Schine a soft berth in the Army.

The Senator gave no definitive reply to Adams, contenting himself with pointing out that Dave should not be used as a whipping boy in any way in the dispute between the committee and the Pentagon.

On the telephone later that night, Senator McCarthy and I agreed upon our answer: We say "no" to the offer and we say it promptly.

In the midst of preparations for the attack came another attempt at appeasement. On February 24, Senator Dirksen invited Senator McCarthy and the other Republicans on the committee to a supposedly secret fried-chicken luncheon at his office. Present was Army Secretary Stevens. Uninvited guests included the Democratic members and about a hundred newsmen, the latter milling round the entrance to Dirksen's suite.

In short order the event was to become famous. The luncheon over, Senator Mundt read a "memorandum of understanding" which began: "There is complete accord between the Department of the

Army and the Special Subcommittee on Investigations that Communism and Communists must be rooted out of the Armed Services wherever and whenever found." In the memo, Stevens agreed to furnish to the committee the names of all the individuals who had a hand in promoting and later honorably discharging Peress. Stevens agreed, moreover, that the committee was within its rights in questioning General Zwicker and other Army officers. When Stevens journeyed back to the Pentagon, his story was that, in return, he had received guarantees from Senator McCarthy that there would be no more "harassment" of Army officers.

Most of the press regarded Stevens' action as a "capitulation" rather than as commendable cooperation with a senatorial committee. The reaction was so strong that White House aides hurried into a huddle and spent hours preparing a statement to blunt the edge of what they considered Stevens' "humiliation." After "long, grueling discussion and arguments," Sherman Adams went out to the south lawn, where President Eisenhower was practicing approach shots with a No. 8 iron, and told him that a face-saving announcement had been worked up. The President listened as he swung at golf balls and said that Stevens ought to make the statement personally.

Stevens read it in Press Secretary James A. Hagerty's office. He denied surrendering to McCarthy, asserting: "I shall never accede to the abuse of Army personnel under any circumstances, including committee hearings. I shall never accede to their being browbeaten or humiliated. . . . From assurances I have received from members of the subcommittee, I am confident that they will not permit such conditions to develop in the future."

Senator McCarthy, replying at once, pointed out he had made it very clear to Stevens that neither military personnel nor anyone else would get special treatment before the committee. If witnesses are not frank and truthful, no matter who they may be, "they will be examined vigorously to get the truth about Communist activities," he said. "If it will be unpleasant to tell the truth, I cannot be responsible. I very carefully explained to the Secretary a number of times that he was Secretary of the Army and not running the committee."

The peace move collapsed.

Puzzling to me was the role in which I suddenly found myself cast. Despite Symington's cryptic "crossfire" warning in our strange interview and the innuendos of the other subcommittee members, I was still unable to picture myself as the principal target. I couldn't accept the fact that I was important enough to have all those officials and political figures plotting to rid Washington of me.

Then, one day I read the answer in the newspaper.

CHAPTER 9

COUNTDOWN

O N SUNDAY MORNING, February 27, I was sitting opposite my father in the library of our apartment when I picked up a copy of *The New York Times* and learned at long last what Senator Syming-ton had meant by "crossfire."

Arthur Krock, *Times* columnist and White House confidant, dis-closed that the Eisenhower wing was counting upon Republican members of the seven-man subcommittee to join with the three minority Democrats to fire me. *The Republican members, who had always supported the committee in its actions, would link with the Democrats, and I would be caught in the crossfire.* Their belief was that I was McCarthy's "supply line"—that I supervised the work that produced the material for hearings and investigations. With me out of the way, presumably the Senator would be unable to continue the investigations, at least at the same pace and on the same subject matter.

Krock was commenting on the decision announced the day before by the Senate Republican Policy Committee "to review the methods of Senate investigators with the object of improving them—notably by ending inquiries by one-man subcommittees." Two facts, Krock reported, had become incontrovertibly clear to the Republican leaders in Congress and the managing party politicians: "One was that the President and the party could not be left in this position without heavy risk of repudiation of the party by the people. The other was that if no disciplinary move against McCarthy were made at the Capitol, the President might take the field against him in person, involving the heavier risk of a Republican split that could not be mended by election day."

To correct the first and forestall the second, Krock wrote, Republican senators led by Michigan's Homer Ferguson moved rapidly. After the resolution was adopted by the Policy Committee, Ferguson canvassed all committee chairmen for their ideas.

Then came the kicker.

"Beneath the surface," Krock wrote "these further moves were made:

"1. The other Republicans on McCarthy's subcommittee that is inquiring into Army matters were urged to view it as their duty, and in their self-interest as well as in the interest of the Senate as a whole, to restrain McCarthy from such outbursts as that against Zwicker. They were urged hereafter, not all to absent themselves from the subcommittee hearings, thus allowing it to be a one-man show by McCarthy. On these counsels progress was reported.

"2. *The leaders further proposed that steps be taken soon to sever Roy Cohn from his post as counsel of the McCarthy subcommittee.* They justified this on the ground that he has encouraged his chief in his attacks on the Army and traced Cohn's animation to his differences with the Army over David Schine, Cohn's young associate who was drafted some time ago. The other Republican subcommitteemen were told that there is a record of Cohn's interventions with the Army with respect to Schine that will become public and will certainly be no asset to them. This record, it is said, shows that McCarthy took care to have no part in Cohn's efforts for Schine. But a Chairman and his group cannot wholly disassociate themselves from criticism of their counsel."

The move to rid the subcommittee of me, Krock reported, was progressing.

And now another major incident occurred which brought the storm closer still.

During the course of an investigation, we discovered evidence that a woman named Annie Lee Moss was an active member of the Communist party. An Annie Lee Moss had been employed in the Pentagon Code Room, and after I personally studied the evidence, we brought the case before the subcommittee. We produced a formidable witness, Mrs. Mary Stalcup Markward, an undercover agent whom the FBI had placed in the Communist party. In executive session and later at

a public hearing, Mrs. Markward testified she had become membership director of the party in Washington and thus knew all members
in the area. She testified that a woman named Annie Lee Moss was
listed as a member in the Washington region in the 1940's.

The evidence appeared entirely convincing, but an extraordinary
thing happened that resulted in a nationwide explosion of headlines.

I called Mrs. Moss to the stand during the public hearing. As I
started to question her, I noticed that Senator McClellan was presiding. I knew Senator McCarthy was unable to attend because of
illness, but I had not realized until that moment that all of the Republican members of the subcommitte were also absent, leaving the chair
to McClellan, as the senior Democrat.

Annie Lee Moss denied that she had been a member of the
Communist party. There must be another Annie Lee Moss, she said.
It must be a case of mistaken identity.

I told the senators: "There is only one Annie Lee Moss FBI file
and only one Annie Lee Moss Department of Justice file." We also
had a second witness who corroborated Mrs. Markward's testimony as
well as other supporting evidence.

At this point, Senator Symington intervened. "I believe you are
telling the truth," he told Mrs. Moss. And if the Pentagon refused to
take her back he would personally give her a job, even though "I may
be sticking my neck out." The *beau geste* brought a storm of applause
from the audience.

Now McClellan began to belabor me. He accused me of preparing
the case improperly. He said it was a disgrace to drag this poor
woman before the committee when there was no basis for any
accusation. There was more applause.

It was a vivid scene and the anti-McCarthy press made the most of
it. Edward R. Murrow, the late radio and television commentator,
made Mrs. Moss the heroine of one of his programs, stressing the
theme that a poor, innocent Negro woman can, through mistaken
identity, be wrongfully accused of Communist ties. John Crosby, then
a television critic, wrote movingly: "The American people fought a
revolution to defend, among other things, the right of Annie Lee
Moss to earn a living, and Senator McCarthy now decided she had no
such right." Liberals castigated Mrs. Markward as an "informer."

I spoke to Senator Symington right after the stormy hearing and
tried to convince him of his mistake. I told him where he could go to

establish the facts for himself. "If you do," I said, "you will realize what a serious error you have committed." But the Senator was satisfied with his *beau geste*.

So matters stood on the Annie Lee Moss case for several years, until 1958.

The Subversive Activities Control Board had been seeking for years to compel the American Communist party to register under the McCarran Act as a subversive organization. On two separate occasions, however, the U.S. Court of Appeals had rejected the SACB's ruling on the ground that the testimony of some of the witnesses, including that of Mrs. Markward, was "tainted." On January 9, 1958, and in a later ruling on April 11, the court ordered the SACB to produce the documents upon which the testimony of the "tainted" witnesses was based.

On September 19 of that year, the SACB conducted a rehearing at which pertinent FBI documents were examined. I quote now from the SACB finding, which, in the light of the tumultuous events of four years earlier, makes fascinating reading:

> The situation that has resulted on the Annie Lee Moss question is that copies of the Communist party's own records, the authenticity of which the party has at no time disputed, were produced to it (Exhibits 499 to 511 inclusive), and show that one Annie Lee Moss, 72 R Street, S.W., Washington, D.C., was a party member in the mid-1940's. Yet, on several occasions before the Court of Appeals and the Board the party charged that witness Markward had committed perjury before the Defense Department in the Moss Security Hearing in testifying to what the party's own records showed to be the fact.
>
> We conclude that upon production of the documents demanded by respondent, the Communist party's charge that Markward gave perjurious testimony was not substained. Consequently, Mrs. Markward's credibility is in no way impaired by the Annie Lee Moss matter.

This story received scant attention in the press. *The Saturday Evening Post* was one of the few publications that reported this final development. It stated in an editorial late in December, 1958: "Thus Mrs. Markward stands vindicated as one who performed a difficult and unrewarding mission for her country. Vindicated also is the FBI which the Communists are sworn to destroy, and—in this instance at least—the labors of a much abused congressional committee."

A couple of days after the Moss outburst, while charges and recriminations were still echoing in the press and over the airwaves, McCarthy received a phone call from Defense Secretary Charles Wilson inviting him to lunch. He hated such affairs, but sensing something was up, I persuaded him to accept. And it was well he went, for that luncheon furnished the tipoff that the campaign against us had gone into its final dramatic phase. The countdown had begun.

McCarthy told me he had barely pulled his chair up to the table when Wilson informed him that a lengthy report had been compiled about me. Its theme was that as chief counsel for the subcommittee I had been exerting pressure on the Army to get favored treatment for David Schine. So shocking was the report, said Wilson, and the information so thoroughly documented, that he would be powerless to keep it from getting out unless I resigned at once.

"What did you tell him?"

"What do you think I told him? I told him to go to hell."

McCarthy said he had asked Wilson to let him see the charges and give me a chance to refute them. Wilson said he would, but he conveniently forgot.

The pieces of the puzzle were beginning to fall into place. After attempts at conciliation and what amounted to offers of bribery had failed, elements in the Army were now resorting to blackmail to force us to drop our investigation.

An hour or two after the luncheon McCarthy and I ran into Symington in the corridor of the Senate Office Building. The Missourian, wearing a conspiratorial air, said in hushed tones that he and the rest of the subcommittee had just received a "strictly confidential" mimeographed report detailing our "improper activities" on behalf of Schine. As he turned to walk away he whispered for my ear his reminder, last made two months before: "Crossfire!"

I was beginning to feel scared and a little sick. We were being hounded, pushed into a blind alley. . . . For a few brief moments I felt that the best thing would be to pack my bags and get away from Washington and its intrigues. But then a contrary emotion took over. When some people feel trapped, they have the instinct to turn on their foes and fight to a finish. The role of underdog, I discovered, can give one courage.

At any rate, twenty steps beyond Symington and his "crossfire" whisper my spirits rose to face the enemy. I spoke to McCarthy. "This 'strictly confidential' report—in another ten minutes the Administration will turn it over to the press."

I was wrong—by about two hours. Later that afternoon friendly newsmen notified us that employees of the White House, Pentagon, and Justice Department were "leaking" out verbatim copies.

One of those not surprised was Sherman Adams. He has in fact admitted that the leak was planned. "Not entirely by accident," he wrote in *Firsthand Report,* "the Army's report on its troubles with Schine fell into the hands of a few newspaper correspondents before it was seen by the subcommittee, and their stories built up a backfire against McCarthy, as intended."

The liaison was a man high in the Administration. His first step was to try to neutralize the newspapers favorable to us. Accordingly, he telephoned a newspaper friend of mine in the latter's New York office. The friend reported the conversation to me as follows.

The Administration spokesman indicated that certain powerful Administration forces were seeking to bring an end to the McCarthy subcommittee investigations. He said that in particular I was "in trouble," that an attempt would be made to put me out of business so far as the McCarthy probes were concerned, and that the White House would like nothing better than an assurance that this particular publisher would abandon me when the bombardment began.

The publisher was frank. He explained that I was his good friend and that, moreover, his organization thought highly of our efforts to combat Communist infiltration.

A White House representative also proposed to Senator Charles Potter of our subcommittee that he write a letter to the Department of Defense, asserting he had heard rumors of the existence of serious charges contained in a report. He was to request a copy of the report forthwith so that the committee could study its allegations. Naturally, then, the Defense Department would "have" to send a copy of the report to each committee member. Naturally, too, it would be "difficult" to keep such an explosive document under wraps. Somehow, someplace, some member of the press corps would manage to glimpse a copy and then the story would be all over Washington and the country. Thus is a leak "engineered."

That night we held a strategy meeting at McCarthy's house. Thrashing the matter out, we decided that as soon as the report was made public we would retaliate by releasing certain memoranda of our own. These recounted in detail the approach to McCarthy by Adams and other attempts by the Pentagon to put the heat on us to drop the Peress case and the whole Army probe. They contained revelations such as the sealing-off of General Lawton in an Army hospital to keep him from cooperating with the subcommittee. In short, these memos would tell a far different story from that put out in the not-so-confidential Administration report. They would show that instead of our pressuring the Army on behalf of Dave Schine, the Army had been using questionable means to silence the subcommittee.

Sleep was difficult that night, with the day's events still whirling in my head. I finally dropped off. In the morning persistent knocking awakened me. It was my friend Anthony Lewis, later a Pulitzer Prize-winning correspondent for *The New York Times*. Tony, who had been a classmate of mine at Horace Mann School in New York, was then working for the Washington *Daily News*.

I was jolted wide awake when Tony handed me the *Times*. There "it" was in black headlines four columns wide at the top of the front page:

ARMY CHARGES McCARTHY AND COHN THREATENED IT IN TRYING TO OBTAIN PREFERRED TREATMENT FOR SCHINE

The story occupied the lead spot in the paper, and covered much of three pages on the inside. It got right to the point: "The Army reported today it had been subjected to direct threats by Senator Joseph McCarthy and his chief counsel Roy Cohn." There followed a detailed recital of what was contained in the thirty-four-page report drawn up by the Army and made available, it seemed, to anyone willing to publicize it.

Tony handed me the other morning papers. All carried similar headline stories. The shooting had begun.

The telephone rang. It was Larry Spivak, inviting me to go on "Meet the Press" a week from that Sunday night.

I had not foreseen the enormity of the move against us. I realized that counterattack was imperative if I was to survive. "I'll go on 'Meet the Press,' but not on a week from Sunday night," I told Spivak. "I want to go on *this* Sunday night."

He said he was booked with a cabinet member for Sunday. I replied, "Larry, I've got to have my forum at once or my version of this story will never get heard."

"Hold it!" he said, and hung up.

In a few minutes he called back. "I've canceled the Secretary. You're on Sunday night."

About five minutes after my talk with Spivak, one of the editors of *Time* called to say that I would appear on their cover and be the subject of the lead article. A *Time* reporter turned up. He said that whether I liked it or not he was going to be my shadow for the next few days. I was aware that Henry Luce was pro-Administration and would see to it that I was cast as the villain in this drama. But I also knew that *Time* would do the story anyway. I had to go along and hope for the best.

Meanwhile, on March 13, the day after the Army charges were published, Senator McCarthy counterattacked. He released the memoranda and disclosed for the first time the behind-the-scenes tactics pursued by Army officials. The charges were sensational:

They told (memo for the files, November 6, 1953) how Secretary Stevens asked us to hold up our public hearings on the Army and go after the Navy, Air Force, and the Defense Department instead. When we pointed out that we had no evidence warranting an investigation of these departments, Adams said not to worry about that "because there was plenty of dirt there."

They told (memo from Roy Cohn to Senator McCarthy, December 9, 1953) how John Adams said he knew about an Air Force base where there were a large number of homosexuals, and that he would trade us this information if we would tell him which Army project we would investigate next.

They told (memo from Frank Carr to Senator McCarthy, December 9, 1953) how the Army was trying to use Schine as a hostage to pressure us to stop our hearings, and that in fact John Adams referred several times to Dave as "our hostage." The Carr memo said: "I am convinced that they will keep right on trying to blackmail us as long as Schine is in the Army."

They told (memo from Roy Cohn to Senator McCarthy, January

14, 1954) of Adams' threat that if we kept on with our Army investigation he would fight us every way he could. They told in the same memo how Adams said "this was the last chance for me to arrange that law partnership in New York which he, Adams, wanted. One would think he was kidding, but his persistence on this subject makes it clear he is serious. He said he had turned down a job in industry at $17,500 and needed a guarantee of $25,000 from a law firm."

Countering the Army charges, these memos made a public test of the question, "Who is telling the truth and who is lying?" a certainty.

My appearance on "Meet the Press" turned out well. The questions asked were to the point and gave me my first opportunity to present my side of the story to a nationwide audience and try to undo the damage caused by the Army report. I termed the Army charges false and accused the Pentagon of trying to use Dave Schine as a "bargaining point" to halt the McCarthy investigation. It felt good after being the target of all those brickbats to have a launching pad for a few of my own. The TV appearance enabled me to give a clearer picture of the Schine issue. I stated:

I did not ask for preferential treatment for Dave Schine at any time . . . He was taken into the Army right in the middle of one of our investigations and just at the time that our committee was preparing, with a deadline facing it, reports based on our investigation during the past year, which he had handled . . . Secretary Stevens offered to give him temporary duty of a couple of weeks or more than that to complete this work. Instead of that, it was decided by all concerned the thing to have him do would be go ahead into the Army and after his training was over, after hours and over weekends when he was not engaged in training, to have him devote himself to completing this committee work in which he was involved. And that is exactly what happened.

What of the charge that I sought to get Schine off Sunday KP duty? I replied:

As a memorandum in our file reflects, that was the weekend before the deadline on filing the Overseas Information Program report which Schine wrote. That was a Sunday and there had been an agreement in advance that he could use that day to work on this report. They reneged on that agreement, and that was the only purpose of the communication with the Army. At no time did I or anybody else on the committee ever suggest that he should be relieved from KP or any other unpleasant duty that any draftee had to go through and I don't think he ever would have wanted us to make such a request.

Mr. Bell of the AP asked me about the charge, which had received wide publicity, that I had threatened to "wreck the Army." I replied, "That statement is ridiculous on its face. Of course I didn't and of course I couldn't."

The public reaction to the program did much to restore my confidence. Letters and telegrams poured in, most of them favorable.

My appearance on "Meet the Press" did not sit well with the subcommittee. It was now openly hostile and made no secret of its wish to fire me. (McCarthy was in Arizona.) When it met a few days later I felt the chill the minute I entered the chamber. Symington, who was incensed by the broadcast, demanded to know why I had not obtained the committee's advance permission.

It was a strange challenge. Here was a group of "statesmen" candidly out to eliminate me en route to stopping McCarthy—and one of them demanded to know why I was defending myself without getting permission from my would-be destroyers!

The majority of the subcommittee had been convinced that publication of the Army report would have such a devastating effect that they could meet behind closed doors and vote for my removal. They had wanted a swift amputation. To accomplish this, they had Senator Potter's vote lined up with the three Democratic members—Symington's "crossfire"—and were hoping to get it over with at an executive session. Then, presumably, McCarthy would no longer have someone to supply him with ammunition and the whole McCarthy problem would just go away.

But things worked out otherwise. The television appearance won enough support from newspapers and individuals that the committee members realized my elimination would not be simple. A secret ouster behind closed doors would be star-chamber work at its worst. The newspapers were calling for an investigation. The committee would have to go through the motions of a hearing and suffer my side of the case to be presented.

Mine turned out to be, however, a Pyrrhic victory. The subcommittee as constituted could not conduct the investigation, since McCarthy, its chairman, was under fire himself and would certainly support me. A special committee would have to be named. Whoever named it would, by his very act of selection, render prejudgment.

A dramatic chain of events had been set in motion. The Army had made its move. The subcommittee had made clear where it stood. For my part I could not resign under fire, nor would Senator McCarthy permit me to do so.

It was too late to stop the countdown.

CHAPTER 10

THE BIG SHOW: The Players Assemble

A SERIES OF FAST-BREAKING EVENTS occurred in the six weeks preceding the Army-McCarthy hearings.

Some members of the Administration, joined by influential Democrats, sought to steer the investigation over to another committee where they could command more support. A formal request was submitted to the Senate by Senator Estes Kefauver that the Armed Services Committee handle the matter, and much behind-the-scenes maneuvering took place to put it there. However, Senator Leverett Saltonstall, chairman of that committee, threw up his hands in horror at the prospect of sitting in judgment on Senator McCarthy and then having to go back to Massachusetts, a pro-McCarthy state, to seek reelection in the fall. Another move to create un "impartial" committee was opposed by Republican leaders who felt the Cohn-Adams-Schine row was our subcommittee's problem and that it must not abdicate its responsibility.

McCarthy, too, insisted the investigation be conducted by his committee, although he was aware of the complexities involved in having his own group sift charges leveled not only against him, as chairman, but against members of his staff. Nevertheless, he, Dirksen, and Potter were confident a solution could be worked out, and it was.

On March 16, the subcommittee reached this decision:

1. A seven-member "special committee" of the subcommittee was created to conduct the investigation.

2. Senator McCarthy would step down as chairman and Senator Mundt, next in seniority, would preside.

3. Members of the special committee would include the original members with the exception of McCarthy, whose place would be taken by Senator Henry Dworshak, a Republican of Idaho who was a member of the full Committee on Government Operations, of which the investigations subcommittee was a part.

4. All other committee matters would be set aside while the special committee sifted the accusations. Outside counsel and a new staff would be engaged. Public hearings would be held at which all witnesses would be sworn.

I heard the details on my car radio in New York. As I listened, I quickly ran through the panel of "judges" in my mind. "Five to two against," I realized—the three Democrats, and Senator Potter and Senator Dirksen who were under strong White House pressure to join in the "crossfire." But maybe things wouldn't be too bad. Senator Mundt, the chairman, was a wise, fair-minded man. He would be an important balancing-point. I had confidence he would handle the proceedings justly. But five to two were formidable odds.

Now counsel had to be chosen and ground rules established. Attorneys were needed to represent the Army, the special committee, and our side.

The man who undertook the task of finding counsel for the Army, I am reliably informed, was former Governor Thomas E. Dewey of New York, twice Republican candidate for the Presidency. Mr. Dewey scouted around among the top law firms, offering the job to several eminent attorneys, who declined with thanks. At length he approached Joseph N. Welch of Hale & Dorr, an old, much-respected Boston firm, and Mr. Welch agreed to serve.

The sixty-three-year-old Mr. Welch was a courtly gentleman with an old-fashioned grace of manner; a deft, sly wit, and an unerring sense for the jugular. Although he was the very picture of the proper Bostonian, Mr. Welch was born on a farm near the prairie town of Primghar in the northwestern corner of Iowa. He graduated with honors from Grinnell College, winning a scholarship to Harvard Law School, where he made an even more brilliant record. At Hale & Dorr, Welch worked standing up at a chest-high desk, an old-fashioned work habit that further endeared him to the public when they heard about it. After the hearings ended, we became friends and

I value a letter I received from him, thanking me for laudatory comments I had made about him to a magazine interviewer.

The Army-McCarthy hearings brought national fame to Joe Welch. At their close, he expressed the hope that he would be permitted to retire into obscurity but neither the American people nor, I suspect, Joe Welch himself, really wanted this to happen, and it didn't. He continued to receive hundreds of fan letters every month, won recognition as 1956 Father of the Year, and even enjoyed a brief career as a television and motion picture performer. He won critical plaudits for his portrayal of the small-town judge in *Anatomy of a Murder,* a role he accepted because, he said, "that was the only way I'd get to be a judge."

Joe Welch's zest for public performance was keen and his talent for it admirable. In one brief exchange during the hearings, I gave voice to this opinion and I am sure Mr. Welch appreciated the observation. He had asked me about a visit I had made to the Stork Club in New York City, at that time one of America's best-known restaurants and supper clubs.

WELCH: By the way, I have never been there. That must be an expensive place, isn't it?

COHN: It depends on how many people you have with you, sir . . .

WELCH: I will bet I couldn't get in, could I, Mr. Cohn?

COHN: Well, they cater to television celebrities, Mr. Welch, and I think you could.

For all his old-fashioned ways and deceptive gentleness, I never underestimated Joe Welch. He was a formidable adversary.

The problem of choosing independent counsel for the special committee was more difficult. The members met, tossed suggestions onto the table, discarded many, accepted some. But one after the other, the lawyers who were approached turned down the offer. After seven men had rejected the job, Samuel B. Sears, a distinguished Boston attorney, accepted. But the Special Committee soon discovered to its discomfiture that Mr. Sears had been a McCarthy supporter in 1952. He bowed out "in the public interest" and the quest resumed.

Senator Dirksen, on a visit to Tennessee, had met a burly, bulldog of a mountaineer lawyer from Knoxville named Ray H. Jenkins. He had a lantern jaw, a tough exterior, and a reputation for sincerity, determination, and fairness. He was a superb criminal lawyer who had tried some 500 cases without losing a client to the electric chair. Senator Dirksen, impressed, recommended that Jenkins be appointed committee's counsel.

I got to know him well in the next few months. Then fifty-seven years old, he had a great craggy head, topped by dull-red hair that he wore in a crew cut. Politically, he was a middle-of-the road Republican of the Taft wing. In 1940, he had served as Tennessee campaign manager for Wendell Willkie. Born poor, the son of a Cherokee County doctor, he worked his way through Maryville Tennessee College and the University of Tennessee Law School, and was admitted to the bar in 1919. He had become one of Tennessee's wealthiest attorneys, and certainly one of the most colorful.

He was a born showman, with a gift for holding an audience or a jury in the palm of his hand. "He's the sort of lawyer," *The New York Times* said in the best description of him I read, "who completely dominates a case and a court. Rising with square jaw set and fire in his eyes, he'll unbutton his collar, loosen his coat, untie his tie and go to work. The gestures of his hands are almost as gripping as his oratory. He reminds one of a boxer dog when he sets his jaw. He laughs, cries, derides, always showing emotion." He made an immediate hit with the committee members.

Meanwhile, our side was still without counsel. The Senator, Frank Carr, and I spent hours on the problem, weighing innumerable candidates. Against the advice of some of my good friends I had come to the conclusion that we should not have anybody represent us at all. And so one evening at the Senator's home I said: "The question we ought to be discussing is not whom to choose, but whether.

"Look," I argued, "I'm a lawyer. I can prepare the case. There is nothing devious here, no complex story to build up, no careful strategy to concoct. We have a simple story to tell. The facts are the facts, and the art of counsel cannot change them." I was young, I was proud and doubtless a little stubborn in my belief that I needed no outside counsel to assist me in telling what I knew was the right side. I succeeded in convincing McCarthy and Carr to enter the lists without counsel, leaving the field to Mr. Welch for the Army and Mr. Jenkins for the committee.

In mid-April began a series of pretrial conferences and on April 20, the rules of procedure were announced.

The plan called for Jenkins, as counsel for the committee, to present both sides of the case—that is, he would act both as prosecutor and defense attorney. Since the Army had filed the charges, it would act as "plaintiff," presenting its case first. Then we, as "defendants," would follow. Jenkins was to prepare the Army's case and present it to the committee in cooperation with Mr. Welch. When this was completed, Jenkins would prepare our defense, in cooperation with me, and present it to the committee.

A unique feature of Jenkins' role was his alternation between direct and cross-examiner. For both sides, he would start by bringing out a witness's story in an encouraging way—then, when his direct questioning was concluded, he would change to a cross- or hostile examination of the same witness. The unique procedure had been used effectively in 1951 in the investigation of the dismissal by President Truman of General of the Army Douglas MacArthur.

The impartial counsel could take as much uninterrupted time as he wished to question witnesses. When he was finished the chairman of the committee would proceed to the questioning for a maximum of ten minutes without interruption. Following this, each senator-member of the special committee would have his ten-minute turn, alternating from Democrat to Republican in order of senatorial seniority.

After the senators had had their round, Senator McCarthy and Mr. Welch, or those associated with them, would have ten-minute turns. Then there would be further go-rounds, starting with Mr. Jenkins, until everyone had had a chance to conclude his interrogation. (See Appendix A for the text of the rules of procedure.)

A few days after his appointment as counsel, Ray Jenkins came to see me in my office in the old Senate Office Building. I awaited the interview with trepidation because I had no notion what he might be like. Would he be friendly or hostile? Would he listen or was his mind made up? The odds against me were long and I didn't want them longer.

Jenkins' bulldog head appeared in the doorway. We shook hands. He sat down at the side of my desk and I got my first real look at the mountaineer lawyer. At close range he seemed less angry than his photographs, probably because of the wide, pleasant smile which now broke upon his face.

Suddenly he rose and went to the door, carefully closing and locking it. He returned, sat down, and asked in the slow drawl that millions of television watchers were to hear so often the next few months:

"What do you think of them—Stevens and Adams?"

I laughed. "I have a great deal to say about both gentlemen," I answered, and we began discussing the preparation of our case. We reviewed the persons whom we would probably call as witnesses in our behalf, one of whom would certainly be Dave Schine. I asked Jenkins: "What should we do about that? He's important to the case, of course, but he's serving in the Army."

Jenkins replied: "Don't worry about that. We'll arrange to get him here for the preparation and the hearings."

I observed: "I hope they won't get you up on charges of asking special privileges for Dave, as they have us."

I liked the man. After that initial interview, I was satisfied that the committee had chosen well. While the majority of the special committee appeared set upon a public lynching, it was good to know that its special counsel would not hold the rope.

Days and nights blurred together in those weeks before the hearings. McCarthy, Jim Juliana, Frank Carr, Dave Schine, and I spent hour after hour, usually at the Senator's home, carefully, methodically setting down our recollections, dredging up from our memories every stray fact that had a bearing on the issues. Sleep was minimal, mealtimes forgotten. Hamburgers and tea, courtesy of Jean McCarthy, appeared at odd hours. We worked, all of us, harder than ever in our lives.

At last we were ready.

On April 22, at 10:35 in the morning, Chairman Mundt banged his glass ashtray on the table, and it began.

CHAPTER 11

THE BIG SHOW: Backstage Notes and Opening Scenes

FROM THE FIRST DAY to the thirty-sixth and last, it was incredible theater, a drama with heroes and villains, excitement and pure corn, suspense and unexpected twists. It was the costliest such extravaganza ever mounted for the American public—costly to the taxpayer, to Congress, to the Armed Forces, and to the Executive branch, costly as well to the television networks who junked several million dollars' worth of advertising to put it on. Two million words of testimony were taken, and printed—enough to make twenty novels of best-seller bulk.

Across the nation twenty million citizens listened and watched on their sets in homes, shops, offices, bars, factories, and even movie houses. In this big show one could be both an actor and a spectator: after some hearings I joined the audience to watch the half-hour midnight summary. Department stores reported a sharp drop in sales. Office managers had a time keeping staffs at work; sales of TV sets zoomed. Dental appointments were shirked. Housewives set up ironing boards before TV screens. Pedestrians clustered about car radios at the curbs. No baseball World Series ever drew so much attention as the game of Army versus McCarthy. It left far behind the previous record-holder for interest, the spectacular Kefauver investigation of crime and the underworld, which ran a mere eight days.

Let me sum up the issues around which the hearings centered. The Army had charged in a bill of particulars filed with our subcommittee that we sought preferential treatment by improper means for David Schine before he was drafted into the Army as a private. We had countercharged with our own bill of particulars that the Army improperly attempted to stop the subcommittee's investigations into the Army.

The Army specifically named Senator McCarthy, our executive director Frank Carr, and myself as chief counsel. We, in turn, cited Secretary Stevens, John Adams, and two days before the hearings opened, Assistant Secretary of Defense H. Struve Hensel. Hensel, we charged, "supervised the attempt to discredit this subcommittee" by issuing the original Army allegations leaked to the press. We maintained that Mr. Hensel, by helping in the attempt to put us out of business, was trying to stop us from investigating certain charges concerning his activities as a Government official in 1942, 1944, and 1945.

There was really but one name that was important, that of Joseph Raymond McCarthy. And one issue, McCarthy vs. his enemies. This is the central fact we must never forget as we recall those tumultuous days.

As I write about the hearing I will, from time to time, quote segments of my observations dictated not long afterward. Many of these observations are merely notes, but they express my feelings at the time clearly and sharply. I will take these bodily from context, without editing. These comments of mine will be set off in italic type in the chapters that follow. Here is the first one:

Here were seven United States senators, all the top brass of the Army, a bunch of lawyers, everything else, all involved in nationally televised hearings lasting months over the question of whether special treatment was given to a private in the United States Army!

What a colossal waste of taxpayers' money! The only redeeming feature of this disgusting spectacle, to me, was the fact that it showed the American people how petty and conniving Washington politics could be and also showed them, and doubtless more importantly, a good many facts about Communist infiltration in the U.S. and the length to which people would go to destroy anyone who was associated with the cause of anti-Communism.

On several occasions, Senator McCarthy referred to the proceedings as a "circus." Apparently, at least one guard in the Caucus Room thought so too. Following one of the morning sessions he called out to the spectators: "Clear the room! We've got to get the tent back up at two o'clock."

Let us be clear on one major point.

The real purpose of the hearings was *not* to determine whether Senator McCarthy and his associates tried to extort preferential treatment from the Army for one private, and *not* to judge whether the Army sought to "blackmail" us into giving up our investigation into Communist infiltration within its ranks.

Actually, the Big Show was nothing more than an unforeseen accident that occurred when the White House and Justice Department totally misjudged Senator McCarthy's reaction to their behind-the-scenes efforts to retire me. When they were forced to leak their catalog of charges—a move that still did not force the hoped-for capitulation—events quickly escalated beyond control. Demands for public hearings became louder and more insistent and they could not go unheeded.

Joe McCarthy, Frank Carr, Jim Juliana, and I formed an inseparable quartet. We met nearly every morning at eight at the Senator's home for a breakfast conference. Joe lived in an old three-story frame house, one of a long row, at No. 20 Third Street in the northeastern section, four blocks from the Senate Office Building. He and his wife Jeannie had had most of the interior scooped out, and had converted the rambling house into a fine residence. A large living room, 35 feet long and 20 feet wide, had been created on the first floor front by ripping out a few walls. At the head of the second floor, a sunken den had been built for Joe, a good-sized room that featured a startling ten-foot-square reproduction of a Jesse James "Wanted" poster on one wall.

Our morning talks took place in the living room, around the fireplace, Joe seated in a large upholstered club chair, I on the edge of a sofa, and the others gathered around. Jean was always there to greet us and served us breakfast, on a tray. We would confer between bites until nine, when we'd start out for the hearing room. I don't recall that Jean ever missed a session.

Each day as we left the house, George B. Danker of Washington's Metropolitan Police Force would be waiting to escort the Senator to the hearing. At the conclusion of each day, Lieutenant Edward Adams would escort him home. Wherever the Senator went during the day, one of the officers would walk ahead while the other followed close behind. They were assigned as bodyguards by the Police Department after he had received threatening letters. He himself made no requests for protection and paid scant attention to his protectors.

The luncheon recess was used mainly for conferences, with food an incidental. About half the time, we would go to the old Carroll Arms across the street, the hotel where the Senator felt so much at ease. We sat at a corner round table. Joe never varied from his noonday order: a medium hamburger, with a slice of raw onion and a tomato. For drinks, there was tea, hot or iced, or milk shakes.

When the hearings recessed for the day, generally around four-thirty or five, we'd proceed to the Senator's office to confer about the next session. There was no time for day-after quarterbacking or looking backward. The work of preparing for the following day occupied all our attention.

The evening conferences lasted from one to three hours, followed by dinner either at the Senator's house or, sometimes, at the Colony Restaurant. Then more planning until, about midnight or one A.M., the day would finally come to an end.

Because of this preoccupation with the business at hand, it was impossible for me to appreciate fully the public's vast involvement. TV camera lights became scarcely noticeable after the first days. We forgot that America was watching and listening. The first time I became sharply aware that so many people were watching came during the incident of the "cropped photograph." Information had been supplied to the committee that the picture in question had been "cut up" at the Colony while Dave Schine and I were having dinner there with staff members. (That was untrue.) At any event the Colony was mentioned several times during the testimony.

It was a fine restaurant that always did good business, but I had rarely known it to be jammed to the door. That night when we went there for dinner I noticed with astonishment that a line of people snaked far out into the street. I couldn't imagine what was happening. Inside, I asked Alex Stewart, the owner, if he was host to some special party. He answered happily: "No party. But we've been getting coast-to-coast television publicity thanks to your hearings, and we've been playing to capacity ever since." He sent over a bottle of champagne. It was the first evidence I'd had that we were that much in the public eye.

Weekends, I would go to New York to see my parents. I would tell my troubles to George Sokolsky, to Ed Weisl, the prominent lawyer, and to his wise and courageous wife, Alice, and to a few other close friends. There was almost no time for socializing, nor, indeed, did I want it. I tried going out on a date or two, but they were sad affairs. Once my companion spent the evening in tears telling me how dreadfully sorry she was for my terrible plight. I went home thoroughly depressed.

Friends did wonderful things. They kept up my parents' spirit throughout. I will always remember gratefully the offer of Robert Morris, who had been elected a judge in New York, to resign his post and come down to help me; and the thoughtful concern of that incomparable couple, Mitzi and Sam Newhouse; the letter Von and Jack O'Brian wrote me from Nassau, the vitamin pills our doctor sent down when he thought I looked tired on television; appellate division justice Martin Frank's after-court trips to Washington—so many evidences of people's kindness.

Distinguished visitors came daily to the hearings, which quickly acquired the status of a major social event. One day Jacqueline Kennedy, recently married to the young senator from Massachusetts, watched the proceedings from a seat behind the witness chairs. When Perle Mesta swept into the chamber with an entourage, Senator McCarthy leaned over to me and whispered, "I've never been to any of her parties but here she is at mine." This former minister to Luxembourg told reporters she was not planning any gala events for a while. "I couldn't compete with this."

Certain "regulars" were the wives of several senators. They were seated directly behind the senators on the committee. They were dynamite as allies. They encouraged me when I was dispirited, and they gave me wise, womanly intuitive as well as soundly practical advice about politics and the men who practice it. These women, such as Mrs. Styles Bridges and Mrs. George Malone and Jean McCarthy, were not only smart and attractive but intelligent, with a wide understanding of politics and the nature of men and events.

If the Democrats on the subcommittee wondered, as I am sure they must have, how I knew in advance the questions they planned to ask or the moves they intended to make, they will learn now that I was gifted, not with extrasensory perception, but with memos from the senatorial wives who would steal glances over the shoulders of the "opposition" senators on the committee. I would get a knowing nod which was a signal for me to send someone over to pick up a note containing the latest information. They put the CIA to shame.

Some of the ladies had a formidable sense of humor which they used to convey their feelings about the hearings. Once, when they were especially put out at Senator Symington, they had a bottle wrapped as though it were a gift of liquor and passed it to the distinguished senator from Missouri. He glanced at it, nodded his thanks to the ladies, and nudged Bobby Kennedy. "After the hearing," he whispered, "we'll have a drink." The Senator, impatient to know what brand the ladies had sent up, tore off part of the wrapper under the table to read the label. It was citrate of magnesia.

We were in our seats that first morning. I felt a tingle in the back of my neck, and a kind of exhilaration born of relief. The preliminaries were over and the moment of truth was at hand.

Soon after we took our seats the Army team marched in as though on regimental parade. In came Mr. Stevens, in came Mr. Adams, in came Mr. Welch, and trailing them in order of seniority marched a glittering file of uniformed and beribboned generals, colonels, and miscellaneous officers. Smartly they took their places at or near the counsel table.

I think this was the Army's first mistake. Because when Mr. and Mrs. America, looking in over the cameras, saw all the brass sitting around the hearing room, I think it occurred to many thousands of people that the taxpayers' money could better be served if these people were left back at the Pentagon to attend to their business instead of coming in daily to appear on television and sit there and watch the hearings in which they had no part.

That entrance! It was like something out of a 1910 comic opera.

Mr. Mundt said, "The hearings will now come to order . . . these charges, as well as their implications are of such a grave and serious nature as to have caused great concern on the part of this subcommittee as well as on the part of the American people. It is therefore the purpose of this investigation to make a full and impartial effort to reveal that which is true and to expose that which is false with respect to said charges and countercharges."

Mr. Jenkins rose and said, "Mr. Chairman, I should like to call as the first witness for Mr. Stevens, Mr. Adams, and Mr. Hensel, Major General Miles Reber."

On the stand, General Reber, a tall, imposing figure, clipped off his title: "Commanding General, Western Area Command, United States Army, Europe, with station at Kaiserslautern in Germany." Before this, he had been chief of legislative liaison of the Department of the Army, stationed in Washington, and it was in this capacity that we had dealt with him in the summer of 1953 in discussing an Army commission for Schine.

On direct examination by Ray Jenkins, the General told of our efforts to obtain a commission for Schine, about "frequent" telephone calls he received from me urging speed (one or two daily over a two-week period, he said), and about several calls from Senator McCarthy on the subject. Ultimately, he testified, Mr. Schine was found to be "unqualified" for a direct commission in a number of branches to which the application was submitted.

General Reber's testimony made it seem as though nothing like this had ever happened before in official Washington—that no senator, representative or person high in the Administration had ever made a request for a commission to the officer who functioned as military liaison between Capitol Hill and the Army.

Perhaps, in the best of all possible worlds, the idyllic condition he implied might exist, but unfortunately, in this imperfect world, things didn't happen that way—as Ray Jenkins soon demonstrated.

After he had questioned the General in a friendly manner on direct examination, Jenkins shifted about in his chair for a few seconds and then launched upon his cross-questioning. It was a remarkable Dr. Jekyll-Mr. Hyde transformation. He became a totally different person. His soft and honeyed voice now took on a buzz-saw edge; his demeanor ceased to be pleasant and became almost menacing. Jenkins was to perform in this astonishing way all through the hearings. I never ceased to marvel at it. Someone made the observation: "He is totally impartial. He is unfair to both sides."

He got a few interesting ones from Reber on cross, and so did other members of the committee.

JENKINS: General Reber, you, in your position with the Army, received many telephone calls from many senators, congressmen, administrative officials, and others, with reference to the inductees, draftees, or those about to become so, did you not?

REBER: Yes, Mr. Jenkins, I did.

JENKINS: And that has been common practice, I would say, since the time to which your memory runneth not to the contrary, is it not?

REBER: Yes, sir.

JENKINS: So that these telephone calls and conversations from Senator McCarthy, we will discuss him first, were not unusual, were they?

REBER: No, sir; telephone calls from senators were not unusual.

JENKINS: Did you at any time feel that Senator McCarthy was high-pressuring you?

REBER: No, sir; I cannot say that I felt that he was high-pressuring me to a great extent. I was sure that he wanted a favorable answer. I could tell that.

A few moments later, Senator Mundt asked the General: "Did you consider any of the calls or conversations that you had with Senator McCarthy to come under the heading of using improper means to induce or intimidate you to give Mr. Schine a commission?"

REBER: No, sir; I was not intimidated or anything like that.

MUNDT: Let me ask you the same question concerning Mr. Cohn. Did you consider any of his calls or conversations to be of a nature to comprise an improper effort to induce or intimidate you to give Private Schine a commission?

REBER: None of Mr. Cohn's calls to me were of that character.

Then Senator McClellan asked the witness: "Now there was nothing unusual or out of the ordinary in any respect that a senator might call you or call any other representative of the Army, or any other branch of the service to ascertain if an applicant might receive a direct commission?"

REBER: Nothing unusual, Senator.

MC CLELLAN: In other words, that is frequently done?

REBER: Yes, sir.

MC CLELLAN: And they are frequently granted, where the applicant can qualify?

REBER: That is correct, sir.

Senator Potter, during his ten-minute questioning, asked: "You have been here about ten years in the liaison division, is that correct?

After hearing of his victory over Robert La Follette in the 1946 Republican senatorial primary, McCarthy posed beside one of his campaign posters. *(Wide World)*

David Schine and the author during their visit to USIS facilities in Germany.
(European Picture Union)

David Schine, the author, Senator McCarthy, and Senator McClellan during the Voice of America investigation in 1953. *(Wide World)*

In February and March of 1954, McCarthy met with Defense Secretary Charles E. Wilson (above) and Army Secretary Robert T. Stevens (right), both of whom promised the McCarthy committee full cooperation.

(Wide World)

Army Counselor John G. Adams   *(UPI)*

Major General Miles Reber   *(UPI)*

Brigadier General Ralph W. Zwicker   *(UPI)*

Dentist Irving Peress.   *(UPI)*

The Army's version (above) and ours (below) of the famous "cropped" photo showing David Schine and Army Secretary Stevens. In the Army's version, Colonel Bradley stands on the left. *(UPI)*

The subcommittee's special counsel, Ray Jenkins, makes a point forcefully. *(UPI)*

Private Schine with Senator McCarthy and the author during the hearings. *(International News Photos)*

The author testifying
before the committee.
(UPI)

Senator McCarthy congratulates the author at the completion of his
testimony.   *(Wide World)*

Senator McCarthy was troubled by severe headaches during the hearings. By the end of the day he often sat with his hand covering his eyes.

(UPI)

The author listens attentively to testimony. *(UPI)*

Senator McCarthy swears to tell the truth as he prepares to testify before the committee. *(Wide World)*

McCarthy shakes a finger. *(Wide World)*

Senator Stuart Symington, on his feet, addresses Senator McCarthy angrily. *(Wide World)*

Francis Carr and Senator McCarthy cover microphones with their hands to talk privately. *(Wide World)*

Fred Fisher, a young lawyer employed by Joseph Welch's Boston law firm. *(UPI)*

Welch weeps outside hearing room after McCarthy's mention of Fisher. *(Wide World)*

Karl Mundt, committee chairman, ignores whispered conversation between Senators John McClellan and Stuart Symington. In background, Robert Kennedy whispers to an unidentified man. *(UPI)*

Senator Charles Potter, a Republican, is congratulated by Democrat John McClellan for demanding the firing of committee personnel. Senator Symington sits in the center. In the background are Senator Mundt and Senator Henry Jackson. *(UPI)*

The author at Biloxi, Mississippi, on summer training the day after testifying at the McCarthy censure hearings. *(U.S. Air Force)*

Senator Ralph Flanders tells a press conference of his plans to strip Senator McCarthy of his committee chairmanship.   *(UPI)*

The Watkins committee, which investigated Senator McCarthy after the Army hearings. Seated around the table, clockwise from lower left, Senators Samuel Ervin, Jr., Francis Case, Edwin Johnson, Arthur V. Watkins, John C. Stennis, and Frank Carlson; Edward B. Williams, McCarthy's counsel, and Senator McCarthy.   *(Wide World)*

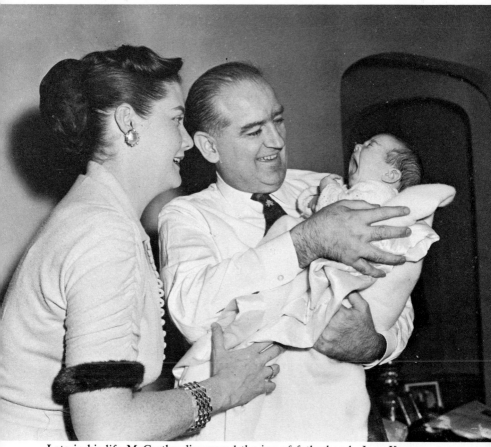

Late in his life McCarthy discovered the joy of fatherhood: Jean Kerr McCarthy looks on as the Senator proudly displays his yawning daughter, Tierney Elizabeth. The couple adopted the baby in January of 1957.

(Wide World)

U.S. Marines served as pallbearers at Senator McCarthy's funeral. Here, with Mrs. McCarthy following, they carry the coffin from the Capitol after a funeral service in the Senate Chamber. *(Wide World)*

Jean McCarthy arrives for funeral mass at St. Mary's Catholic Church in Appleton, Wisconsin, May 7, 1957.

(Wide World)

REBER: Approximately, yes, sir.

POTTER: Can you tell the committee approximately how many members of Congress have asked or made similar requests for commissions for persons, either constituents or friends that they might have?

REBER: Senator Potter, I couldn't possibly estimate a number of cases that I have been asked to look into with reference to things like commissions over the past ten years. It is a sizable number.

POTTER: It is a sizable number?

REBER: A sizable number.

Still the General emphasized continually that while neither Mc-Carthy nor I "intimidated or threatened" him in any way, the frequency of my telephone calls in Schine's behalf did, in his opinion, constitute "unusual pressure."

Then, almost casually, Joe McCarthy dropped his first bombshell of the hearings.

"Is Sam Reber your brother?" he asked.

"Yes, sir," replied the General.

At once the entire room stiffened with a rising tension. Samuel Reber had been the Acting Deputy U.S. High Commissioner in Germany. Theodore Kaghan, who had labeled Schine and me "junketeering gumshoes," had worked for him as a public affairs officer. Following an open hearing a month after our European trip, the State Department requested Mr. Kaghan's resignation. In the summer of 1953, Commissioner Reber himself submitted his resignation. Now Senator McCarthy, seeking to establish a motive for General Reber's hostility toward us, asked him: "General, at the time that you were processing the application of this young man, Schine, for a commission, were you aware of the fact that he had had a very unpleasant experience with your brother, who was the Acting High Commissioner in Germany?"

REBER: I was not aware, Senator, of any specific experience with my brother. I knew that Mr. Cohn and Mr. Schine had had specific difficulties with the Department of State during their trip to Europe in the spring of 1953 but I was not aware of any specific difficulty with my brother.

MC CARTHY: You, of course, knew that your brother was the Acting Commissioner of Germany at the time.

REBER: I did, sir.

MC CARTHY: And had you read the newspaper stories about the statements that your brother, Sam Reber, had made about Mr. Cohn and Mr. Schine?

REBER: I do not, to the best of my ability, recall seeing any specific statement attributed to my brother in the newspapers about Mr. Cohn and Mr. Schine.

MC CARTHY: From your brother's office, then?

REBER: I do recall statements, yes, from the office of the High Commissioner.

At the afternoon session, considerable time was spent over the manner in which Sam Reber was separated from his State Department post. Senator McCarthy asked if the General knew that the Commissioner "was allowed to resign when charges that he was a bad security risk were made against him as a result of the investigations of this committee." General Reber stated he did not know and had never heard that his brother retired as a result of any action by the committee.

Senator McCarthy's question caused a furor at the hearing. The Senator pointed out that he had asked it "on the grounds of motive," to determine all the essential facts that might have bearing on the credibility of the General's testimony. After bitter exchanges, Counsel Jenkins said the question was perfectly valid: "It is my opinion that Senator McCarthy, or any other party or witnesses, is always entitled to show motive on the part of a witness."

Late in the afternoon, the testimony of the second witness, Secretary of the Army Stevens, was interrupted to give General Walter Bedell Smith an opportunity to appear. General Smith, friend of the President, distinguished statesman, Eisenhower's chief of staff in Europe during World War II, former ambassador to the Soviet Union, was now Undersecretary of State. He had taken time out from preparing for a forthcoming Geneva conference to come to the hearing room.

As he was called, I scratched my head because I could not actually remember, at first, why Secretary Smith could be a witness at these hearings. Then it suddenly hit me. I had gone to General Smith after Dave was drafted when it became apparent that the Army was going to give him the foot and not use him in any useful way. I had telephoned and then gone to see General Smith, who formerly had been director of the Central Intelligence Agency, to ask him whether or not he could find a spot for Dave connected with investigative or intelligence work which could utilize his talents and his knowledge gained with the committee a little better than in some post for which he was unqualified.

I had a most pleasant talk with General Smith, in which I put the situation very bluntly and he told me he would certainly look into it and see if there were such a spot and if there were, he would be happy to recommend Dave for it. . . .

General Smith took the stand. I was nervous as to what he would say. I need not have been. General Smith testified that neither Senator McCarthy nor I had done anything unusual or improper.

He had been on the stand less than a minute when he told the hearing that the Senator had never, either in person or by telephone, approached him about Schine. Then he read a letter he had sent to Secretary of Defense Wilson twelve days before which spelled out the substance of our telephone talk and interview, and the action he had taken. He had called John E. Hull, vice chief of staff of the Army, who informed him that Schine's qualifications did not justify his direct commissioning in any of the technical services where such commissions were being issued. Then this exchange followed:

JENKINS: How long were you actively connected with the Army?
SMITH: Forty-one years, sir.
JENKINS: State whether or not, during all of your years of experience with the Army you have been contacted from time to time by United States senators, congressmen, administrative officials, and others, with reference to procuring or causing to be given a commission to an inductee, or a member of the Armed Forces.
SMITH: I have been contacted many, many times, on a number of occasions by members of Congress.
JENKINS: Did you regard these requests by Mr. Cohn on behalf of Schine as extraordinary or unusual or improper?
SMITH: I did not.
JENKINS: State whether or not on either of those occasions you felt that Mr. Cohn was being too persistent or was trying to high-pressure anyone.

The General was silent a moment. Then he looked up, stuck out his jaw, and boomed, "Not me, sir!" The Caucus Room broke into laughter at his answer. Later Jenkins asked, "Do you regard anything said by Mr. Cohn to you on either of the two occasions you mentioned as being improper?" General Smith replied, "I do not."

Senator McClellan thereupon asked, "There is nothing improper in the individual himself or any member of Congress, any other friend, requesting a direct commission for an individual in the armed services, is there?" To which the General answered: "If he believes that the individual is qualified, willing to bear arms, and to serve, there is not. I have done so myself."

A prominent member of the Eisenhower Administration had told the hearing there was nothing wrong in my trying to see that Dave Schine was placed where he could do some good.

It was an excellent beginning.

CHAPTER 12

THE BIG SHOW: The Dirksen Compromise

FOR FOURTEEN DAYS, Robert T. Stevens, impeccably attired in gray flannel, occupied the witness chair flanked by unsmiling generals in full regalia, most of the time under a revealing cross-examination that reduced him to incoherence and ultimately to exhaustion.

Bob Stevens was the first important witness for the Army, and an unqualified disaster for his side. Fifty-four years of age at the time of the hearings, he was a graduate of Phillips Andover Academy and Yale, served as a lieutenant in World War I, a colonel in World War II, and was decorated with the Legion of Merit and the Distinguished Service Medal. He was a gentlemanly, essentially kindly man—an innocent in the man-eating Washington jungle. Despite his attractive personal attributes, it was hard to make out his qualifications for the high office of Secretary of the Army. He had always been a prominent Republican, was the head of the J. P. Stevens textile firm which his family founded, and undoubtedly active in Republican activities. But he lacked the essential toughness of mind to handle the hard politicians running the Pentagon.

He went through his direct examination and told his story, which was little more than a monotonous reading out loud of the already published Army charges. He told about requests we made to give

Dave special assignments and see that he was put in a particular place. His direct examination was not eventful.

Jenkins then changed roles and cross-examined. That cross-examination was devastating. It revealed Bob Stevens not as a man threatened by Senator McCarthy and his associates, as the Army charged, but as a top-level Government official who saw nothing unusual or improper in anything the committee staff did, and who, in point of fact, went far out of his way socially and officially to win the favor of McCarthy, Schine, and myself—the very persons he was accusing.

Stevens was revealed as having gone through three phases. He first cooperated with the Senate Investigating Committee, in the expressed and probably sincere belief that it was his duty as a cabinet officer to cooperate with a duly constituted congressional committee, which in this case was investigating subversion in the defense establishment and the breakdown in security that made it possible. The second phase was a series of private attempts, using the personal relationships he had established with McCarthy, Schine, and myself, to get the committee to stop the investigation, because he was being pressured by the military bureaucrats to stop us. When this failed he entered the final phase, which was the use of private threats and public allegations to halt the committee's investigation. Stevens was brought into the third phase by the anti-McCarthy cabal.

All during phases two and three, and up to the time of his cross-examination, Stevens had maintained his cooperation with the investigation and denied any attempt to stifle it.

But under cross-examination Stevens admitted that his one clear aim during the tumultuous months of phases two and three was to stop the committee's investigation of Communist infiltration into the Army—exactly as we charged in our forty-six-point bill of particulars.

According to his own testimony, he proposed that our committee suspend its investigation and let the Army take over. When Counsel Jenkins coldly pointed out: "I think you wanted as long a suspension as possible, didn't you?" Stevens replied candidly: "Well, I suppose I probably did." The Pentagon must have shuddered.

The day after this admission, McCarthy reopened the question. The Army secretary ducked and dodged sixteen of the Senator's pointed requests to clarify his attitude. On the seventeenth try McCarthy finally got this admission:

MC CARTHY: Now, can you tell us today, whether or not you wanted the hearings at Fort Monmouth suspended?

STEVENS: I wanted them suspended in order that the Army could carry out the hearings themselves and make progress reports to your committee and stop the panic that was being created in the mind of the public about Fort Monmouth on a basis not justified by the facts.

MC CARTHY: How did you finally succeed in getting the hearings suspended?

STEVENS: How did I finally succeed?

MC CARTHY: Yes. They are suspended as of today. We both agree to that, I believe. How did you finally succeed?

STEVENS: They aren't suspended, as far as I know.

Anger rose within the Senator. His voice dripped sarcasm as he asked: "Are the hearings still going on?" Stevens' reply was fatuous. "Are they still going on?" he repeated. "You know about that."

McCarthy thereupon snapped: "You know that the hearings were suspended the day you or someone filed your charges against Mr. Cohn, Mr. Carr, and myself. You know that, don't you? Let's not be coy." Thus the Senator early scored one of his most telling points.

Stevens was to admit a great deal more. Far from showing indignation at the "improper pressures" supposedly exerted, the Secretary of the Army had displayed affable indulgence toward all members of our staff; for example:

Item: Testimony disclosed he had made arrangements at the elegant Merchants Club in downtown New York for the McCarthy subcommittee to be entertained there while the New York hearings were in progress. We could order whatever we pleased, whenever we pleased, he decreed, with the bill sent to him. Counsel Jenkins was incredulous. "Did you think, Mr. Secretary, that it was within bounds of propriety for you to do that?" Stevens thought it was. "That was not done for the purpose of mollifying or pacifying him or anything?" Jenkins pursued. Stevens said it was not, that he did it as "a friendly matter of convenience."

Item: On October 13, during the Monmouth hearings, Stevens invited the Senator and his staff to luncheon, and later he was entertained at dinner at the Waldorf-Astoria Hotel by Mr. and Mrs. J. Myer Schine, David's parents. I was present with my father and Senator McCarthy. It was a pleasant party, much laughter and good talk.

Item: Next morning, Stevens rode down to the hearings, held in Foley Square, in Dave Schine's car. During the ride, they talked over Dave's Army status, then approaching the draft stage. Stevens' recollection is that Dave suggested he might become a special assistant to the Army Secretary and that Stevens countered with the observation that "if he would face up to his forthcoming induction . . . he would look back on it all his life as one of the great experiences that he had had." It was all very friendly.

Item: On November 16, Frank Carr and I went to see Stevens, informing him that McCarthy was disturbed about comments the Army Secretary had made at a press conference. He had said that, so far as the Army was concerned, it had no proof of espionage at Fort Monmouth. Next day, Secretary Stevens flew to New York to see McCarthy. He invited the Senator and his staff to lunch at the Merchants Club to talk over the situation. "After a few preliminaries," he testified, "I said to Senator McCarthy or inquired of him as to why he was so provoked with me, and he indicated that he thought that my press conference had been badly handled, shall we say; that I hadn't given a correct picture as to the situation at Fort Monmouth, and he was quite put out about it. So then we discussed the question of what should be done about it. I indicated that I would be willing to consider issuing a clarifying statement if there was one that appropriately could be issued."

By the end of the lunch, newspaper reporters, having gotten wind of the conference, were at the club in droves; a clarifying statement was thereupon issued by the Secretary, who said he meant he had no evidence of current espionage at Monmouth and that he spoke, not for the committee, but for the Army. The statement, he felt, was substantially the same as the preceding one but worded differently.

"Designed for the purpose of, shall we say, pacifying or mollifying the Senator?" asked Jenkins.

"I have been cooperating right along with the Senator and his committee and I wanted to continue to do it," Stevens replied.

As the meeting was about to adjourn, Stevens learned that McCarthy, Carr, and I were planning to hold hearings in the Boston area the following day. I also happened to mention that I was hoping to see Dave Schine at Fort Dix on a business matter before the Boston trip.

Stevens thereupon flew us all to McGuire Air Base, which adjoins Dix, in his official plane. Then he offered us the plane to fly to

Boston, while he himself returned to Washington in another craft. On the way to Boston, McCarthy remarked dryly: "He's turning handsprings to make us stop, isn't he?"

Item: He posed willingly for a smiling photograph with Private Schine at Fort Dix. And he did so at the time he later claimed in the Army charges that we were improperly pressuring him to give preferential treatment to Dave. The photo, placed in evidence by Counsel Jenkins on April 26, became a national sensation because Mr. Welch charged it had been "doctored." The day after it was introduced, he showed the committee another picture. The one placed in evidence, he said, "was an altered, shamefully cut-down version intended to show only Stevens and Schine together. Actually, he insisted, the two were pictured in a group but the rest of the group had been cropped out. Others in the original picture were Frank Carr and the commander of the base.

A series of witnesses took the stand—Jim Juliana, George Anastos, a staff aide, a couple of others, and I—to testify about the difference in the pictures. The explanation was incredibly simple and did not alter in the slightest the importance of the exhibit.

I had recalled seeing such a photograph and asked Dave Schine about it. He replied that he had the photo framed on the wall of his office. I asked him if he could get it; he made a special trip to New York and brought it down, arriving with it in the midst of the first day's hearing. When Jim Juliana whispered to me that it had come, I whispered back instructions to get copies made of the picture showing Stevens and Schine. I did not see the original picture and did not know that this base commander was in it, nor would I have considered it of the slightest importance.

Juliana passed the assignment along to Don Surine of our staff. Don was on friendly terms with the technicians manning the photocopying unit in the basement of the Senate Office Building and got the job done quickly: blown-up pictures—one of Stevens and Schine and one of the entire group. He received two copies of each and brought them back to Juliana. There was no thought in my mind, in Juliana's mind, in anybody's mind, of trickery, fakery, or any of the hanky-panky later attributed to us.

MUNDT: Was there some uncertainty in your mind at that time as to whether the subcommittee wanted the group of three or the group of two? I was wondering why you asked him to make two of each.

JULIANA: There was no uncertainty at all in my mind. Senator, I was under instructions to get the picture of the two individuals in it; and no one had given me instructions to make any number of copies.

When Senator Dirksen asked Juliana why he had not delivered a blowup of each one of the photographs to Jenkins, he answered, "The only reason I did not, Senator, was because in discussing this picture with Mr. Cohn and Mr. Jenkins at the original meeting, there was never any mention of another party, and I was under the continual instruction to furnish a picture of Secretary Stevens and Private Schine." Juliana further testified he had no thought that removing the base commander and Carr from the picture would make the slightest difference to anybody, nor did it alter one whit the fact that Stevens had flown down to Fort Dix in his plane and had on that occasion been photographed with Schine, which Stevens had denied. The fact that the base commander was there with Schine to meet the plane hardly changed anything.

Nevertheless Joe Welch, with his sense of drama and excellent timing, managed to create a major event out of an essentially trivial incident and thus divert people's attention from the central issue.

I concede that cropping can alter a picture's meaning. Say two couples are dining in a restaurant. They are ushered to a banquette and seat themselves, left to right, as follows: Husband A, Wife A, Husband B, Wife B.

Now suppose the two on either end are cropped from a picture taken by the restaurant's photographer and a blowup is made of the two in the center. It would seem that the two were dining tête-à-tête. The photograph would lie.

But the deletion of two irrelevant persons from the end of this much-discussed picture did not alter the basic meaning—*that Bob Stevens willingly posed for a photograph with Dave Schine at a time when he was supposed to be bitterly angry at him for using so-called improper pressure.*

The maneuverings, the backings and filings of Secretary Stevens and his cohorts were puzzling. They alleged improper pressures by me and McCarthy on behalf of Schine, while the record showed that during the relevant period Stevens and his men were making overtures to us. On a day when a "threat" was made, Stevens would be found entertaining us at lunch. The entire chronology of the Army and its interpretation of events was phony—a tailored afterthought.

After listening in pained astonishment to Stevens' lengthy, and unhappily still unfinished, account of his humiliating efforts to pacify McCarthy, the Senator from Illinois concluded that the public interest was not being served and that the Administration was cutting a sorry figure in the country's eyes. Something had to be done, and quickly.

The politically attuned Dirksen mind worked fast. At this stage, he reasoned, some method must be devised of closing the public hearings before too many citizens began to wonder what manner of men they had steering the ship of state. And Everett Dirksen was a supremely practical man and a statesman who knew when to make the smart moves. He felt the continuation of the hearings was tying up the military, stymieing the work of the committee—and doing the country no good.

Accordingly, he engineered a series of steps designed to end or curtail the hearings, whichever the committee and principals would accept. Some of the moves were presented to the committee at open hearings and published at length in the newspapers.

But the most intriguing elements, as well as the astonishing aftermath, were never revealed.

The initial phase of Dirksen's plan, which called for the hearings to be shortened by limiting the number of witnesses, was well publicized. At the opening of the May 4 session, Counsel Jenkins announced that a meeting had been held in the subcommittee's chambers the night before and the proposal explored. The assumption was that all parties were in agreement.

But Mr. Welch announced as the hearing opened that this was not so. He told the committee that he and Mr. Jenkins had conferred at 9:15 that morning. "We were unable to invent a magic formula for shortening the hearings," he said. ". . . I have been forced to say that I think the American people will demand and should have the long, hard furrow plowed."

Dirksen was not giving up. He began work on a second plan which called for the public hearings to end at once. Further witnesses would be heard in closed session, with public release of all testimony. This proposal included a secret feature which could have exploded a bombshell. But the fuse fizzled. The result was an episode with mystery-story overtones, involving a young man in a hotel room awaiting a telephone call that never came. . . .

One day in early May, a prominent friend of mine who is a business executive was approached by Tom Coleman, a powerful Republican leader from Wisconsin, acting as an Administration intermediary. Coleman, an original McCarthy backer, remained close to the Senator and at the same time stood well with other segments of the Republican party, including the White House.

Coleman asked the executive: "Would Roy agree to a plan, involving him personally, that would result in ending the hearings at once, or at the very least, shortening them considerably?" Coleman then outlined the proposal:

John Adams and I were to resign simultaneously, he as counselor for the Army, I as chief counsel to the subcommittee. We were to announce that we were taking the step at a personal sacrifice to end hearings that were promising to run a long and stormy course. Thus we would save the taxpayers' money and serve the nation.

The executive telephoned me and explained the plan. "How does it sound to you?" he asked. I was realistic. We were doing well at the time, but wasn't this only because the Army's showing thus far was so poor? Who could foresee the turn events might take in the days to come? Moreover, the hearings had already become a nuisance, a colossal bore, possibly the most monumental absurdity in our history.

I told my friend I had no desire to see the proceedings prolonged, but I would have to obtain Senator McCarthy's approval. A staff discussion followed. McCarthy saw the wisdom of stopping the public show, which he wasn't enjoying despite the points he had made against Stevens. He would hate to have our association end, but the alternative was a chaotic mess up ahead for the whole country. "Besides, nobody is going to win this thing," he said prophetically, "and it may continue till God knows when. Meanwhile all that work is piling up undone."

So one morning when the hearings were in recess, I was installed in a suite at the Mayflower and told to remain there until I received a phone call informing me that the deal was accepted by the Army. I was to spend the time preparing a letter and a statement of resignation to match similar documents by John Adams.

That was a lonely, day-long wait at the Mayflower. I ordered lunch sent up, ate it with no appetite, and paced around the room. During the afternoon the phone rang with "progress reports" . . . Pentagon chiefs in a huddle . . . Adams undecided but would do as his bosses wished . . . Stevens thought the plan had merit, but . . . things look bad . . . things look good . . .

In between calls, I began drafting my statements on a yellow legal pad, read them over many times, making change upon change.

The afternoon waned. Toward six, I ordered dinner. I left most of it untouched. Time passed. It began to grow dark. The telephone rang again. It was my friend. The Army, he told me, had rejected the proposal. "It's very poor judgment on the part of the Army people," he said. "But they did it and that's that. You may as well go home."

I hung up, tore my resignation and the accompanying statement into tiny bits, tossed them in the wastebasket, and returned to my less luxurious quarters at the Carroll Arms.

Dirksen was furious. He went to the White House, the Army's letter in his hand, and asked that the Administration insist on the Army's agreeing to the plan. But despite his eloquence, the White House refused to bring any pressure to bear on the military. If that was how the Army wanted it, Dirksen was told, that's the way it had to be.

Dirksen still didn't give up. He spent the evening of May 10 and the next morning polishing his proposal, hoping to make it more inviting to the Army. The opening of the hearing was delayed for an hour after Chairman Mundt received a call from Dirksen advising him that his revised blueprint to close the show was even then being typed up.

So, fresh from the typewriter, Senator Dirksen's modifications were read to the special committee. He proposed 1) that Stevens' testimony be concluded, Senator McCarthy be summoned to the stand, and the public hearings be recessed upon conclusion of the Senator's testimony; 2) that other witnesses requested by any principal for rebuttal be called into executive session forthwith and such testimony be made public immediately; 3) that Counsel Jenkins review the testimony and interview all prospective witnesses, then report on whether any other persons should be heard in public sessions; and 4) that Senator McCarthy, at the conclusion of his testimony, be authorized to resume the regular hearings on matters not related to the present controversy.

A vigorous debate on the motion followed. Secretary Stevens stood fast. "It goes without saying," he said, "that whatever decision may be taken by this committee, the Army will abide by it. But insofar as the Army is concerned, at the present time we do not subscribe to the idea of putting witnesses into executive session."

Close to the noon adjournment hour, Chairman Mundt made an impassioned plea to all principals and committee members. He implored us all to "go to your respective shops" and hold ourselves in readiness to consult with Senator Dirksen or Counsel Jenkins. "I hope and I pray," he said, "that during the noon hour men will search their souls and their consciences to determine whether there is not something more important than trying to protract these things in public as we have been, and still without doing violence to justice, find some other way to adjudicate the controversy."

Then, he added: "The chair says now, so that all parties will know, if you say to me at two-thirty you think this is unfair to take off television and off the air and change the rules, the chairman is going to vote to provide for those who insist upon it that which they consider to be equity and justice and fairness in the form of procedure." In other words, Senator Mundt would vote "no" if any one of us directly involved felt the proposal was unjust to him.

At the afternoon session, Joseph Welch announced that Secretary Stevens, suffering from a virus infection, had gone home. Was he still opposed to the Dirksen resolution? Welch would try to reach him by telephone. Chairman Mundt offered the use of a private telephone, but the Army counsel said he would use a pay phone. There was a brief recess while Welch made his call.

"Mr. Chairman," the Bostonian reported a few minutes later, "due to the wonderful invention of television, the Secretary was able to follow what had happened."

"That is the best compliment TV has had yet," Senator Mundt commented.

"He was therefore ready to talk," continued Mr. Welch.

"Wonderful. And what was Mr. Stevens ready to say?"

"He said 'No.' "

Chairman Mundt wanted clarification. Did the "no" mean that the Army Secretary felt the Dirksen proposal would be unfair and unjust to him, if passed? Mr. Welch wouldn't answer for Mr. Stevens, so again the hearings were recessed while he put another dime in a pay telephone to find out.

Upon his return, Mr. Welch quoted the secretary: " 'I continue in my view that the proposed resolution would not result in fairness.' "

Came the vote.

McClellan, no. Dirksen, aye. Jackson, no. Potter, aye. Symington, no. Dworshak, aye.

A 3-to-3 tie. Chairman Mundt had already announced his intention to vote against the shutdown if any principal considered it unfair to him.

"The chair votes no," he announced. "The motion fails."

The fiasco had one important development: Administration, White House, and Army lost a valuable ally in the hearings—Everett Dirksen.

The senator from Illinois had become disenchanted with the proceedings. He saw clearly that the emotional upheaval the clash was causing was dividing the country. He admitted at the hearing that some of the letters and telegrams he was receiving daily "are so intemperate and abusive and so unrestrained that my office force is afraid they might affect my finer sensibilities and they try to hide them from me."

The Army's refusal to get the ridiculous show off the road made him decide to review his position.

When they turned him down on that, Senator Dirksen, who has a good deal of guts and is with you when he is with you and against you when he is against you, notified them that he had had it and that he did not regard them as having the first degree of intelligence and that from then on he was not going to do their bidding in these hearings any longer.

Late on May 11, the very day his proposal was defeated, I received a message that Senator Dirksen wanted to see me. Could I be at his office in the morning before the session began?

When I arrived, I could tell by the way he ran his fingers through his tousled hair that he was upset. He summarized his efforts to persuade the Administration and the Army to accept his plan, and their rejection. Then, his voice rising, he said, "Roy, I've just about had it with those people. I'm fed up with them. I offered them a chance to get off the hook and they were stupid enough not to take it."

Dirksen paused a moment, then continued speaking, his mellifluous voice rising from deep within his chest. I have always marveled at the wonderful organlike tones Everett Dirksen could produce. But now I was not hearing the tones but the words.

The Senator was telling me that he had certain facts in his possession that directly contradicted some of the Army's charges. They covered incidents that would destroy completely a number of the points upon which the Army case rested.

"Gerald Morgan and John Adams came to see me on the afternoon of January 22." The day previous, I knew, John Adams, at Sherman Adams' request, had been instructed to draw up the details of the Army's charges.

"Adams," Senator Dirksen went on, "wanted me to use all my influence to stop the subpoenas for the loyalty board members." During the Monmouth hearings, Senator McCarthy and I had considered it essential to summon certain members of this board to shed light on the Communist infiltration we had discovered, to answer such questions as, "How did these individuals obtain security clearances? Why were they cleared?" The Army had objected strenuously to our proposed questioning of the loyalty board members, and, through John Adams, had refused to produce the members when they were summoned. Our alternative was to issue subpoenas, a move to which the Army reacted violently. Strong efforts were made to stop the issuance of those subpoenas. Here, in Senator Dirksen's office, I was learning what those efforts were.

" 'Kill those subpoenas,' they said to me. They said more. If those subpoenas were not stopped, charges about you and all the others would be made public."

"Did they actually make that threat?"

"Not openly. But the implication was plain. They spoke about how the entire subcommittee might be made to look in the eyes of the nation if those charges came out."

"That's blackmail, Senator," I said. "How can these facts be brought out at the hearing?"

The Senator said: "In the interests of the country and all the participants I tried to stop this fiasco. I knew if it continued I would be honor-bound to give facts within my knowledge. The Stevens group has demanded continuance of the hearings, and it is at their peril that the facts must now emerge."

Two days later Senator Dirksen himself stepped to the witness stand, took the oath and told his story. His failure to ring down the curtain on the hearings, he said, "will be one of the greatest regrets in my legislative career." And he added: "But now that it has got to be in the open, we might just as well have the whole story so that nobody can take umbrage and say that the junior senator from Illinois departed from a straight line."

Dirksen then told of the conference with Morgan and Adams:

> Frankly, as I reconstruct the conversation in my office on that afternoon, Mr. Adams came to my office for the purpose of enlisting my influence to kill those subpoenas and to stop them. I can place no other interpretation upon that action. And in pursuance of that, wanting to do what I thought was the right thing, being interested in the Army and the maintenance of its morale, I promptly called Frank Carr of the committee and I could not get him because it was evidently too late.
>
> I went to my office early the next morning, because I was thoroughly agitated about it. I should go back for a moment to say that in connection with this effort, to stop those subpoenas, that is the first time, Mr. Chairman, that I heard about the Cohn-Schine controversy.

Next morning, he had telephoned Carr and requested him to hold the subpoenas, if they had not already been issued. That afternoon, Dirksen, Potter, Mundt, and McCarthy met at the latter's office. Dirksen pointed out that charges existed that could destroy the effectiveness of the subcommittee, which he called "an important instrument of Government in ferreting out subversion and communism." If what he had heard the day before was true, he said, then Roy Cohn should be fired forthwith—and perhaps John Adams as well. Nothing specific was decided upon at the meeting, but the subject was aired thoroughly. In Senator Dirksen's words: "I just left it at this: that Mr. Adams came to my office on the afternoon of January 22 for the purpose of enlisting my interest, and my influence, if possible, to at least suspend the issuance of those subpoenas for members of the loyalty board and perhaps to kill them."

Once Senator Dirksen had gone on the stand and told the story, the other two senators at the meeting with McCarthy had to follow suit.

Karl Mundt went first. He too was visited by John Adams on January 22, he said. He, too, was told about my alleged efforts to win preferential treatment for Schine. He, too, was asked to use his influence to stop issuance of the subpoenas.

Even Charles Potter admitted he was approached by a close friend, Deputy Army Counsel Louis Berry, on the evening of January 22, for the same purpose. Berry coupled the request to stop the issuance of the subpoenas with an account of the Cohn-Schine matter.

Three United States senators, one after the other, told the nation how top Army representatives sought to halt an important phase of the Army investigations by bringing influence to bear upon a congressional committee. And in the process, the same Army officials carefully planted the notion that one Roy Cohn was doing terrible things and that charges describing them could find their way to the newspapers.

There were many tempests in this particular teapot, but none matched the weird episode of the monitored telephone calls.

It started as a mystery story and ended as a farce. Before the hearings opened, rumors skittered around Washington that the Army had tapped all our telephones and transcribed every conversation. The rumors also said that we, in turn, had had taps on the Army's phones. I say categorically: never at any time in all my work for the Government, either in the Justice Department or on Capitol Hill, did I ever authorize or in any way contribute toward the tapping of any telephone. I don't believe in wiretapping, except in espionage (national security) or kidnapping cases. As a prosecutor and investigator, I found it perfectly feasible to successfully carry out my work without resort to wiretapping or electronic devices. I feel that the technique is about as base an invasion of privacy as could ever occur, totally inconsistent with the American system of justice.

But our Army opponents believed otherwise. Even though it might have been in violation of the Federal Communications Act, the Army had a secretary listening on an extension to take down the talks. I discovered that this was almost standard practice in the Army Secretary's office. Army counsel John Adams transcribed only one or two calls, but Secretary Stevens monitored not only every phone conversation with Senator McCarthy and me but with other senators on the committee, with senators on Capitol Hill, and with officials of the Administration.

Broad hints were dropped that these transcriptions fully confirmed the Army charges that we had exerted pressure on Schine's behalf. The build-up was dramatic; the denouement, a grave disappointment for the Army. Even though these transcripts were tainted, I was ready to agree to their admission in evidence provided I could make sure we would be hearing all the transcripts the Army had made and not just those that would help their case. I asked for, and finally received, permission to examine them in private. As I surmised there was nothing in them—with the possible exception of one—that could damage us. Most, in fact, were helpful.

There were twenty-one transcriptions of conversations between Stevens and Adams on the Army side, and McCarthy, Carr, and me. There was one in which I requested Stevens to ask Allen W. Dulles if Schine would fit into the CIA. In another, Stevens himself suggested that Schine be granted two weeks of temporary duty before his induction in order to wind up his subcommittee work. When I thanked him for this unusual procedure, Stevens replied that he was "accustomed to trying to do very unusual things." In others, Stevens said he had taken up the Schine case with Secretary Wilson, and reported that he had talked long-distance with Schine to assure him he and Wilson had "reviewed the whole situation" and "after going over the situation three times now," they had decided Dave had better take basic training. Small wonder the New York *World-Telegram* said that the calls "reveal an incredible concern on the part of the Army Secretary for the single private. He practically fawned on the boy."

The one damaging conversation, monitored the preceding November, was between Stevens and McCarthy. "For God's sake," the Senator had said, "don't put Dave in service and assign him back to my committee. If he could get off weekends—Roy—it is one of the few things I have seen him completely unreasonable about. He thinks Dave should be a general and work from the penthouse of the Waldorf . . . I think for Roy's sake if you can let him come back for weekends or something so his girls won't get too lonesome— maybe if they shave his hair off, he won't want to come back."

I suspect that the one person who was chagrined over the release of the monitored calls was Senator Symington. They showed the Missouri senator deeply involved in machinations to use the hearings as a device to destroy McCarthy. Participating in the "crossfire" himself, he gave Stevens copious advice on how to deal with the subcommittee chairman, at one point counseling the Army Secretary: "If you are going to play with McCarthy, you have got to forget about any of these Marquis of Queensberry rules" because "this boy [McCarthy] gets awfully rough." McCarthy pointed out that by the comment, Symington disqualified himself as a judge in the controversy and demanded he step down. Symington refused, but stood revealed before the nation as an accuser sitting as a judge. This incident gave rise to the "Sanctimonious Stu" cognomen.

CHAPTER 13

THE BIG SHOW: The "Purloined" Document

FOR AN ENTIRE YEAR, a document had been locked in Senator McCarthy's office files.

In the form of a letter addressed to Major General A. R. Bolling, chief of Army Intelligence, it bore the typewritten closing: "Sincerely yours, J. Edgar Hoover, Director." At the top were the words: "Personal and confidential, via liaison." The document disclosed that persons with known Communist records were employed at the Fort Monmouth radar and research laboratory, one of the country's most sensitive and secret installations.

The letter created a sensation at the hearings, but for the wrong reasons. Not for a moment were the "crossfire" senators interested in the warnings and if anything had been done about them. They pursued, instead, the line of inquiry begun by Mr. Welch, who told Senator McCarthy: "I have an absorbing curiosity to know how in the dickens you got it." At the height of the angry debate that followed, Senator McCarthy leaned over to me and whispered: "It's grisly. They're yelling at the cop who got the goods on the murderer. They don't give a damn about the murder—they only want to know how the cop got the proof."

Indeed, this was almost a pattern at the hearings. The question wasn't whether Stevens and Schine were together at Fort Dix when Stevens took us there in his Army plane. It became whether the commander of the base was cut off the other side of the picture. The question here was to become not whether the Army had with gross laxity ignored the FBI's written warnings about security risks at the Monmouth radar laboratory but how McCarthy got a copy of the FBI warning. These diversions were certainly astute dramatic tactics by Joe Welch, but they hardly disposed of the basic issues.

The bitter and lengthy controversy over the document could have had a salutary effect had it resulted in a thorough discussion of a question that the episode brought into focus: how far a committee of Congress may go to obtain information it requires for its Constitutional function as a legislative brake upon the Executive branch.

This question lay at the core of the dispute over the document. In my opinion, it overshadowed all other aspects of the incident and, indeed, was one of the key points raised by the hearings themselves. The problem is not new; it emerged when the nation was in its infancy and has been recurring since in almost every Administration. Rarely, however, has the issue received a thorough airing, and never in full view of the entire country.

Unfortunately, the chance for constructive talk was allowed to pass and nothing developed but acrimonious argument, glaring headlines, and a footnote to history known as the "Case of the 'Purloined' FBI Document."

The document was produced late in the afternoon of May 4 by Senator McCarthy to support his contention that the Army had failed to act despite strong evidence that subversive elements had seeped into the Monmouth laboratory. The FBI director, he testified, had sent a series of reports to Army Intelligence, citing the Communist records of persons employed there, for whatever measures the Army deemed necessary.

The document now submitted by the Senator was one of these. It contained thirty-four names, many of them linked in some way with the Rosenberg-Sobell spy ring. When we started our investigation at Fort Monmouth, we discovered that about half were still employed at the radar laboratory. The bulk of the letter dealt with one Aaron L. Coleman, a section chief, who was allowed to remain at the center two years and eight months after the report had been submitted by Mr. Hoover. Coleman had admitted under oath at our subcommittee hearings that he had gone to a Communist party meeting with Julius Rosenberg. A raid on his home in 1953 had uncovered a total of forty-three documents that he had taken from the laboratory, some containing secret information. Coleman insisted that he had taken the material with the approval of his superiors. Coleman was suspended from his job in September of that year but was ultimately reinstated.

After the hearings, Coleman instituted a $600,000 action against a New Jersey newspaper for publishing McCarthy's statements about him, which he alleged were libelous and defamatory. The case was thrown out by a jury, and on March 9, 1959, by a 6 to 1 decision, the New Jersey Supreme Court upheld the dismissal. Coleman had brought suit following statements made to reporters by Senator McCarthy at Fort Monmouth in 1953 and published in the Newark *Star-Ledger*. One statement was made after a closed hearing of the subcommittee, the other after an open session. On October 23, after the closed hearing, the newspaper reported McCarthy as saying that "an ex-Marine officer"—Coleman had served as a radar officer in the Marine Corps in the Pacific—"may have been the direct link between the laboratories and the Rosenberg spy ring." On December 9, the *Star-Ledger* had stated: "Senator McCarthy (R–Wis.) yesterday moved to have a suspended Fort Monmouth, N.J., radar scientist cited for perjury after his public denials did not jibe with testimony given by executed atom spy Julius Rosenberg."

The majority opinion delivered by Justice Harry Heher stated that newspapers accurately reporting statements on the subject of hearings held by congressional members outside hearing rooms are not exposed to libel, providing no malice was intended.

"The jury could have found," Justice Heher wrote, "as it no doubt did find, that the communication was honestly made in the pursuit of what was reasonably conceived to be a public responsibility, an exercise of the basic right of freedom of speech and of press. Here, the evidence of a committee-authorized publication stood uncontradicted; and even if the proofs be open to contradictory interpretations, then the issue was within the exclusive province of the jury."

The fact that a jury in New Jersey unanimously threw out Aaron Coleman's case seems not to have been considered worthy of mention by the Rovere school when it vilifies McCarthy for the Monmouth hearings.

Oddly, the introduction of the document was not a planned maneuver, as people thought, but an impulsive gesture by the Senator, not unlike the one in which he was to blurt out the Fisher story a month later. The testimony of Secretary Stevens was now in its ninth day. The thrust of our examination at this point aimed at proving that the Army had hampered our subcommittee's investigation at Fort

Monmouth. The questioning droned on, with little of consequence developing. During one of the interminable quibbles over a minor point, the Senator reached into his briefcase and withdrew a document.

Leaning over to Frank Carr at his left, he whispered, "Shall I hit them with this one?" Carr glanced at the paper, recognized it, and quickly replied, "Oh no, put it back." Frank foresaw the result: the opposition would use the FBI report to divert the issue.

"You're probably right," McCarthy agreed, and stuffed the paper back into his briefcase. But in less than fifteen minutes, it was in his hands again. Stevens' answers were getting nowhere and McCarthy had become impatient. Now, holding the document, he asked the Army Secretary:

"Do you recall ever seeing or getting a report from any of your subordinates in regard to certain Fort Monmouth personnel, before our committee started its investigation?" And then: "Mr. Secretary, I would like to give you a letter, one which was written, incidentally, before you took office but which was in the file, I understand, all during the time you are in office—I understand it is in the file as of today—from the FBI, pointing out the urgency in connection with certain cases, listing the fact, for example, that Coleman had been in direct connection with espionage agents . . ."

Frank Carr had foreseen the effects accurately. The document started a major controversy—not over the Army's disregard of an FBI warning of subversive activity, but over the question of "how in the dickens" McCarthy had got hold of it.

There was no secret. One year earlier, an officer in G–2 made a telephone call from a pay station to our subcommittee office and asked if he could meet the Senator. A secret meeting was arranged, at which he told McCarthy he was "disgusted" and "alarmed" because nothing was being done about a memorandum the FBI had sent to the Army. The memorandum had been filed away and ignored, he said. He handed it over to the Senator, who turned it over to the investigative staff.

The long discussion over the authenticity of the paper produced the following:

A fifteen-page memorandum had been sent by the FBI to Major General Bolling on January 26, 1951, warning about subversives employed at Fort Monmouth. The document produced by Senator McCarthy, the Army claimed, differed in form, was materially shorter, did not bear the same opening and closing, lacked Hoover's signature, and, in sum, was not the actual memorandum sent by the FBI director nor even an exact copy. But the substance was deadly accurate.

All of this was true and once again the McCarthy team was accused of producing doctored evidence.

What were the facts?

While the letter produced by McCarthy was neither the exact document Mr. Hoover's office had sent to G–2 nor a copy, the information in it was contained word for word in the original letter. Omitted was the detailed account of security and loyalty data about each of the thirty-four individuals mentioned, in place of which the words "derogatory" or "not derogatory" appeared. Except for this and the salutation and closing, the language of the two documents was identical.

Moreover, Mr. Hoover never at any time repudiated the contents of the letter, which had been labeled "spurious," "false," and "bogus" by our opponents. Robert A. Collier, assistant to Mr. Jenkins, made a hurried trip to FBI headquarters to interview the director and returned with Mr. Hoover's carefully weighed opinion: the letter was not an exact copy of the document, as it differed in the respects mentioned above. But Mr. Hoover never stated that the information it contained was unfaithful to the text of his memorandum. It was not.

Further, the letter was not "purloined" by any member of the subcommittee staff, an impression many critics have sought to create and which, I am sure, many still believe. It was evidence that came to us from an outside source.

The question over which the committee argued so hard and so long—"Was this the document Hoover sent?"—was largely irrelevant to the core issue and almost totally obscured it. To debate Joe Welch's charge that the letter was "a carbon copy of precisely nothing" was to make the whole affair go skittering wildly down a side road, which, for all its interesting scenery, was a side road nonetheless. The discussion should have centered around the far more significant point: Was this the information Hoover sent? Was the substance true or was it concocted?

It should be noted that at the time Senator McCarthy introduced this two-and-a-quarter-page letter, he believed it to be a true copy of an Army document circulated within the Intelligence Department as a result of an FBI report. We all assumed this to be the case. As the Senator told the committee: "If the FBI reports to the head of G–2 on some thirty individuals, as they did here, the normal thing would be that G–2 would, I assume, either send a complete copy or a summary of this to be put into the files of each individual concerned."

The Case of the "Purloined" Document involves an even larger question: To what extent was Senator McCarthy justified in possessing it at all, and in using the information it contained?

Part of the answer lies in understanding the true function of the FBI. There is a great misconception about this which extends as far as the floor of Congress itself. People often say, Why do we need congressional committees?—the FBI can get rid of the Communists and put the spies in jail. Actually, the FBI is not a prosecuting agency at all. It has no subpoena power; it may only investigate and report its findings in secret to the appropriate arm of Government. The bureau states in one of its own publications: "Charged with the duty of investigating violations of the laws of the United States and collecting evidence in cases in which the United States is or may be a party of interest, the FBI functions as a purely fact-finding agency. It does not evaluate, adjudicate, or prosecute cases."

Once the FBI obtains the available facts, it may only transmit the information to the head of the agency employing the person. If the agency chief decides to ignore the report, that ends the matter. The findings will lie in the files and the individual—whether a spy or a Communist or an embezzler—remains at his post. The FBI has done its job and is silenced. It cannot act unless specifically authorized by the Department of Justice.

It is precisely here—when Government agencies fail to act—that duly constituted investigating committees of Congress play an indispensable role.

These committees may not conduct criminal trials or send anyone to jail, but they possess subpoena powers and can call hearings to bring to the public attention situations that otherwise might never come to light or might emerge only after extensive damage has been done.

Perhaps the most eloquent definition of the function of a legislative committee was offered in 1900 by Woodrow Wilson. I read this statement at the Army-McCarthy hearings, and it is worth recording here: "Unless Congress have and use every means of acquainting itself with the acts and the disposition of the administrative agents of the government, the country must be helpless to learn how it is being served; and unless Congress both scrutinize these things and sift them by every form of discussion, the country must remain in embarrassing, crippling ignorance of the very affairs which it is most important that it should understand and direct. The informing function of Congress should be preferred even to its legislative function. The argument is not only that discussed and interrogated administration is the only pure and efficient administration, but, more than that, that the only really self-governing people is that people which discusses and interrogates its administration."

Senator McCarthy considered the function of his subcommittee in these terms. The committee, under the Legislative Reorganization Act, had a mandate to investigate instances of dereliction of duty, laxity, and failure to act on the part of Government agencies. This act specifically stated that the Committee on Government Operations of which the McCarthy subcommittee was a part, "shall have the duty of studying the operation of Government activities at all levels with a view to determining its economy and efficiency." McCarthy's reasoning was A-B-C simple: a) if the FBI warns a Government agency about the existence of Communist cells and espionage activity within its very offices, and b) if these warnings are consistently ignored, then c) this constitutes a strong indication of inefficiency. Therefore the subcommittee is not only privileged but has a duty to investigate.

Recent history has shown that if it were not for the probing of a congressional committee, the Alger Hiss espionage case would still be a mystery. It was first aired in 1939, but no action was taken. Later, the House Committee on Un-American Activities looked into the Hiss case, but President Truman was not only unimpressed—he denounced the committee's probe into the Hiss and other cases as "red-herring diversions." Four months later, on December 16, 1948, the day after Hiss was indicted for perjury in connection with spying activities on the basis of evidence uncovered by the House Committee, the President told a press conference he still thought the whole thing a red herring.

Harry Dexter White, Secretary Morgenthau's top aide, was established as being a Communist agent in FBI reports submitted to the White House on down—but they remained covered up until the story was exposed by a congressional committee. William Remington would never have been exposed were it not for an investigation of his Communist activities conducted by a similar committee. Many more cases could be cited to underscore the point. *Yet for merely possessing evidence of subversion in his capacity as a senator and then chairman of a Senate investigating committee, McCarthy was subjected to bitter criticism—called a seditionist, a revolutionary, an inciter to rebellion, and an enemy of the established order.*

I am indebted to David Lawrence for providing a fascinating parallel involving another Wisconsin senator, the elder Robert M. La Follette. Toward the close of his first term La Follette interested himself in the plight of postal employees who were dissatisfied with their working conditions. The *Congressional Record* for August 10, 1912, contains an article that appeared originally in *La Follette's Weekly,* published for the Senator's constituents:

> Denied the right to petition Congress for relief . . . the mail clerks determined to protect themselves by organizing. This drew from the Administration a series of persecutions almost unparalleled. The men were told, in effect, that activity along these lines would mean the loss of their jobs. Sen. La Follette took hold of this situation. He addressed letters to all the mail clerks asking for the facts. From the pile of correspondence he received, a most appalling mistreatment of government employees and American citizens is revealed.

He took this step despite two executive orders issued in 1906 and 1909 by Presidents Roosevelt and Taft respectively, which barred U.S. employees from passing any information along to any member of Congress. "The gag rule is un-American, unjust," La Follette wrote. "It is a slap at the Constitution and an affront to our citizens." For so saying, La Follette was not accused of breaking the law or fomenting sedition, nor was any censure move made against him. He is now enshrined as a great liberal senator!

At the hearings Senator McClellan suggested that Senator McCarthy himself had broken the law on espionage by accepting a classified document. Subsequently the charge was echoed by a number of others. The Department of Justice was thoroughly aware of the circumstances. Had the Senator been guilty of breaking Federal law that Department could be expected to say so and take action. But there was no case and no action. The intelligence officer who turned the paper over to McCarthy was hardly a "subversive," as Senator Potter asserted, nor was he guilty of a law violation.

Once again, when the facts and merits were all with McCarthy, a case can be made against the manner in which he defended himself. He blundered badly when he explained his stand.

Under Welch's questioning, McCarthy adopted an unyielding attitude startlingly like that of close-mouthed witnesses who had refused to answer *his* questions when he was the interrogator. When Welch reminded him that the oath he took before testifying included "a solemn promise by you to tell the truth, comma, the whole truth, comma, and nothing but the truth"* the Senator replied, "Mr. Welch, you are not the first individual that tried to get me to betray the confidence and give out the names of my informants. You will be no more successful than those who have tried in the past, period."

The Senator said he had no mental reservation about telling the entire truth, but when he was asked who delivered the document to him, he answered, "The answer is no. You will not get that information."

WELCH: You wish, then, to put your own interpretation on your oath and tell us less than the truth?

MC CARTHY: Mr. Welch, I think I made it very clear to you that neither you nor anyone else will ever get me to violate the confidence of loyal people in this Government who give me information about Communist infiltration. I repeat, you will not get their names, you will not get any information which will allow you to identify them so that you or anyone else can get their jobs.

A moment later, Senator McCarthy was sounding like the many dozens of witnesses he himself had criticized for being unresponsive at subcommittee hearings.

WELCH: How soon after you got it did you show it to anyone?

MC CARTHY: I don't recall.

* This is an old courtroom histrionic, which the distinguished trial lawyer Frank Raichle always responds to by yawning and saying, "Oh, come on, we all have heard him take the oath. Why don't you just ask the question?"

WELCH: Can you think of the name of anyone to whom you
showed it?

MC CARTHY: I assume that it was passed on to my staff, most
likely.

WELCH: Name the ones on your staff who had it.

MC CARTHY: I wouldn't know.

WELCH: You wouldn't know?

MC CARTHY: No.

WELCH: Well, would it include Mr. Cohn?

MC CARTHY: It might.

WELCH: It would, wouldn't it?

MC CARTHY: I say it might.

WELCH: Would it include Mr. Carr?

MC CARTHY: It might.

There was no need for McCarthy to defend so violently, and even
with truculence, a right he so obviously possessed. This right was
upheld by Counsel Jenkins and Chairman Mundt the very day the
question was raised.

Chairman Mundt halted all demands to have McCarthy name the
informant when he said, "The chair unhesitatingly and unequivocally
rules that in his opinion, and this is sustained by an unbroken
precedent so far as he knows before Senate investigating committees,
law-enforcement officers, investigators, any of those engaged in the
investigating field, who come in contact with confidential information,
are not required to disclose the source of their information."

The President had the authority to permit disclosure of the original
FBI document and thus establish conclusively the accuracy or inaccuracy of what McCarthy said it contained. Would the Administration do so, or would it invoke the secrecy directive? The answer was
not long in forthcoming. Chairman Mundt sent the Attorney General
a request for permission to make the letter public, but this official, on
orders from the White House, refused to declassify it. The ruling was
politically tailored to hurt McCarthy, and hypocritical in view of the
same Administration's handling of a confidential FBI report only six
months before in the Harry Dexter White case, when that served its
political purpose. This episode is worth recalling.

Appearing before the Executive's Club on November 6, 1953, in
Chicago, Attorney General Herbert Brownell stated that in the course
of reviewing data on White, he discovered that a detailed FBI file
included evidence that White was a Communist underground agent

engaged in espionage for the Soviet Government. President Truman, Brownell said, knew about the file and the charges. Nevertheless, in January of 1946, Truman sent White's name to the Senate as director of the United States Mission to the International Monetary Fund. White had been an assistant secretary of the treasury. "Harry Dexter White was a Russian spy," Brownell told the Chicago group. "He smuggled secret documents to Russian agents for transmission to Moscow . . . I can now announce officially . . . that the records in my department show that White's spying activities . . . were reported in detail by the FBI."

What did President Eisenhower say about this "disclosure" of information in the FBI files? As expected, a storm broke over the Brownell revelations, with the Administration severely attacked on the grounds that it was making a political issue of the case.

Eisenhower, however, deplored the view of the "partisan critics." He said that the central point in the case was "this shocking FBI evidence . . ." He added: "The Attorney General made these facts known to awaken the public, as well as many uninformed people in government, to the existence of the Communist threat from within and to show that any individual, even though high in Government, if found to be a security risk, should be promptly and without apology dismissed."

When Senator McCarthy urged that the contents of the letter be made public, citing these very reasons, the President refused. It is difficult to avoid the conclusion that political considerations dictated this blackout—and the one that followed.

The next secrecy order by the Administration was designed to cover up the behind-the-scenes cloak-and-dagger moves within the Administration to "get" McCarthy.

To this end, on May 17 President Eisenhower forbade all Defense Department personnel from testifying at hearings about private conferences and telephone calls within the Executive branch. He told Republican leaders that members of the White House staff were "under no obligation to the Legislative branch of government" and embodied the order in a letter to Secretary Wilson.

"Because it is essential to efficient and effective administration that employees of the Executive Branch be in a position to be completely candid in advising with each other on official matters," he wrote, "and because it is not in the public interest that any of their conversations or communications, or any documents or reproductions, concerning such advice be disclosed, you will instruct employees of your Department that in all of their appearances before the Subcommittee of the Senate Committee on Government Operations regarding the inquiry now before it they are not to testify to any such conversations or communications or to produce any such documents or reproductions. This principle must be maintained regardless of who would be benefited by such disclosures."

The order came in the midst of testimony by Counselor Adams on the January 21 meeting in the Attorney General's office when plans were made to draw up the chronology of charges against us. It stopped the hearings at once because much of the controversy centered around what was said and done at this and other executive meetings.

Why did Eisenhower issue the order? There was no doubt in McCarthy's mind: "Too much was coming out and he had to stop the show," he told me that evening at his home. He handed me an article he had ripped from the Sunday issue of *The New York Times*. It was dated May 16—the day before the Eisenhower letter to Wilson—and was written by Arthur Krock, an opponent of the Senator. Krock had said:

> It may be that when the testimony has been completed, Senator Joseph R. McCarthy's national influence will have suffered the heavy injury which is the hope of many. But if that is dependent on proof that his investigation of security risks in the Army was unusually ruthless, was the direct consequence of the Army's refusal of certain favors for Private G. D. Schine, and was pursued for the purpose of discrediting the Army's former commander, now in the White House—whatever the cost to national security—the testimony so far has not supplied it.

The Krock view of the evidence simply makes clear what the Administration doubtless knew already: the hearings were going against it and the wisest course might be to cut them short before matters grew worse. We could not help noting, moreover, that the blackout came when the Army's case was almost concluded and we were ready to begin ours.

Senator McCarthy felt deeply about the issue. If the order is allowed to stand, he told the committee, the truth about the origin of the charges against us and the motives of those who brought them will be forever hidden from the American people. Senator McClellan agreed that the executive order was a "serious mistake." He said, "If such an order was to be issued, I think it should have been issued long ago and we could have known then that a part of the truth possibly would never be available to this committee. We could have determined then whether we would undertake these hearings under those conditions."

Senator Dirksen said that if the hearings continued under the order, at their close "we would be in the unhappy position of litigants in a lawsuit where proof on one side could not be fully established. The result would be inconclusive indeed. . . . I do not see how this committee sitting as investigators and judge and jurors could finally make a finding and make a report with the proof incomplete. . . . I earnestly admonish the committee that the prudent and the reasonable thing to do at the moment is to take enough time to explore the full impact of the executive order to determine whether or not there are any modifications or exceptions to it . . ."

And so, at 3:50 on May 17, the hearings were recessed for a week. Senator Dirksen went to the White House to try to convince the President to change his mind. But the President refused to allow us to establish for the record the full truth about that fateful January 21 meeting when plans were drawn to destroy Joseph McCarthy.

When I visited McCarthy in the late winter of 1956, two years later, we sat before the fireplace in his living room and talked.

"Have you noticed," he said, "that all these years there has been a kind of double standard in the country concerning me? If I do something—anything—it is viewed in one light; but if anyone else does the same thing, it is taken entirely differently.

"Now you take that incident during the hearings about the purloined letter. For having that letter, which clearly showed dereliction on the part of a Government agency in failing to get the Communists out, I was called all kinds of names. But the very people who shouted the loudest didn't hesitate for a moment to raise a war chest to steal official documents from my files for their own ends. Now you take the Hughes case—"

I had been fascinated by that case. It was so fantastic that no novelist would venture to use it for a plot. It was, indeed, a perfect example of what McCarthy meant by the "double standard."

In 1953, a man named Paul H. Hughes applied for a job with our subcommittee. He told Frank Carr, Don Surine, and Dick O'Melia of our staff that he had just resigned from the Air Force after sixteen years' service and had information that one of our bases in Saudi Arabia was riddled with security risks. Carr made inquiries, determined to his satisfaction that the charges were groundless, and forgot about the man and the matter. He was never hired, and never saw Senator McCarthy in his life.

Hughes next turned up at the office of Clayton Fritchey, then deputy chairman of the Democratic National Committee and editor of a publication called *Democratic Digest*. Posing as a "secret" investigator on Senator McCarthy's staff, Hughes told Fritchey he could provide a mass of documentary "proof" in the form of affidavits and minutes of secret meetings that McCarthy was engaged in a wide variety of illegal activities. Over a period of two months, Fritchey paid Hughes a total of $2,300, encouraging him to remain a McCarthy "investigator" while he compiled reports on the Senator, his staff, and all the supposedly dreadful things that were going on.

At the beginning of 1954, when the Army-McCarthy controversy was at the boil, Hughes called on Joseph L. Rauh, Jr., a well-known ultra-liberal Washington lawyer who was, at the time, chairman of the Americans for Democratic Action. Hughes told his story to Rauh, who was just as entranced as Fritchey and even more eager to part with cash to obtain documentary evidence that would "expose" McCarthy. Rauh spent a total of $8,500 for "expenses" Hughes would incur as he pursued his task of purloining documents from the McCarthy files.

For the money he received, Hughes provided Rauh with a fat file of "proof" which contained such sensational items as:

——Senator McCarthy maintained a veritable arsenal of weapons in the basement of the Senate Office Building, including revolvers, Lugers, and submachine guns.

——The McCarthy staff extorted stories of subversion from witnesses, in one case threatening to expose a Syracuse University professor's illegitimate son if he did not cooperate.

———A list of the names of McCarthy's secret informants within the White House.

———A lurid story of McCarthy's marital troubles.

There was much more—all fabricated by Hughes' fertile imagination. Later, Hughes and his attorney admitted in court that the notes, documents, minutes of meetings, the whole lot, were completely fraudulent. His attorney conceded that Hughes was "base, venal . . . a louse engaged in filthy practice."

The story now accelerates. Hughes told Rauh he needed an investigator, a friend from the service named Bill Decker, to help him extend the exposures. Decker was put on Rauh's payroll. His name appeared on vouchers and memos, but he himself never appeared anywhere. He was, in point of fact, as fictitious as the documents Hughes dug up. There was no Bill Decker, and Hughes pocketed his "salary."

Rauh now went to Philip Graham, publisher of the Washington *Post,* who introduced Hughes to James Russell Wiggins and Alfred Friendly, managing editor and assistant managing editor, with a view to preparing a series of articles on the explosive disclosures. Rauh left for a summer in Europe, while the editors and Hughes conferred over the story. Hughes continued to "discover" material throughout the summer and early fall, finally announcing in October that he had "resigned" from our staff.

At this point, Friendly and Hughes began collaboration upon the articles, based upon the "documents" the latter had collected. But now the plan, so remarkable for its brazenness, began to fall apart. The *Post* assigned one of its top reporters, Murray Marder, to get more details. He discovered that investigator "Decker" had provided affidavits from six persons who testified to reprehensible activities on the part of Senator McCarthy and his staff. The signers, Marder found, were, like Decker himself, phantoms. The Syracuse University professor had no illegitimate son and hadn't ever been in touch with McCarthy nor McCarthy with him. And so on.

The *Post* tore up the series without publishing a line. Equally embarrassed but thousands of dollars poorer, Fritchey and Rauh wanted to end the whole thing. The tale might have been lost to history if Hughes had not come up with another story in an obvious attempt to revenge himself upon Rauh.

This concerned Harvey Matusow, a former member of the Communist party and later an undercover agent for the FBI, who had testified before the Senate Internal Security Committee about the Communist activities of a number of individuals. In a reversal that understandably commanded a good deal of attention, Matusow said he had offered false testimony.

Hughes went to the FBI and charged that Rauh and a number of alleged co-conspirators had persuaded Matusow to recant, asserting that he had overheard a number of suspicious remarks that could lead to no other conclusion. Hughes was taken before the grand jury hearing the Matusow case, where he repeated his charges. When Rauh and the others were summoned to offer their side of the story they told how they had been duped by Hughes. The entire plot, at once repugnant and comic, came to light.

Under questioning by Thomas A. Bolan, then an assistant Federal attorney, Hughes admitted that he had sold trumped-up evidence and forged documents. He did insist, though, that he thought Rauh knew all along that the evidence was fake and encouraged him to provide as much as he could in order to discredit McCarthy.

Hughes admitted faking evidence from McCarthy's files, and McCarthy's enemies did not hesitate to accept these "purloined" documents at face value and pay large sums of money for more.

Hughes was indicted on charges that he had perjured himself before the grand jury concerning his Matusow testimony. He was acquitted on some of the charges because the trial jury obviously refused to believe the testimony of Rauh and the others; subsequently the Government dropped the case. The trial established the fact that McCarthy's enemies paid more than $10,000 in expenses for documents and information which they believed to have been purloined from his files. Rovere's book on McCarthy contains not one word on the Hughes case, although he had publicly promised to discuss it. All other critics on McCarthy have maintained a similar silence.

CHAPTER 14

THE BIG SHOW: On the Stand

M Y FIRST APPEARANCE on the witness stand came at mid-morning of April 27, the fourth hearing-day. It was a disaster. Summoned to testify about the "cropped" picture and Dave Schine's contributions to the work of the subcommittee, I committed virtually every possible blunder. I was rambling, garrulous, repetitious. I was brash, smug, and smart-alecky. I was pompous and petulant. Worst of all, I tried to match quips with the rapier-minded Joe Welch, who had behind him some forty years of courtroom experience in the art of impaling a legal opponent on his verbal foil. I was neatly skewered a number of times.

From the transcript, I have chosen some of my choicer utterances and listed the traits they unhappily projected during that brief initial session. It should be noted that on the witness stand as in life, often it isn't what you say so much as how you say it. Thus, while the words alone may not appear too damaging read in cold print, a certain tone and attitude accompanied them that made me appear somewhat less than self-effacing.

Arrogance—"Roy Cohn is here speaking for Roy Cohn, to give the facts." (I still grimace at the recollection of that grand pronunciamento.)

Self-importance—Asked if I could produce the original photograph, I replied I could but indicated the committee had to understand that "I have an awful lot of papers and stuff to attend to and it is not in my possession." I added confidently (and pompously): "I am sure it is under my control."

Condescension—"I will be glad to answer any question that any member of the committee wants to ask."

Once I advised Mr. Jenkins how to conduct his examination of me. ("I wonder if we could do it this way: Could I give you my recollection as to exactly what I did do?") Surprised but courteous, he replied that that would be fine. Several times, I corrected him unnecessarily. ("Excuse me, Mr. Jenkins. You say the day before yesterday? I believe it was the end of last week.") He acknowledged I was right but the time made no particular difference. I kept making the same points over and over.

My attempts to trade jibes with Joe Welch were dismal failures. At one point, we clashed over whether Stevens and Schine were smiling and looking at each other in the picture. I said they were; Welch disagreed, calling Stevens' expression "grim." He handed me the photo, which showed Stevens on the right, Schine in the center, and Colonel Bradley on the left.

Welch began by suggesting that the Army Secretary may have been directing his gaze at the colonel, rather than at Schine. "It would take someone with clairvoyance to know at whom Secretary Stevens is looking, would it not?" he asked.

"No sir," I replied, "I don't think so. It would take somebody with common sense who can look at a picture and see what's in it."

Welch pursued the point. "I think I observe on Colonel Bradley's face a faint little look of pleasure. Do you, sir?"

"I would say I know that Colonel Bradley had a good steak dinner shortly afterward," I replied. "Perhaps he was anticipating it."

My attempt at humor gave Welch a golden opportunity for a line that brought down the house. "If Bradley is feeling good about a steak dinner," he said, "Schine must be considering a whole haunch of beef!"

Earlier, after I had announced that I was not represented by an attorney, Welch said, "Mr. Cohn, I assume you would like it understood that although I sit at the same table, I am not your counsel."

"There is not a statement that has been made at this hearing with which I am in more complete agreement," I answered. ". . . I have no counsel here . . ."

"In all modesty, sir," the Bostonian replied, "I am content that it should appear from my end that I am not your counsel."

It was a neat thrust, slyly implying I would do better if he were my lawyer. The remark drew a wave of laughter but my unfunny rejoinder did not. "I might say," I said, "that you are certainly not going to get any fee from me." Mr. Welch went on to other matters; he knew when to leave a point after scoring.

During the luncheon recess, I walked to the elevator with Senator McCarthy for a conference in his fourth-floor suite. "You were about the worst witness I ever heard in my life," he said, and proceeded to catalog my faults. He was reeling them off as the elevator came and we stepped inside. Senator Symington, standing near us, overheard McCarthy's criticisms and felt sorry for me. "Don't be so hard on him, Joe," he said "I'll give you fifty dollars for his brain any day." At the moment, I felt he would be overpaying.

My first-day debacle reopened the question of legal representation: Should I now get a lawyer for my future appearances before the committee? Before I was summoned, practically all my close friends and advisers had pressed me to obtain counsel. They argued there was no disgrace in being represented; that every other witness had his lawyer sitting with him, even John Adams, the Army's own lawyer; that since I was a principal in the controversy, I needed a cool, objective individual at my side to help me maintain perspective. I lost count of the times I heard the adage, quoted earnestly into my ear, that the man who acts as his own lawyer has a fool for a client.

My father pressed me to obtain counsel. "Get Charlie Lockwood or Paul Windels," he urged. Mr. Lockwood was a retired Supreme Court justice and Mr. Windels was former Corporation Counsel of New York City, both men of integrity and courage. Senator Mc-Carthy told me in his office that very noontime: "Roy, run, don't walk, to a lawyer! Get Eddie Williams." Edward Bennett Williams, still in his early thirties, was already earning a reputation as a brilliant trial counsel. That night, I spoke by telephone to George Sokolsky and some other good friends. Their advice: "Get a lawyer."

But I decided the other way. Despite my poor preliminary performance, I would go it alone. I would embark upon an intensive campaign to prepare myself for my next appearance, intended to present myself less awkwardly before the twenty-million-member jury judging the case.

I had come to the realization that the Senate hearings were less a search for truth than a gigantic personality play, with the "winner" or "loser" to be ultimately chosen on the basis of impressions built up during the sessions rather than on the evidence. Originally conceived as part trial and part fact-finding mission, the investigation had quickly become mostly show and image-building. The older and more experienced principals, I saw, understood this from the beginning and were playing shamelessly to the grandstand. They all knew that you don't have to be wrong up there in the hearing room in order to lose—you just have to sound wrong.

Yes, the old pros understood. Wily Joe Welch, though protesting he was only a country boy new to the ways of Washington, knew the score, and so did Senator Symington. They constantly played for effects. Curiously, Senator McCarthy understood the game too. Many times he told me that nobody would be adjudged guilty or not guilty when the hearings ended, except in the eyes of the people. But although he was able to perceive flaws in the performances of others—mine, for example—he lacked the critical insight to evaluate his own. This shortcoming, discussed more fully in a later chapter, proved to be his Achilles' heel. Matters would have turned out better for Joe McCarthy had he possessed the ability to see himself as others saw him.

My plan called for an objective appraisal of my initial appearance. Studying the transcript, I recalled the manner of my replies, and forced myself to write down each fault as I discovered it. I made a long list. Reviewing it, I determined to work hard to change each debit into a credit.

Instead of being talkative, I would speak to the point.

Instead of being aggressive, I would be withdrawn.

Instead of being smart-alecky, I would be deferential.

Instead of being excitable, I would be unruffled.

Most important, instead of surrounding myself with a host of advisers on the stand, I would sit there all alone. When Stevens and Adams testified, there were so many high-ranking military officers sitting behind them, one wondered who was left to run the Pentagon! I felt that the contrast between the lonely figure on the stand and the brass-engulfed Army witnesses would be striking and could not help engendering sympathy for our side.

From that time on, I utilized all my free moments to rehearse my next appearance. I tried to anticipate every possible question that would be hurled at me, and hour after hour, I practiced my answers. At night, I sat before the mirror in my hotel room, studying my demeanor and listening to the inflection of my voice as I answered my own questions. I probed for any characteristics that might be interpreted unfavorably and, when I found them, rooted them out with practice. People who saw me walking on the streets, my lips moving, wondered if I had begun talking to myself. In a sense, I had; I was rehearsing.

It was not easy to convince Senator McCarthy. "Roy," he said again, "you're making a serious mistake. You're in a dogfight with a lot of sharp characters who have made up their minds to rip you to pieces. I'm older than you and I've been through the mill. Take my advice. For the sake of your own survival, get a lawyer."

"Senator," I argued, "I respect your judgment and experience, and every day that I spend in this jungle I become more and more aware of my own inexperience to cope with the in-fighting. But I've grown a lot older in a very short time, and I am beginning to see how the game is played.

"These hearings are not being held behind closed doors. The whole country's watching and listening, and they can't land any low blows, at least ones that are too obvious, in full view of millions. I understand the situation better than any lawyer I could get. I'm sure that if I go up there, without counsel, without aides, without briefcases full of documents, and tell the truth, answering all the questions put to me simply and directly, the country will believe me."

Reluctantly, the Senator agreed. However, to make certain I would not fumble seriously, he asked me to his home for a full-dress rehearsal. On May 25, a small group gathered in the McCarthy living room. Present to test me were the Senator and his wife, Frank Carr and Jim Juliana of the committee staff, my colleague from prosecuting days, John M. Foley, and Willard Edwards, Chicago *Tribune* correspondent.

I sat in the center of the living room, facing the questioners. Before the barrage began, Edwards told the group: "Roy's greatest handicap is the general feeling that he's a cocky young bastard, and he should strive to remove that impression." I caught McCarthy's eye. Neither of us bothered to say how acutely I was aware of this and how I had been working to correct it.

From the vantage point of thirteen extra years, I can entertain with a degree of detachment Mr. Edwards' characterization of the impression I made, as well as criticism leveled at me during those turbulent months. I was elected by President Truman to membership in his private S.O.B. Club, denounced by Defense Secretary Wilson in impressive though unprintable profanities, accused by Vermont's Senator Ralph Flanders of being "engaged in some devious, mysterious, unexplained conspiracy to destroy civil liberties," and excoriated by some forgotten journalist as a "Jewish spy who sold out to the Communists." Indeed, "cocky young bastard" was the least of the lot. Willard Edwards wrote a detailed memo about the evening of my rehearsal and filed it. He found it in his files on the story and agreed to its reproduction in this book.

The hour of the meeting was set for 8 P.M. I finished my story about 8:30 P.M. but was not worried, knowing the tardy habits of all those scheduled to be present. True enough, when Jean answered my ring, she and the Senator and her mother were just finishing dinner. It was fried chicken, for a change, not one of the usual pickup meals which seem to be popular in the family. Joe was in the living room, on the telephone. Jean made coffee and I joined the Senator.

He was in a serious mood. I remarked that Senator Dirksen appeared to have swung over completely to his side. He had during the day offered an excuse for Cohn's alleged threat to "wreck the army," remarking that it was in the great American tradition to sound off in that manner when displeased, uttering threats which were not to be taken seriously. Joe repeated what I have heard him say on many occasions—that he had no ambitions whatever to take over the leadership of the section of the Republican party that is dissatisfied with President Eisenhower, that it was incredible that he could be the one to assemble a cohesive force.

"I am perfectly willing to be the hatchet man," Joe remarked. "I can see that things are developing to the point that it will appear to be all Eisenhower on one side and all McCarthy on the other. But I am not the man to become the leader of the one side." I am still unable to determine and I don't think anyone knows, even he himself, if Joe has serious White House ambitions but feels it is good strategy to conceal them at this time.

Roy arrived at 8:50 P.M. which is punctuality for him. He was accompanied by Frank Carr, Jack Foley, and Jim Juliana.

The next two hours were occupied by Roy's running over his proposed testimony. There were numerous distractions, some of them irritating, others humorous, and I remember thinking at the time that this was one of the most unusual groups I have ever seen in action. The amazing fact is that they are the most efficient investigating group I have observed in twenty years of experience on the Washington scene despite what seems at times to be a most haphazard method of functioning.

Roy sat on a chair with Juliana and Foley taking turns at asking him the questions. McCarthy constantly interrupted. I reserved my advice to suggesting that Roy assume the attitude he had adopted on his "Meet the Press" program some months ago—modest, almost humble, self-effacing, with references at times to older heads with more wisdom than his. There was some banter about this being a difficult role. I suggested that Roy's greatest handicap was a general feeling that he was a cocky young so-and-so and he should strive to remove that impression. He said simply, "I am one," but agreed to do his best.

McCarthy's theory was that Roy would be telling the greatest spy story ever told in describing the preliminary history of his record as a criminal prosecutor in communism cases. He wanted this gone into great detail, with documentary reading at times. It would all be familiar to us, he noted, but the TV audience would find it new and thrilling.

As the story continued, Joe wandered off, returning at times to interrupt with suggestions. So did the others and after the first hour I was the one listening. Meanwhile the telephone was ringing constantly, the McCarthy hound was barking its head off at intervals, and Roy was continually distracted. He was entitled to quiet attention as he faced a climactic role in his life, one that may swerve the direction of his future career, and he earned my sympathy. It is at times like these when he was obviously perturbed at the repeated distractions that I realize he is only twenty-seven, a fact one is inclined to forget because of his brilliance of mind and apparent superb confidence in himself. He is still only a young man, the center of one of the most frenzied spectacles of our times, and I have a good idea that when he is by himself, his inward anxieties are heavy. I discovered that evening that he sleeps badly and has been taking pills.

Frank Carr revealed that the committee has subpoenaed and questioned Miss Iris Flores, a stunning young brunette, who is one of Dave Schine's girl friends, No. 1 on the list at the present time. She is the one to whom Dave made several phone calls a day during his Ft. Dix stay and the committee obtained her name thru subpoena of the telephone records. The Army has insisted upon questioning her to determine if Dave misused his pass privileges for feminine entertainment when he was supposed to be engaged on committee business.

There was much discussion of whether her testimony would help or harm the McCarthy case. She was Dave's companion on New Year's eve and her testimony would be that she fretted the evening away while Dave pored over committee records in preparation for the annual report. This was fine but would anyone believe it? During the evening a call came from Senator Mundt, and McCarthy reported Mundt thought the girl's testimony was not pertinent. This, however, was undecided and the beauteous Iris was present in the hearing room this morning. From what I heard, if she testifies, it will be a field day for the press.

(When I left that evening, I phoned the office and dictated a three-paragraph story about Iris being questioned. I was aware that Walter Winchell had been informed of the incident and was hunting for a picture of her.)

Dave called up and said he was with Iris. Joe asked them to come over but Dave said his companion was dead tired and was retiring. He showed up an hour later himself. He was due back in Ft. Myer at 1 A.M. and wanted someone to call up his colonel and get him an all-night leave. He interrupted Roy in the middle of his story and asked for action.

"Dave, for God's sake," responded Roy. "Do you realize that I'm going on trial before 20 million people tomorrow and am trying to get my thoughts organized?"

Carr flatly refused to make any call and Dave was told to get his pass from Jenkins, the subcommittee counsel, if he wanted one.

At 11 P.M., Joe broke up the conference. He insisted that Roy be fresh for tomorrow's ordeal and go home and get some sleep. . . .

JENKINS: Now, Mr. Chairman and members of the committee, I very happily announce that we have concluded with the Army's case, and I now desire to call as first witness for the Senator McCarthy staff, Mr. Roy M. Cohn.

Now, after twenty-one days of hearing the Army's side, it was our turn. When my name was called, I walked around the long coffin-shaped table, behind which the principals were seated, to the witness chair opposite. Beside and behind it were many other chairs, occupied in the weeks preceding by the colonels and generals who served as aides to Stevens and Adams. I sat down in the middle of the front row.

Ray Jenkins looked down at me from across the table and, sympathy in his voice, said, "Mr. Cohn, you are quite alone there, sitting there by yourself." I felt forlorn in the middle of emptiness. The thought crossed my mind that whatever planning I had done to *appear* subdued had been a waste of time—I never felt less "aggressive" in my entire life.

Mr. Jenkins began by developing my career in the Justice Department and my qualifications for serving as chief counsel to the subcommittee.

JENKINS: Have you made a considerable study of Communism, Mr. Cohn?

COHN: I have, sir.

JENKINS: And particularly as it related to the infiltration of Communists in the United States and into the various governmental branches and agencies?

COHN: Yes, sir.

JENKINS: Could you give us a short definition of what a Communist is?

COHN: A Communist, sir, is one who is under the discipline of the movement which stands for the overthrow by force and violence of the Government of the United States and of every other free government throughout the world, and the movement which works by criminal, illegal means, by espionage and sabotage and every other foul way known to man, to bring about the day when the world will be under the control of the international Communist movement, and when free governments will no longer exist.

JENKINS: I take it you are not on the friendliest terms, then, with the Communist party, is that right, Mr. Cohn?

COHN: I am not, sir.

JENKINS: You have not been nominated as editor of the *Daily Worker?*

COHN: No, sir, I have been referred to in the *Daily Worker* very considerably, sir, but I have not been nominated by them for any favorable offers.

JENKINS: Could you give us a short definition of espionage?

COHN: I would say espionage, sir, is defined by law in title 18 of the United States Code and involves generally the possession of or transmission of information vital to the national

> defense of the United States to a foreign power with intent
> that it be used against the interests of the United States . . .
>
> JENKINS: What is a subversive?
>
> COHN: . . . A person who is dedicated to interests unfavorable
> to the continuation of the free government under which we
> live in this country.

Under further questioning I explained that my duties as committee
counsel included the questioning of witnesses at executive sessions
and public hearings, working with the staff to develop information on
the infiltration of Communists into the United States Government and
corruption in office, and the assembling of facts gathered for presentation to the committeee.

Mr. Jenkins asked me if, without divulging names, I could reveal
the sources from which the committee obtained its information on
spies, Communists, and subversives in the Army or any Government
agency. I have been asked this question many times and the answer
was not a secret. Here is what I told Mr. Jenkins:

> First of all, we get a good deal of information from people out-
> side of Government, people who have been in the Communist
> movement and who are in the best position to know what the
> Communists are up to. We get information from certain people
> in Government who point out instances where Communists are
> being covered up and where no action is being taken against
> Communists despite FBI warnings. We get information, sir, by
> going over old files, old records, documentations of people who
> have signed Communist petitions and who might later turn up in
> Government, from communications received by us from many
> patriotic organizations, from Americans all around the country
> who gain this information and who see fit to furnish it to this
> committee, to the investigating committee of the United States
> Senate. Those are just a few of the sources.

During the rest of the morning session, I described in detail matters
with which the reader is already familiar—how the investigation into
Communist infiltration of the Army got started, my initial meetings
with Stevens and Adams, their general unhappiness with the Fort
Monmouth probes. I felt at ease and told my story simply.

Next day, the direct examination ended and Ray Jenkins proceeded to change hats. Now he went after me hard, searching for

chinks and contradictions in my account. I answered his probing questions as best I could, and nothing eventful developed. Whenever possible, I gave simple "yes" or "no" answers. It's often said that this is difficult for a witness to do. Actually, it's the wisest course to follow and I recommend it to anyone who is ever put under cross-examination. By talking too much the witness only opens new areas of inquiry to a hostile attorney. I can't count the number of points I made as a lawyer and investigator because witnesses could not keep their mouths shut.

The major charges of the inquiry came up during my long interrogation. I answered them all.

Did I make the statement that "Stevens is through as Secretary of the Army?" "I did not."

Did I say, "We will wreck the Army?" "No, I didn't."

Did I use improper pressure to get a commission for Schine? "I did not."

"Did Adams refer to Schine as a 'hostage' in the Army's efforts to halt the McCarthy investigation of Fort Monmouth?" "He called him by that name, as the hostage, more frequently than he called him by the name of Schine."

Did I use vituperative language in my dealings with Army officials? "In my opinion the statement that I used vituperative language is false. I think the language I used is the same as anybody else uses. There might be an occasional word I would not want to repeat on television."

Was it true that I lost my head when Schine was not given special privileges, such as being kept off KP duty? "That is completely untrue."

What was my relationship with Dave Schine? I answered that I had met him at a luncheon arranged by a mutual friend two years before and we soon became warm personal friends. Mr. Jenkins developed the subject of our friendship fully before the committee:

JENKINS: In all fairness, Mr. Cohn, isn't it a fact that he is one of your best friends? We all have our best friends. There is no criticism of you on that account.

COHN: No, of course not, sir.

JENKINS: We have friends whom we love. I do. And the relationship between you and Dave Schine has been very close for the past two years, hasn't it?

COHN: Yes, sir. He is one of a number of good friends I am proud
to have.

JENKINS: Have you known him socially?

COHN: I have.

JENKINS: Visited in his home?

COHN: Yes, sir.

JENKINS: He has visited in your home?

COHN: Yes, sir.

JENKINS: And perhaps you have double-dated together. There
is no reflection on anything about that. You are both single
men as we understand it.

COHN: We have been on double dates, sir . . .

I explained that Schine joined the McCarthy committee two or
three weeks after my appointment, having been recommended by a
number of persons, including me, and that he continued to work
actively with the committee until his induction into the Army.

What did Schine do, actually, for the committee? I said, "Dave
Schine came with the committee as an unpaid consultant originally to
work on an investigation of the United States information program
and the Voice of America, matters to which Dave had given a
number of years' study and writing before he did come with our
committee. The type of work he did, to answer your question, was
this: he interviewed personally and on many occasions, in fact most
occasions, alone, I would say hundreds of witnesses working at the
Voice of America and the information program. He checked out the
facts obtained from these witnesses, obtained documentation, participated in the setting up of what were a large number of executive
sessions and public hearings held by this committee in connection
with that investigation."

Mr. Jenkins, on the first day of my appearance, brought up what he
termed "the most serious charge made by you and Senator McCarthy
against the Army or Mr. Stevens and Mr. Adams"—that the latter
had sought to have the committee ease up on the Army and shift its
attention instead to the Air Force and Navy. I testified that the
suggestion was first made by Mr. Adams on October 21 in New
York. On that day we had dinner at my home and attended a
prizefight at Madison Square Garden. Afterward we went on to a
supper club or two.

The special counsel quickly noted that he would draw no unfavorable inference from my visit to a so-called late spot. "I understand you are a single man," he explained.

"Yes, sir."

"And Mr. Adams is a good talker and he probably will be able to talk himself out of any domestic difficulties," Mr. Jenkins observed.

"Based on that night," I replied, "there is nothing he has to talk himself out of."

Next Mr. Jenkins wanted to know about the suggestion that we "go after the Navy or the Air Force."

"I want to emphasize," I said, "there was no great dramatic thing about saying, 'Stop the investigation about us and go ahead and blow up the Navy and the Air Force.'

"The idea which Mr. Adams was trying to project was that if we were to investigate Communist infiltration in the Navy and the Air Force at the same time, at that time, that would sort of take some of the onus off the Army, and if we could leave the Army alone and give some attention to the Communist infiltration in the Navy and the Air Force, it would not put the Army in a bad light or it would not leave the Army all alone in a bad light." I added that neither Adams nor Stevens had ever suggested "that we pursue any false information or anything of that kind about the Navy and Air Force."

I went on to tell how on December 9, during the Fort Monmouth investigation, Mr. Adams spoke to me outside the hearing room in the Senate Office Building and the conversation continued inside room 101, the committee's staff headquarters. Mr. Adams then said he knew where we planned to investigate after the Monmouth probe was finished and asked me to let him in on the details. I replied that I had no idea what project he had in mind, and that when the time came I would certainly tell him about it. Nonetheless, he thought I was holding something back.

"I'll tell you what I'll do," he said. We were still outside in the corridor. He took out a pad and paper and drew a map of the United States, dividing the country into nine areas. He told me: "You mark on this map the location of the Army place which you are going to investigate next, and I am going to mark down the location of an Air Force base where there are a large number of sex deviates which will make some good hearings for your committee." We walked into my office and the talk went on.

JENKINS: What did he say, Mr. Cohn, about your going after the Air Force or after these homosexuals?

COHN: I don't remember any extended discussion about that. He was just going to trade in this piece of information for something that he wanted.

JENKINS: Did you then have any information about homosexuals in the Air Force?

COHN: No.

JENKINS: Did you trade with him?

COHN: No, sir.

JENKINS: Was Mr. Carr with you on that occasion?

COHN: Yes.

JENKINS: Mr. Cohn, as I recall your testimony, that is the third time that this man Adams suggested to you to go after the Air Force or the Navy?

COHN: That is right.

Finally, it was Joe Welch's turn to ask the questions.

Now his demeanor underwent a complete transformation. Gone was the benign old-fashioned New England lawyer. His gentle voice took on a new sharpness; the courtly manner disappeared. His questions came faster, his voice grew edgier, his sarcasm became more biting.

The tension began rising as we faced each other across the broad table. And then the Fisher incident exploded in the hearing room and throughout the nation.

CHAPTER 15

THE BIG SHOW: The
Ninth of June

I T WAS ON THE THIRTIETH DAY of the hearings. Who among the watchers of that incredible performance can forget it? Though lasting scarcely fifteen minutes, the Fisher episode was the emotional climax of the proceedings.

While the event itself was enacted in full view of millions, the complete story is here told for the first time. The gaps in the public's understanding of the Fisher case are many and wide. Here is the way it was:

On the late afternoon of June 9, Joe Welch was demanding to know if our subcommittee was routing out spies and Communists from their roosting places as swiftly as they could be detected.

"Mr. Cohn," he asked, "if I told you now that we had a bad situation at Monmouth [Ft. Monmouth, N.J.], you would want to cure it by sundown, if you could, wouldn't you?"

And again: "Mr. Cohn, tell me once more. Every time you learn of a Communist or a spy somewhere, is it your policy to get them out as fast as possible?"

And still again: "May I add my small voice, sir, and say whenever you know about a subversive or a Communist or a spy, please hurry. Will you remember those words?"

Senator McCarthy was growing angrier by the moment at what he later excoriated as "baiting" of the witness and "filibustering" of the hearing. Finally, his patience exhausted, he spoke up from his place at the end of the long table:

"Mr. Chairman, in view of that question . . ."

"Have you a point of order?" asked Chairman Mundt.

"Not exactly, Mr. Chairman," angrily replied the Senator, "but in view of Mr. Welch's request that the information be given, once we know of anyone who might be performing any work for the Communist party, I think we should tell him that he has in his law firm a young man named Fisher whom he recommended, incidentally, to do work on this committee, who has been for a number of years a member of an organization which was named, oh, years and years ago, as the legal bulwark of the Communist party . . ."

Senator McCarthy was referring to Frederick G. Fisher, Jr., thirty-two years old at the time and a law associate of Mr. Welch. Fisher, McCarthy pointed out, had been a member of the National Lawyers Guild, an organization described by the Attorney General as "the legal bulwark of the Communist party."

"I have hesitated bringing that up," the Senator said, "but I have been rather bored with your phony requests to Mr. Cohn here that he personally get every Communist out of Government before sundown."

McCarthy pointed out that Welch had recommended Fisher to assist him as special counsel. "I am not asking you at this time to explain why you tried to foist him on this committee," the Senator said. "Whether you knew he was a member of that Communist organization or not, I don't know. I assume you did not, Mr. Welch, because I get the impression that, while you are quite an actor, you play for a laugh, I don't think you have any conception of the danger of the Communist party. I don't think you yourself would ever knowingly aid the Communist cause. I think you are unknowingly aiding it when you try to burlesque this hearing in which we are attempting to bring out the facts, however."

During the Senator's remarks, Lawyer Welch had remained seated, staring fixedly at the counsel table. Now, close to tears, he spoke slowly and feelingly as millions watched.

"Until this moment, Senator, I think I never really gauged your cruelty or your recklessness. Fred Fisher is a young man who went to the Harvard Law School and came into my firm and is starting what looks to be a brilliant career with us . . ."

He went on to explain that he had indeed intended to name Fisher to assist him as special counsel on the committee but, at dinner one night in Washington, had asked him point-blank if there was "anything funny" in his background. Fisher, Welch said, had replied that when he was in law school "and for a period of months after" he had belonged to the Lawyers Guild. "I said," Welch told the committee, " 'Fred, I just don't think I am going to ask you to work on the case. If I do, one of these days that will come out and go over national television and it will just hurt like the dickens.' So, Senator, I asked him to go back to Boston."

The audience in the great Senate Caucus Room was hushed, all eyes on the elderly lawyer as he continued to talk, his voice heavy with emotion.

"Little did I dream you could be so reckless and so cruel as to do an injury to that lad. It is true he is still with Hale & Dorr. It is true that he will continue to be with Hale & Dorr. It is, I regret to say, equally true that I fear he shall always bear a scar needlessly inflicted by you."

A moment later, he uttered what is perhaps the most remembered line of the hearing: "Let us not assassinate this lad further, Senator. You have done enough. Have you no sense of decency, sir, at long last? Have you left no sense of decency?"

Mr. Welch, tears now glistening in his eyes, refused to discuss the subject further and took his seat. Suddenly the tension in the room snapped. Spectators and even newsmen burst into applause despite Chairman Mundt's frequent warnings against any demonstrations.

No dramatist could hope to write a more eloquent and moving scene.

What were the facts?

The first thing that needs to be said is that the impression that McCarthy exploded a deep, dark secret for the very first time was by no means the case. The Fisher story had been in the newspapers on April 15 and 16, almost two months before. For example, *The New York Times* had published a photograph of Mr. Fisher on page 12 of its April 16 issue. In an accompanying news story was the following: "Mr. Welch today confirmed news reports that he had relieved from duty his original second assistant, Frederick G. Fisher, Jr., of his own Boston law office, because of admitted previous membership in the

National Lawyers Guild, referred to by Herbert Brownell, Jr., the Attorney General, as 'the legal mouthpiece of the Communist party.' "

But there remains an important part of the background of this story hitherto untold.

Welch was employing a basic courtroom tactic carefully designed to make a witness lose composure. The object of such a technique is to make a witness expose himself emotionally and therefore be made to appear as the kind of individual who might be capable of committing a particular offense even though no actual evidence has been shown that he did, in fact, commit anything. If a man is charged with beating his wife in a fit of temper, a telling point could be made if the prosecutor can needle the defendant into exploding on the stand.

Day after day, Joe Welch bore down on me, badgering and baiting, needling and taunting, demanding yes or no answers to questions that obviously could not be answered in one clipped word, ridiculing with every histrionic means in his repertoire the work of the investigations subcommittee. The transcript is studded with passages like this:

> WELCH: . . . I just want a straight yes or no answer.
> MUNDT: Give him a chance, Mr. Welch.
> WELCH: I say, can't he answer it quite simply?
> MUNDT: We will never find out unless you give him a chance to try.

Mr. Welch sought to show that I did not bring certain information about subversives to the attention of Secretary of the Army Stevens as quickly as he thought I should.

> WELCH: If you had gone over to the Pentagon and got inside the door and yelled to the first receptionist you saw, "We got some hot dope on some Communists in the Army," don't you think you would have landed at the top?
> COHN: Sir, that is not the way I do things.

And later:

> WELCH: I think it is really dramatic to see how these Communist-hunters will sit on this document when they could have brought it to the attention of Bob Stevens in twenty minutes

and they let month after month go by without going to the
head and saying, "Sic 'em, Stevens."

COHN: May I answer that last statement?

WELCH: I only said you didn't say, "Sic 'em, Stevens," and you
didn't, did you?

COHN: Mr. Welch, you said a few days ago that you wanted to be
fair. If you do want to be fair, sir, you will let me correct
what is an erroneous impression which you are trying to
convey here.

WELCH: I am not trying to convey the impression that you
actually said, "Sic 'em, Stevens," you understand that, don't
you?

COHN: I think I understand what you are trying to do, sir.

With these and other jibes, Mr. Welch obviously intended to
provoke me into losing my temper and thereby showing, in full view
of the subcommittee and, of course, the American people, that I was
indeed an "irresponsible young upstart," a "hot-headed young crusader," to use some of the choice descriptions carried by some segments of the press. However, I had foreseen Mr. Welch's line of attack
and remained calm through all his thrusts.

Even my sharpest critics noted that Lawyer Welch had been unable
to prove much of anything during the eight trying days I spent on the
stand. Wrote Michael Straight in *Trial by Television:* "Roy Cohn had
proved an excellent and persuasive witness." Mr. Welch himself was
so deluged with letters and telegrams protesting the violence of his
cross-examination that one day he acknowledged it before the committee. "Mr. Cohn," he said on the sixth day of my testimony, "my
mail and my telegrams reflect, sir, that you are held in gratifyingly high
esteem in this country. There apparently are a good many people who
think I was unfair to you yesterday."

It was clear that by June 9, Welch desperately needed to pull a
rabbit from his hat in order to alter the image now left with the
committee and the millions who had watched the hearings all through
the late spring and early summer. It was, by and large, not a bad
image. No members of our staff had been proved anything but
perhaps overzealous at times in doing our jobs. Most observers
agreed. I have chosen to reproduce Michael Straight's analysis of the
hearings to this point, because nobody could allege that this editor of
the *New Republic* was favorably biased toward the Senator or me.

Mr. Welch had conceded that the Army could not hope for complete vindication. The public reaction that had risen against Senator McCarthy had reached its high point and begun to ebb. From now on, if he could control himself and appear as a moderate, responsible leader, that might be the final image left on ten million television screens. It would have gone far to obscure earlier impressions of brutality. It might once more have opened the door of welcome to the White House and the Republican high command. With the patronage of a great party behind him, Senator McCarthy could rise to new heights following this trial. Without that patronage he might be left an outlaw.

Welch found the rabbit in his hat in the form of the Fisher incident—one that, in truth, none of us wanted to bring up—not Mr. Welch; not I, and not Joe McCarthy, who had agreed not to use the matter over television.

Early in the hearings, I sized up Joe Welch as a horse trader. I mean no disrespect; this is an art commonly practiced in the legal profession, business, and politics. I felt strongly that Mr. Welch would not be averse to a fair swap somewhere along the line if opportunity arose, and integrity permitted.

Neither, in truth, would I. And this is the way it happened.

On June 7, two days before the Fisher blowup, the session adjourned at 5:40. Slowly the large room began to clear. I lingered behind to put my papers in order. On the way out, I fell in step with Mr. Welch.

"There's a little matter I'd like to talk to you about sometime," Welch said. "I think you're the sort of person to whom I can talk off the record about it."

"Coincidentally," I replied, "there is something I would like to talk to you about privately."

"Well then," he said, "let us make 'sometime' now."

Down the hall, Welch spotted the open door of an empty committee room. We entered and shut the door.

"This whole thing is a shame," Welch said. "I have no love for a great many things on my side, but we're both lawyers and we have a job to do. Nevertheless, we don't have to hurt one another unnecessarily while we are doing it."

He paused, then resumed: "Do you want to go first, or shall I?"

I said I would begin.

Three days before, early on June 4, I said, he had started to question me about my draft status, pointing out that a number of news stories had appeared on the subject. I had told him from the stand that I would be willing to answer any questions he'd care to put. He replied, and I now refer to the transcript: "I understand that. But I hope I won't ask any. I hope before we go into this matter that you will consult your file or bring it to the stand with you, so you can reel that off to us, what your whole story has been."

I said: "Whatever you want, Mr. Welch."

Now, in the empty committee room, I told him: "From the thrust of your questions, I can see where you are going. I assure you, however, that your bottom line is wrong. But in trying to get there, I think you would be hurting me unnecessarily. The facts have no bearing upon anything with which the hearings are concerned. I can produce them and they will satisfy you, but the very process of explanation could create an impression that something *might* be there. Frankly, the matter would be personally embarrassing to me. Do you have to go into it?"

I thereupon told him the facts. Briefly, this was the story:

In my sophomore year at Columbia College, when I was eighteen years old, I succeeded in obtaining an appointment to West Point. I had visited there many times with my parents, and loved the place. I was, of course, overjoyed. I was scheduled to take the entrance examinations on the first Tuesday of March in 1945. It was to be a three-day ordeal, and I prepared long and hard, studying far into the night.

I had to pass qualifying examinations in mathematics and English as well as a West Point aptitude test; I had to present an acceptable scholastic background; and, finally, I had to undergo a rigid medical examination and physical aptitude test.

The educational part of the testing I passed without difficulty. But alas, I came a cropper on physical aptitude, which measured among other things muscular power and endurance.

I took the test again the following year. Meanwhile, I was placed, according to the law, on a deferred draft status. But in 1946, sad to say, I was again unable to get through the stiff West Point physical aptitude exam which called for, among other things: 16 push-ups; 28 squat jumps; 30 sit-ups; a 65-foot basketball throw; a 140-foot softball throw; a 300-yard run at 46.7 seconds; and a 100-yard run in 27 seconds carrying a partner on my back! I was no weakling—but I wasn't up to that kind of performance.

Following the West Point rejection, I was classified 1-A, and shortly afterward drafting was stopped in the New York area. It was resumed in June of 1948, but by that time I had enlisted in the National Guard's 953rd Coast Artillery Battalion as a private. In a few months, I was transferred to the 259th Coast Artillery Battalion and later to headquarters, New York National Guard, where on September 6, 1949, I was promoted to sergeant and two years later moved up to warrant officer. In February of 1952, I was commissioned a first lieutenant in the Judge Advocate General's corps.

I told Mr. Welch as I finished my story: "I know there have been imputations that I attempted to dodge the draft. I believe these stories have been planted in newspapers by persons who are attempting to stop my work. I have told you the truth as it was. The bottom line to which I think you were leading in your questioning—that I was some kind of a draft dodger—was wrong."

Welch said, "I think you're quite correct that the 'bottom line' is wrong, but I'm under very heavy pressure from my client to try it anyway. But let me suggest a trade. I'll tell you my *quid pro quo.*"

Welch then reminded me about Fred Fisher, who, he said, had belonged to a Communist-front organization for a while. Welch acknowledged that he planned originally to have Fisher serve as his assistant at the hearing and had processed his name. He reminded me that this was known to us, and that if it became public over television and was brought to the attention of millions of viewers, it would have a twofold negative result. First, it would be given undue importance by many, and "we would all end up looking like Communist sympathizers." Second, the television magnification might be misunderstood by a number of the clients of Welch's Boston law firm.

The incident, in short, was something he would like left out. "If you will omit any reference to the Fisher case," he told me, "I will not return to the topic you want me to stay away from."

I replied that unless he heard from me to the contrary by the next morning, the arrangement was satisfactory and he could consider it an agreement. He replied that it was satisfactory so far as he was concerned, adding, "If any similar situations arise, let us meet privately and deal with them in this manner."

We shook hands and Joe Welch left the room. I waited in the gloom of the chamber for about ten minutes, then left.

That evening, I went to Senator McCarthy's home and gave him a full account of my conversation with Welch and the agreement into which I had entered. *McCarthy approved the trade.*

Why, after all that, did Senator McCarthy bring up the Fisher case at the hearings?

The answer is starkly simple: he lost his temper and blurted out the story.

Recall that Lawyer Welch, by turns sarcastic, sneering, coaxing, taunting, had been insisting day after day that we rush to find Communists "before the sun goes down." Recall that he had been taunting me "as a patriotic American citizen" to turn over names "tonight." Recall that he had demanded to know why we didn't tell the Secretary of the Army to "sic 'em, Stevens" on the Communists.

The jibes did not get too deeply under my skin, but Senator McCarthy could not stand them. When he started to speak, I was horrified. *Time* magazine reported later: "Roy Cohn grimaced toward McCarthy, shook his head and his lips seemed to form the words 'No! No!' " Swiftly I scribbled out a note and sent it over to him by page: It read: "This is the subject which I have committed to Welch we would not go into. Please respect our agreement as an agreement because this is not going to do any good." Television and motion picture films of the event clearly show the note being written, delivered, and read. The Senator, in fact, paused during his speech to say: "I know Mr. Cohn would rather not have me go into this." Welch himself, incidentally, obliquely but publicly acknowledged the agreement when he told the hearing the day before, "Mr. Cohn has my assurance that one large item of his cross-examination is going to be dropped, and, Mr. Cohn, I now make good on that arrangement with you." In my reply, I stated, "You and I have talked from time to time after the session about the elimination of various matters . . ."

I realized at once that the Senator had played squarely into Joe Welch's hands. Dramatically, the Army's counsel, who had been unable to score even the smallest points in nearly eight days, closed his cross-examination of me with a final emotional line: Speaking directly to McCarthy, he said: "You have brought it [the Fisher incident] out. If there is a God in heaven, it will do neither you nor your cause any good. I will not discuss it further. I will not ask Mr. Cohn any more questions."

The blow was terribly damaging to Senator McCarthy. He was pictured before the nation as a cruel man who deliberately sought to wreck a fine young lawyer's life. Many critics, in high glee, seized upon the incident to discuss, in clinical detail, the Senator's alleged heartlessness toward all who stood in his path.

It was pure nonsense, of course, and I suspect Joe Welch knew it. At worst, the disclosure might have been temporarily embarrassing to Fisher and to his conservative law firm, but it was not reasonable to assume that the young attorney would bear a lifelong "scar" as a result. After all, the whole story had run in *The New York Times* two months previously. If Welch seriously believed Fisher would suffer grievously, why did he deliberately use the incident to create a major emotional explosion?

Joe Welch, with his superb instinct for drama, knowing a good thing when it came his way, played the scene for all it was worth. Later, when the hearing adjourned for the day, he wept in the marble corridor outside the Senate Caucus Room and the moment was duly captured by a dozen press photographers. Next morning, large pictures of the weeping Mr. Welch, a handkerchief lifted to his streaming eyes, appeared in newspapers across the country.

It was a masterful final touch. That it was an act from start to finish does not, of course, detract from its brilliance as a maneuver to reverse a losing momentum. Welch's stunt scored well for his client, but nobody should be fooled into thinking that it was anything else.

I had a good feeling about my role. Public reaction was astonishing: my mail grew from ten to fifteen letters daily to between two and three thousand. Sacks of mail jammed our staff headquarters. I was only able to dip into a few each day, but my associates read enough to know that the vast majority were in my favor. The first day they began to arrive I turned to one of the girls and said, "I want every one of these to get a personal reply. I'll start dictating tomorrow . . ." Then I paused because she was giving me a funny look. "Not possible," she said. But we answered as many as we could.

The letters were amusing, touching, encouraging, enlightening, odd. One woman said candidly she had been a strong anti-Semite until she heard my testimony about my work and the fight against Communism. Now she no longer believed that all Jews were Communists—which meant she was still anti-Semitic but maybe not so much so. Another woman wrote that she had not spoken to her son for years, ever since he had married a Jewish girl. After hearing my testimony, she said, she was welcoming the girl into her home! I received many invitations to lecture, some business offers, and even a number of marriage proposals.

At the Washington Airport, en route to New York the first weekend after I began testifying, dozens of strangers came over to shake hands. My father's old friend Judge Samuel I. Rosenman, the New Deal braintruster, said to me, "The general opinion is that you are making by far the best witness in the entire hearings."

On the plane, I read in a copy of the Washington *Daily News,* a Scripps-Howard newspaper often hostile to our side, a column by the late Fred Othman:

> You either like Roy Cohn or you don't. You can't ignore him.
>
> He strikes me as being one of the most intelligent young men I have ever met and maybe that's one of the troubles. Some of those who hate the 27-year-old chief counsel of the McCarthy Investigating Committee, I'm afraid, are inclined to resent the fact that he's accomplished so much more than they have—and in so many fewer years.
>
> So there was Mr. Cohn as witness at the hearings into the Army-McCarthy fracas and impressive he was. He was without doubt the most coherent witness yet to be heard in these generally incoherent proceedings.
>
> He'd obviously done his homework. He knew the dates and the details. They all were in his head and he had to confer with nobody. He was properly modest when committee counsel Ray Jenkins asked him to list his accomplishments and polite he consistently was. The word "sir" got into almost every sentence he uttered. . . .
>
> Perhaps Mr. Cohn's main fault was—and is—the fact that life to him is serious always. He has trouble smiling at jokes involving himself and sometimes I fear he has difficulties smiling about anything.
>
> Take Mr. Jenkins' introductory examination. He wondered about Mr. Cohn's career in the Justice Department after he graduated from Columbia University. Mr. Cohn listed all the cases in which he's participated, including those of the spies Julius and Ethel Rosenberg.
>
> "What was the final result of that case?" inquired counsel Jenkins.

"Very final, sir," replied Mr. Cohn. "They were executed."

The whole room smiled at what seemed to be a gory witticism, but Mr. Cohn remained dead-pan. . . .

No doubt I have treasured my favorable notices. I dimly recollect that there were other commentators and columnists not champing at the bit to run me for President. Still, the hard work, the preparation that had gone into my testimony, had paid off. I had made a passable witness.

CHAPTER 16

AFTERMATH

$\mathbb{A}$ PERSISTENT BELIEF to emerge from the McCarthy era is that the Senator's decline and fall can be traced to the poor television image he projected in the hearings.

According to this theory, Americans at last came to know the "real McCarthy," who stood revealed in his true colors, mostly black. The editor of a Sauk City, Wisconsin, weekly asserted that McCarthy's soul began to show up in his face "and it wasn't a pretty soul." Rovere said the hearings "created an image of the destructive personality." Straight said they unmasked McCarthy's "fanaticism." Others reported the Senator displayed for all to see such qualities as "cold hate," "implacable cruelty," "utter nastiness," "animal viciousness," and so on. Former Senator Potter even offered the view that his "nervous giggle" helped do him in. All stated or implied that McCarthy slowly committed political hara-kiri before the television cameras.

How much truth is there in this? Let us examine the "image" McCarthy created and assess its impact upon his political career.

I must begin by agreeing that McCarthy did indeed make a poor impression. He came into American homes as humorless, demanding, dictatorial, and obstructive. That this was not his true personality is beside the point. Actually, he was warm, possessed of a good sense of humor, and forgiving almost beyond the bounds of reasonableness. But his onstage self is the one remembered.

"You can't fool the television camera," we've been told. Its relentless, probing eye will reveal the true individual no matter what. According to this view, the McCarthy everyone saw on the screen was the real man. I do not pretend any expertise on projection of personality via television but I feel the single illustration of President Lyndon Johnson may be enough to cast a reasonable doubt on the soundness of the argument. Mr. Johnson's television personality has been variously described as that of a gentle schoolmaster, a country parson, and, recently by Jack Paar, as an old folk-singer whose feet hurt. That the television Johnson is not the real Johnson is a fact nobody who has ever known him will deny. None of the man's dynamism and vigorous, restless energy comes over on the screen.

McCarthy's performance at the hearings was miserable. He complained bitterly of being interrupted ("I get awfully sick and tired of sitting down here at the end of the table and having whoever wants to interrupt in the middle of a sentence") and yet he came charging in on everyone else's testimony time and again with his "point of order, Mr. Chairman, point of order." He used the words so often they were taken up by countless comedians and had a vogue as a national catch-phrase. His language toward his opponents was often less than parliamentarian.

He was verbally brutal where he should have been dexterous and light; he was stubbornly unwilling to yield points where a little yielding might have gained him advantage; he frequently spoke before thinking of the effect of his words; he was repetitious to the point of boredom. As one friend observed after a session: "Joe was not only redundant this afternoon, he said the same thing twice."

With his easily erupting temper, his menacing monotone, his unsmiling mien, and his perpetual 5-o'clock shadow, he did seem the perfect stock villain. Central casting could not have come up with a better one.

All this raises important questions: Didn't his staff realize McCarthy was not producing a good impression before the nation? If so, why didn't they advise him to change? Why didn't McCarthy have an attorney sitting beside him to counsel him and act as a brake? And why did he interrupt so often with those points of order?

His staff was aware that McCarthy was not going over well, but at the time, it was not our main concern—although hindsight tells me it should have been. Countless details inundated us. Every evening had to be spent in careful preparation for the following session. We had little time for postmortem discussions of demeanor and even less to watch and study the kinescopes of the hearings broadcast at night.

After my own experience on the stand, I became fully aware of the importance of public impressions. But I felt it would have been presumptuous on the part of a man so much younger to offer his senior unasked-for instruction on deportment. How do you tell a United States Senator he looks and sounds unpleasant? All of us tried from time to time to ease the tensions we felt were largely responsible for his behavior. "Act as though you're enjoying it," Jim Juliana told him once. The television audience often saw Frank Carr, Juliana, or me in earnest whispered conversation with the Senator. When we weren't talking about the testimony, we were pleading with him to "take it easy."

As for representation by counsel, it may now be told that McCarthy did have unofficial legal advice from Edward Bennett Williams.

Mr. Williams in his book, *One Man's Freedom,* states that he refused the Senator's invitation to act as his attorney because "he wanted me for a role no trial lawyer would accept. He was to conduct the cross-examination and retain ultimate control over the manner of presentation of his side of the case. I was to be present solely in an advisory capacity."

It is true that McCarthy had asked Williams to serve, but the invitation was not pressed, principally because of Jean's strong views. Mrs. McCarthy felt that when a man is fighting for his political life he should have someone alongside in sympathy and accord with his crusade. McCarthy heeded Jean's advice to the extent of not engaging Williams as full-time counsel. Nevertheless, he respected Williams' ability and during the hearings they had several evening sessions at the Senator's home.

Some misconceptions about the "point of order" phrase that has become identified with McCarthy should be set straight. Most persons think he invented this device to get the floor. I was amazed to read that former Senator Potter, in describing the sessions to President Eisenhower, said about McCarthy: "He has what he calls point of order, Mr. President. He brings up a point of order and then he makes a speech." Potter should have known that McCarthy neither created the gambit nor was he the only one to use it for the purpose of "making a speech." Actually, at the pre-hearing discussions to set the ground rules, the question arose on how a principal or his counsel could bring relevant matters to the chairman's attention when it was not his turn to speak. It was decided this could be done by raising a point of order.

The first session on April 22 was only minutes old when McCarthy broke into General Reber's testimony with: "Mr. Chairman, may I raise a point?" Senator Mundt thereupon provided McCarthy with his cue: "Do you have a point of order?" he asked. McCarthy quickly caught the suggestion. "As a point of order," he said, "I assume these hearings are going to continue for quite some time, and the thought occurred to me now as to whether or not we will allow hearsay evidence. . . ." One minute later, when the matter he raised was concluded, Senator McClellan broke in with a point of order, and thereafter practically every principal figure in the case used the device to get the attention of the chair, although none so often as McCarthy. Indeed, once McClellan called out: "A point of order, Mr. Chairman." When Mundt asked what he wanted, McClellan replied, "That is the way to get the floor." Senator Symington interrupted McCarthy on a point of order, and once when Mr. Welch wanted the floor, Mundt asked if he had a point of order. "I don't know what it is," Welch answered, "but it's a point of something." Whereupon he launched into the something he had in mind.

One may wonder how it was that Senator McCarthy, so quick to recognize my poor initial performance, could have failed to see the flaws in his own. Certainly he knew the hearings were less a search for the truth than a gigantic personality play. Frank Carr said it best: "You don't have to be wrong up there in the hearing room—you just have to be made to look like a jackass."

McCarthy knew this. Almost from the beginning, he perceived that public opinion would deliver the real verdict. During one luncheon recess he said to me: "People aren't going to remember the things we say on the issues here, our logic, our common sense, our facts. They're only going to remember the impressions." Years afterward, those who watched that spring and summer can now recall only the *impression* of the droll Mr. Welch, the *impression* of a terrible thing done to Mr. Fisher, the *impression* of bumbling Army brass, the *impression* of the rugged but honest mountaineer lawyer—and, unfortunately, the *impression* of an inquisitorial arm-twister furious at having his own arm twisted.

It seems paradoxical that a man of his experience in controversy lacked the critical insight to evaluate his own performance. Yet how human it is! In a recent Broadway farce, a child psychiatrist finds himself unable to control his own rampaging teen-age daughter. Presumably an expert in the principles of handling the young, he is helpless before her wild entanglements. Emotional involvement weakens our perceptions and warps our judgment. We see clearly the mistakes our friends make but develop blind spots that make us unaware of our own behavior in similar circumstances.

So it was with Joe McCarthy in those thirty-six crucial days of his life.

Bad as was his performance, how damaging was it to his political career? Did it "kill him off," as people have told me time and again, and as many now believe?

Undoubtedly the hearings were a setback. But there were other perhaps more fundamental reasons for his decline. By the time the hearings ended, McCarthy had been the center of the national and world spotlight for three and a half years. He had an urgent universal message, and people, whether they idolized or hated him, listened. Almost everything he said or did was chronicled.

Human nature being what it is, any outstanding actor on the stage of public affairs—and especially a holder of high office—cannot remain indefinitely at the center of controversy. The public must eventually lose interest in him and his cause. And Joe McCarthy had nothing to offer but more of the same. The public sought new thrills. The extent to which the problem of subversive influences had faded may be gauged by the fact that Nixon, whose political fortune was made by the issue, did not even mention it in his 1960 campaign for the Presidency. This is not to deny that espionage and subversion were not going on: they were; they still are. But the public could no longer be stirred. It wasn't so much that the phenomenon had disappeared, as that the point had been made. The surprise, the drama, were gone.

Let it be clear that in spite of all this, McCarthy, after the hearings and to his death, had the support of millions who understood the seriousness of the Communist issue. These millions were not discouraged by his lack of TV personality, but continued in their belief in him and his dedication to that cause. Those who were adversely affected were the fence-sitters. The actual swing as a result of the hearings was not great. The pro stayed pro, the anti, anti. And they do to this day.

If McCarthy declined because he had had his time in the sun, the cause of his falling so precipitately is another matter—to be discussed in the chapter "The Final Years." Popular myth-making will probably for years to come insist that he was eclipsed because his "villainy" shone in his face for all America to see on television screens. Why our folklore makes heroes of some and blackguards of others is a subject for social psychologists or pathologists—related, I suspect, to our need to idolize and to release hostility. It is as easy to hobgoblinize Joe McCarthy as to beatify John Kennedy. That the former was no more a devil than the latter was a saint doesn't seem to matter—a basic human need is satisfied.

Our love for oversimplification, for pigeonholing, enshrined Harry Truman as a "scrappy little guy" who knew doggone well what he wanted and wasted no time in getting it. Actually a case could be made to show that he was not really all that decisive. To many, Dwight Eisenhower was a benign figure who, like Father, could do no wrong. Others judged him a fumbling mediocrity. Both views are extremes.

The fact that the greater part of the press was opposed to McCarthy—some of it violently—may be largely responsible for furthering the myth. As Rovere calls the roll: *"The New York Times,* the New York *Herald-Tribune,* the Washington *Post,* the Cowles newspapers, the Knight newspapers, the Luce publications—all were anti-McCarthy." He lists the influential journalists with a national readership who were solidly arrayed against McCarthy: Walter Lippmann, the Alsops, Doris Fleeson, Marquis Childs, Drew Pearson, Thomas L. Stokes. And the radio-television broadcasters: Edward R. Murrow, Elmer Davis, Quincy Howe, Martin Agronsky, Edward P. Morgan. So many willing and able hands can easily create a myth.

An important myth-making factor was the ninety-seven-minute "documentary" film, "Point of Order," put together from TV kinescopes of the hearings and nationally distributed in recent years. I sat through this motion picture twice and was amazed. Virtually every incident favorable to our side was cropped, nearly every unfavorable one was included. None of the important points we scored, and they were many, was there. McCarthy came through as the heavy villain, and I as his apprentice in the black arts—seeking to destroy everything from mere reputations to the armed forces of the nation. It was, I regret to say, a cropped movie.

There was, of course, a "verdict," but it need not detain us long. It was entirely predictable. I would wish I could be as certain of verdicts in my legal cases as I was of the decision that came down that August 31.

It was strictly a party-line ruling: The Republican majority cleared McCarthy of charges that he brought "improper influence" to bear on Schine's behalf, while the Democratic minority attributed "inexcusable actions" to both the Senator and me.

While the Republicans found that the charge of improper influence had not been established as a deliberate and personal act of Senator McCarthy's, they stated that he should have displayed "more vigorous discipline in stopping any member of his staff" from attempting to make such a move. They found that I was "unduly persistent and aggressive" on Schine's behalf and that Stevens and Adams did try to "terminate or influence" the Fort Monmouth hearings.

The three Democrats concluded that McCarthy had "fully acquiesced in and condoned" the "improper actions" of Roy Cohn. Thus: "For these inexcusable actions, Senator McCarthy and Mr. Cohn merit severe criticism on the ground that they had sought preferential treatment for Private Schine." The Democrats also stated that Stevens "demonstrated an inexcusable indecisiveness," and that both he and Adams merit "severe criticism" for "appeasement."

Ex-Senator Potter, in a separate "plague on both your houses" statement, said he believed the chief charges made by both sides were "borne out." On the day the hearings closed, Potter issued a statement that he believed there "may have been subornation of perjury." He said, "I believe a criminal case against some of the principals might be developed if the case were taken to a grand jury room where the testimony would have to be repeated without others being present" (whatever that means). The statement was ill-conceived and unwarranted and nobody paid much attention to it—nobody paid much attention to anything this one-term senator did or said, least of all the Attorney General, who never brought charges of perjury against anybody connected with the hearings.

Potter's propensity for self-contradiction is almost comic. Recently there emerged under his imprimatur a book in which McCarthy is excoriated. And of course Potter was shocked at all the terrible features of McCarthy and McCarthyism as he sat on the subcommittee with McCarthy. So how come he subsequently delivered a eulogy of McCarthy, hailing him and his great contributions to America?

And in the original preface to his recent book, he gave credit for assistance in preparing it to Stanley Faulkner, a gentleman who happened also to have been the lawyer for none other than Major Irving (who promoted?) Peress; and Harvey Matusow, when Matusow was on trial for perjury resulting from his efforts to upset the convictions of the second-string leaders of the Communist party of the United States. The credit to Faulkner on the book mysteriously vanished from the preface before the book went to press. I kept trying to debate publicly with Potter, but he declined consistently. Finally, John Madigan, the host of Chicago's popular CBS television show "At Random," arranged for my surprise appearance on a program with Potter, and I was able to bring out the Faulkner story.

What did the hearings prove?

Here are my notes just as I dictated them at the time:

The only redeeming feature to this disgusting spectacle, to me, was the fact that it showed the American people how petty and conniving Washington politics could be and also showed them, and probably more importantly so, a good many facts about Communism infiltration in the United States and the lengths to which people would go to destroy politically and otherwise anyone who was associated with the cause of anti-Communism. Further, it got across to the millions of Americans the sincerity and I believe the correctness of our position and the fact that we were dealing with the greatest menace known to mankind and that what we were dealing with was infinitely more important than good treatment for a private in the United States Army and that this whole thing was part of a "discredit McCarthy" movement coming from high places.

It demonstrated another very important thing to me. It demonstrated the greatness of America and the American public because here I found a situation where both political parties, everybody in effect, with minor exceptions, had ganged up to destroy me, not because I was important but because of the team to which I belonged and the work we were doing. As somebody put it in the course of the hearings, all we had against us was "the White House, the Administration, the Democratic party, and the Republican party."

But perhaps this answer isn't really responsive to the question, so let us try again.

What did the hearings really prove?

They "alerted the country as never before to the dangers of Communism."

These are not my words nor Senator McCarthy's, though we believed them fully. This was the judgment of Ray Jenkins, the impartial counsel to the committee, one year later, after he had returned to the practice of law in Knoxville and all the fuss and fury had died down.

Some poet, or maybe I should say "doggerelist," summed up the comic aspects of McCarthy vs. the Army in these ten deathless stanzas widely circulated around the Pentagon during the hearings. Understandably, he signed his work only "Anon. Around the Pentagon."

SMALL ODE FROM A FELLOW WHO WOULD LIKE TO READ
ABOUT SOMETHING BESIDES MC CARTHY

McCarthy came down to Camp Kilmer, and to the Army's
    distress
He uncovered a pink-tinted dentist, by the name of Irving Peress.
That was the start of the struggle, that was the start of the strife
And look at the uproar resulting; O take to the hills for your life!

TIME Magazine's having hysterics, the Alsops are chewing their
    nails,
And Pearson and Drummond and Murrow, like puppies are
    chasing their tails.
For Joseph spoke rough to the Army—he wounded a famous
    brass hat.
And blood may be thicker than Zwicker, but Zwicker proved
    thicker than that.

The Pundits gave vent to this chorus: "The Republic may totter
    and fall,
Our Allies soon will depart us, and Joe is the cause of it all.
So haste to the Pentagon, brothers, and send a detachment to Ike;
Summon a Cabinet session, get Nixon in front of a mike!

"Let everyone stir up this ruckus, let all of us get in the act
Let's blow up the battle with rumor, and never obscure it with
fact.
It's time to kill off McCarthy, it's time to turn out his light
It's time to say to the White House, "Now Ike, let's you and him
fight."

"And how can this best be accomplished? How can the nation be
shown?
How can we cripple McCarthy? Why, hit at McCarthy through
Cohn!
Like Caesar and Pompey and Crassus, we'll topple them all in
the line,
For Joseph speaks only to Roy, and Roy speaks only to Schine!"

Thus did the Pentagon counter, and thus the plot thickened and
grew.
From Stevens to Flanders to Dirksen, remarkable epithets flew.
The Army would tackle young Roy, their records would soon lay
him low;
But who would bell McCarthy—who would investigate Joe?

An opponent was found from Dakota, and soon we get on with
the hunt!
Joe will interrogate Roy, but Joe will then get it from Mundt.
Stevens will look after Zwicker, and Adams will probe into
Schine
Wilson will speak for the White House: No witness here will
decline!

Oh, call up the shade of great Vergil, bring poets in from afar:
Let Joseph be girded for battle, like Ivan Skavinsky Skavar.
Trace down the cause of the struggle, sing out without favor or
fear:
Joe stepped on the toe of the Army, the Abdul Abulbul Amir.

Well, on with the terrible combat, let them wrangle it out for this
bone.
The Army can have handsome David, the wolves can have Mr.
Cohn.
But spare us sweet Joseph McCarthy—and reader, if you must
know why:
Without a Joe to belabor, the press would curl up and die.

Think of the frustrated Pearson, with no McCarthy to damn;
Think of a starving Ed Murrow, deprived of this eminent ham.
Oh, a world with McCarthy is trying, but to come to the end of
    this verse
He keeps our adrenalin pumping—and a world without Joe
    would be worse! ! ! ! ! !

After the hearings, I went down to Keesler Air Force Base in
Biloxi, Mississippi, for two weeks' summer training with the National
Guard, in which I was a first lieutenant.

Sitting in a jammed hearing room during the day and poring over
papers until far into every night is not the best way to prepare for
Army training; nevertheless, despite sore muscles, I enjoyed my
Keesler experience. But even down there, I was unable to escape
my recent past.

One day, I heard that Major General Lewis B. Hershey, the very
able director of Selective Service, was visiting the area. Someone,
either from Army public relations or a local newspaper, told the
General I was on the base and asked him if he would pose for a
picture with me. General Hershey, I was told, recoiled as though
stung by a wasp. Secretary Stevens, he said, had done just that thing
with another young member of our Armed Forces, and he wasn't
about to fall into the same trap!

Then there was the weekend when some Army buddies (Colonel
Jesse Reese and Lieutenant Colonel Lewis Weinberg of South Carolina) and I inadvertently dispossessed General Matthew B. Ridgway,
the Army Chief of Staff, of his suite at the Roosevelt Hotel in New
Orleans. I had telephoned the hotel for a reservation but was told
there wasn't a room in the place. I got through to Seymour Weiss, the
owner of the hotel, whom I knew and who has a soft spot for any
Communist fighter, and asked if he had some "house" rooms available such as are generally set aside by the management. Weiss told us
to come on over at once—he had a fine suite for us.

Next morning I was dismayed to learn what had happened. Weiss
had assigned us to the suite reserved for General Ridgway and placed
the general in less desirable quarters! The last thing I wanted at the
time was another run-in with high military officials. And now I, a
lieutenant, had innocently displaced none other than the Chief of

Staff. I met the General a number of times in the lobby and once we sat at adjoining tables in a restaurant, but between us the silence was thick.

On my return from Biloxi, I had several meetings with Senator McCarthy to discuss future plans. The newspapers were predicting my ouster as counsel to the subcommittee. And not without reason. It became increasingly evident that this was much in the minds of the three Democratic senators who, with Senator Potter, could "crossfire" me out. But in official Washington few people are fired directly. It's done by strategy. The plan, in my case, was to introduce a resolution that all members of the subcommittee staff must be resubmitted and reapproved by the committee. Those who did not receive approval would be dropped. Since this was clearly a violation of the long-standing rule that the chairman select the subcommittee staff, I knew it was aimed at me.

Senator Potter made the motion at an executive session. "Why don't you just kick me out?" I asked. "Why go about it in this devious way? Just make a motion to fire me, take a vote on it, and that will be that." Potter characteristically denied he was aiming his resolution at me.

In New York, I talked with my family and friends. I explained that Senator McCarthy wanted me to stay, and that, anticipating a 4-to-3 vote against me, he would offer me a post as his administrative assistant or arrange a job with another committee.

I wanted to remain in Washington. There was much unfinished business and many challenges still to meet. I was also moved by a very human apprehension of the future. In other words, I felt like anybody else who is about to lose his job.

My family felt that I ought to leave Washington, arguing that I had done well, that my reputation was intact, that by and large the public was sympathetic. And so, after days of soul-searching, I made up my mind that I would not take another post on Capitol Hill.

With my going decided, the only question remaining was on the manner of my exit. The comic relief came from a suggestion of my father. He said, "Why don't you just quietly resign?" The chances of my being permitted to do anything quietly range from slim to none. Should I resign or let them vote me out? I made a decision—a bad one. I decided to quit, on the theory that if one makes the *beau geste*—"You can't fire me, I quit!"—one thereby avoids the stigma of being ignominiously bounced. Ordinarily, it's a good theory, but in this case it demonstrated a lack of courage to face the inevitable ordeal. I have regretted it ever since.

Resign I did. In my letter to the committee I said:

> I feel that my helpfulness to the subcommittee has been brought to the vanishing point. In any future investigation in which I appeared as chief counsel, all the slanders voiced against me would be repeated to minimize the evidence presented.
>
> It has been a bitter lesson to come to Washington and see a reputation, gained at some effort, torn to shreds merely because I was associated with Senator McCarthy, who has become the symbol of hatred for all who fear the exposure of Communism.
>
> My father and mother have been almost heartbroken and have been urging me to quit for months. My closest friends tell me that it would be foolish to stay on. Yet I would have continued to fight on against odds if it had not become apparent that I was to become a political sacrifice.

McCarthy, Mundt, and Dirksen issued statements praising my services; the other four senators remained silent. And that, after nineteen of the most incredible months I would ever live through, was that.

CHAPTER 17

CENSURE

O N AUGUST 31, 1954, the same day the subcommittee handed down its verdict in the Army controversy, a special committee opened hearings on a resolution to censure McCarthy for allegedly unethical behavior toward the United States Senate.*

Doubtless the senators had not planned their inquiries to dovetail quite so precisely, but the somewhat startling continuity of investigative action was not lost on the junior senator from Wisconsin, who was now facing his fifth set of probers in four years. He expressed himself bitterly to me: "It's a kind of political relay race. They're not letting the baton drop. One group gets finished and hands the job over to the next one."

The hearings were conducted by Senator Arthur V. Watkins, a sixty-six-year-old austere Mormon from Utah who said at the outset he would tolerate no nonsense, and didn't. An authority on senatorial practices has said that Watkins was the "perfect type figure of one of the Senate's moods, its mood of judgment." He was also a dedicated Republican "regular," devoted to Eisenhower and his Administration.

It has been said that the censure hearings were open but not televised at the specific insistence of Senator Watkins and his committee. (Watkins told newsmen: "Let us get off the front pages and back among the obituaries. That would suit us fine.") Actually, had Senator McCarthy insisted, he could have had these hearings broadcast and telecast, but he was persuaded by his counsel, Edward Bennett Williams, to agree to the exclusion of the cameras and microphones.

* The text of the resolution appears at the end of this chapter.

During the censure hearings I detected for the first time that the mental and emotional pressures of the past several years were beginning to have a measurable effect on Senator McCarthy. In the months I had known him, he had been resilient under attack, buoyant, willing to fight back, at times overly belligerent and eager, and never unconfident. Now, however, with another inquiry before him, his spirit was being eroded.

This became clear to me during a number of conversations I had with him following my resignation. I spoke with him over a static-filled long-distance wire from a post-exchange phone booth at Keesler Field in Biloxi, Mississippi, and later saw him from time to time in Washington and New York. I found him an unhappy man, tense, preoccupied, and most pronounced of all, filled with a sense of futility. His conversation returned constantly to his growing feeling of frustration.

"What can I do?" he said once in his Washington home. "I'm putting in damn near every minute defending myself. I go from one of these nuisances to the next, with absolutely no time to do what we *should* be doing. I fight these things in my sleep. Hell, Roy, what's the use? Should I quit? Be a good little Administration senator? Keep my big mouth shut? Vote the way the White House wants? Stop embarrassing Ike and the gang? And pick up my little rewards—a post office here, a few roads there, and invitations to White House shindigs?

"Damn it! Instead of a senator I feel like a delinquent hounded for a new crime every year."

These are the historical, recorded facts about the censure of Joe McCarthy:

On July 30, Senate Resolution 301 was introduced by the Vermont Republican, Ralph E. Flanders, charging McCarthy with "personal contempt" of the Senate and "habitual contempt of people." It concluded: "Resolved, that the conduct of the senator from Wisconsin, Mr. McCarthy, is unbecoming a member of the United States Senate, is contrary to senatorial traditions, and tends to bring the Senate into disrepute, and such conduct is hereby condemned."

Three days later, the Senate referred the resolution to a special select committee consisting of members of both parties. On August 5, Vice-President Nixon announced the appointment of six senators to this Select Committee to Study Censure Charges: Republicans: Arthur V. Watkins, Utah; Frank Carlson, Kansas; Francis Case, South Dakota. Democrats: Edwin C. Johnson, Colorado; John C. Stennis, Mississippi; Samuel J. Ervin, Jr., North Carolina. Watkins was made chairman.

On August 9, Senator Watkins said he would conduct the forthcoming hearings strictly as in a court of law, adhering to legal rules of evidence and allowing only testimony that was material, relevant, and competent. One week before the hearings opened, he issued these five categories of charges, embodying forty-six separate specifications of alleged wrongdoing:

1. Incidents of contempt of the Senate or a senatorial committee.
2. Incidents of encouragement of United States employees to violate the law and their oaths of office or executive orders.
3. Incidents involving receipt or use of confidential or classified documents or other confidential information from executive files.
4. Incidents involving abuses of colleagues in the Senate.
5. Incidents relating to Ralph Zwicker, a general officer of the Army of the United States.

After the hearings, during which the entire story was recounted once again in minutest detail, the committee issued a 40,000-word report recommending censure in two of the five categories, holding 1) that the Senator's conduct toward the Senate Subcommittee on Privileges and Elections during the 82nd Congress was "contemptuous, contumacious, and denunciatory, without reason or justification, and was obstructive to the legislative processes," and 2) that McCarthy's conduct toward General Zwicker during the hearings on the promotion and honorable discharge of Major Peress was "reprehensible." On the other charges, McCarthy was criticized, but the committee withheld a recommendation of censure.

On November 8, the day after the elections, the Senate met to consider the censure resolution. It was debated for nine days. A ten-day halt was called while Senator McCarthy was treated for bursitis in his right elbow. Four more days of debate, starting November 29, followed. Then, on December 2, the Senate "condemned" the conduct of Senator McCarthy on the first count. The Zwicker count was replaced by a new one, abuse of the Watkins Committee. He thereby became the fourth United States senator to be censured by his colleagues in the history of the upper house. The word "censure" does not appear in the resolution; it was pointed out that the historical term employed in censure resolutions is "condemned."

How just were the hearings and how fair the verdict?

I want not to overstate the case. I have pointed out in preceding parts of this book that Joe McCarthy was not without sin in the four and a half years that preceded his censure trial. His statements were frequently hasty and ill-prepared. He was addicted to dramatic techniques in presenting information that sometimes had troublesome by-products.

I have said all this once, and repeat it. Now, years later, a measured review of all aspects of the historic censure; a recollection of conversations I had with persons closely involved in the event, including the principal figure; a rereading of the voluminous testimony; an examination of the historical background and the laws pertaining to senatorial misbehavior and punishment—all this restudy leads me to these conclusions:

That the verdict was in before the jury heard the evidence, and was strictly political.

That the legality of the case is open to serious question.

That Senator McCarthy was tried, convicted, and punished for offenses that many other legislators had committed a number of times on and off the floor of Congress without being called to account.

Let us examine each.

First, the verdict of guilt had been decided before any testimony was taken.

To start, consider this statement from William S. White's informed analysis of the United States Senate, *Citadel.* Discussing the August 2 decision to name a select committee of inquiry to hold censure hearings and the identity of the "judges" who were picked to serve on it, Mr. White states: "What was not generally understood then was the important fact that on the day that the Senate made provision for this select committee it made all but inevitable the eventual condemnation of Senator McCarthy. . . ."

In other words the Senate club had made up its mind to punish McCarthy for transgressing the unwritten rules of behavior expected of members. Some things simply are not done in that exclusive organization, and McCarthy apparently had done them and had to be called to account. Donald R. Matthews, associate professor of political science at the University of North Carolina, in *U.S. Senators and Their World,* sums it up well: "There are unwritten rules of behavior, which we have called folkways, in the Senate. These rules are normative, that is, they define how a senator ought to behave. Nonconformity is met with moral condemnation, while senators who conform to the folkways are rewarded with high esteem by their colleagues." The conformity must be public, and the dirty work must be done behind the scenes.

McCarthy did not conform. He was not a hypocrite who acted one part publicly and wielded his brass knuckles in the cloakroom. He was the maverick, the unpolished one who did not speak softly, who upset hallowed traditions. Senator William E. Jenner, the quick-witted Indiana Republican, phrased it best: "Joe," he once told McCarthy, "you're the kid who came to the party and pee'd in the lemonade."

However, it would be wrong to assume that the censure can be explained entirely in terms of anger at the contamination of the senatorial beverage.

Senator McCarthy in his bitterness called it a "lynch party." He meant that the move was politically inspired, politically led, and politically executed. Nothing that has happened since has altered my conviction that he was essentially right.

Members of the United States Senate are convivial persons off the floor, much like opposing attorneys who are foes in the courtroom and friends in private. Thus it was that an eminent senator, an Eisenhower Republican, told me at a Washington party one night: "We can't strike out this time. Unless we get rid of your boy, he's going to be a mighty big thorn in our side."

His meaning was clear. The Army-McCarthy hearings, as previous chapters have cited, were a move to eliminate the rambunctious senator. When that dreary, repetitive, quarrelsome, and ludicrous exercise proved little more than that McCarthy was not a very good television performer, the movement to censure him got under way.

No matter who thought up the idea, it was born and carried out as a means of dealing with the "McCarthy problem." As Sokolsky wrote: "This was a political maneuver to eliminate McCarthy's importance . . . to make his name abhorrent and to frighten off any senator, journalist, or radio commentator who chose to support him or his cause."

What was the urgency? Why, exactly, was the Senator considered such a menace to the Eisenhower Republicans as well as to the Democrats? There are a number of reasons:

1. McCarthy had charged the Democratic Party with "twenty years of treason," an unfair generalization that infuriated the forty-seven Democratic senators.

2. A year after Dwight Eisenhower entered the White House, McCarthy was accusing his own party of "appeasement, retreat, and surrender" in the ideological conflict with Communism. Adding one Republican year, he maintained that America had now been subjected to "twenty-one years of treason."

3. President Eisenhower, devoted to the armed services, was personally furious with McCarthy for attacking his close friend General Marshall, for investigating the Army, and for "browbeating and humiliating" army officers.

4. If the Republicans should win control of the Senate in 1954, then under the unalterable seniority rules McCarthy would once more be chairman of the Committee on Government Operations, commanding a large budget and staff with unlimited powers of investigation. Understandably, they dreaded the prospect of more McCarthy "probes."

5. McCarthy had terrorized the Eisenhower contingent. The extent to which this was true was vividly and amusingly described by Rovere: "In 1953, the very thought of Joe McCarthy could shiver the White House timbers and send panic through the whole Executive branch." Once Rovere interviewed an Eisenhower assistant on an unrelated subject. When McCarthy's name was uttered, something startling happened. "At the mention of McCarthy, his [the presidential assistant's] whole manner and expression changed; though he did not move from his chair or put his palms together, he assumed, figuratively, and on his face quite literally, a supplicating mien. I have no record of the exact words he used, but I have a painfully vivid memory of them. 'Don't ask me,' he said. 'For God's sake, please

don't ask me to discuss this. Not now. I'll help you as much as I possibly can, I'll talk about anything else you want. Anything. Just don't press me on this. Don't even ask me why I don't want to talk about it. Maybe someday we can talk it all over, but not now. Accept my word that my reasons are good.' I have not before or since seen a grown man in a responsible position behave in such a fashion. I had the feeling that if I had made an issue of it, I might have persuaded him to see what he could do—in exchange for my promise not again to say 'McCarthy' in his presence—to get me an ambassadorship or even to declassify the recipe for the hydrogen bomb. The mere mention of the senator from Wisconsin, the mere possibility of being compelled to discuss him, had reduced this sturdy man to jelly." One does not have to belabor the point: an Administration that so reacts to a senator has a special interest in removing that senator.

6. Our leaders had made inexcusable mistakes in—

(a) misunderstanding the scope and peril of international Communism, and making one diplomatic blunder after another.

(b) permitting infiltration of Communists high up in the Establishment despite warnings, as in the cases of Hiss, Harry Dexter White, et al.

(c) attempting to cover up past misjudgments and thus compounding them.

(d) personal involvement in the above three points by so many in Government, so that they had a vested interest in concealment and a basic antagonism toward the "cop" on the beat who had discovered them.

7. Because, though McCarthy's national popularity had slipped between January and May of 1954, he was still considered a formidable force on the political scene. Recall that 35 percent of the country, as reported in the May, 1954, Gallup Poll, backed him. In January that year, 50 percent of the population had expressed itself as pro-McCarthy.

The Eisenhower Republicans knew well that, granting the decline, McCarthy still commanded a large, vigorous, and highly vocal public, and the backing of important men in elective office. The political powers behind the President were aware of the havoc that McCarthy could create if he broke away from the party in 1956. The Eisenhower people had only to look back to 1912, to the disaffection of the Progressive section of the party, and the disaster that followed. Theodore Roosevelt built the Bull Moose party, and ran against his fellow Republican, William Howard Taft—and the White House was lost to the Democrats for the next eight years.

Could this have happened in 1954, with Joseph McCarthy heading the dissident branch of the party? After the censure, William S. White reported in *The New York Times* concerning "a current spate of speculation about the possibility in 1956 of some sort of a far Right Wing third party, possibly headed by Senator McCarthy."

For these reasons, it had become necessary to purge Senator McCarthy, and this the Senate proceeded to do in a vote that went strictly along political lines. Note:

Every Democrat in the Senate but one voted for the censure resolution. The lone exception was John F. Kennedy, ill in a hospital at the time.

The Eisenhower Republicans voted for censure.

With a very few exceptions, the conservative Republicans voted against condemning McCarthy.

The final vote was: *For condemnation:* Republicans, 22; Democrats, 44; Independents, 1. *Against condemnation:* Republicans, 22. Total: 67 to 22.

HOW THE SENATE VOTED ON CENSURING MC CARTHY

CENSURE

Republicans—22

Abel (Neb.)	Flanders (Vt.)
Aiken (Vt.)	Hendrickson (N.J.)
Beall (Md.)	Ives (N.Y.)
Bennett (Utah)	Payne (Me.)
Bush (Conn.)	Potter (Mich.)
Carlson (Kans.)	Saltonstall (Mass.)
Case (S. Dak.)	Smith (Me.)
Cooper (Ky.)	Smith (N.J.)
Cotton (N.H.)	Thye (Minn.)
Duff (Pa.)	Watkins (Utah)
Ferguson (Mich.)	Williams (Del.)

Democrats—44

Anderson (N. Mex.)
Burke (Ohio)
Byrd (Va.)
Chavez (N. Mex.)
Clements (Ky.)
Daniel (S.C.)
Daniel (Texas)
Douglas (Ill.)
Eastland (Miss.)
Ellender (La.)
Ervin (N.C.)
Frear (Del.)
Fulbright (Ark.)
George (Ga.)
Gillette (Iowa)
Green (R.I.)
Hayden (Ariz.)
Hennings (Mo.)
Hill (Ala.)
Holland (Fla.)
Humphrey (Minn.)
Jackson (Wash.)

Johnson (Colo.)
Johnson (Texas)
Johnston (S.C.)
Kefauver (Tenn.)
Kerr (Okla.)
Kilgore (W. Va.)
Lehman (N.Y.)
Long (La.)
Magnuson (Wash.)
Mansfield (Mont.)
McClellan (Ark.)
Monroney (Okla.)
Murray (Mont.)
Neely (W. Va.)
O'Mahoney (Wyo.)
Pastore (R.I.)
Robertson (Va.)
Russell (Ga.)
Scott (N.C.)
Sparkman (Ala.)
Stennis (Miss.)
Symington (Mo.)

Independents—1
Morse (Ore.)

AGAINST CENSURE

Republicans—22

Barrett (Wyo.)
Bridges (N.H.)
Brown (Nev.)
Butler (Md.)
Cordon (Ore.)
Dirksen (Ill.)
Dworshak (Idaho)
Goldwater (Ariz.)
Hickenlooper (Iowa)
Hruska (Neb.)
Jenner (Ind.)

Knowland (Calif.)
Kuchel (Calif.)
Langer (N. Dak.)
Malone (Nev.)
Martin (Pa.)
Millikin (Colo.)
Mundt (S. Dak.)
Purtell (Conn.)
Schoeppel (Kans.)
Welker (Idaho)
Young (N.Dak.)

Voting Present: McCarthy (R., Wis.). Not voting but announced as paired: Gore (D., Tenn.) for, and Bricker (R., Ohio) against; Smathers (D., Fla.) for, and Capehart (R., Ind.) against. Not present and not announced: Wiley (R., Wis.) and Kennedy (D., Mass.).

Can anyone seriously contend after studying the lists that the senators were voting on a matter of principle, that they had earnestly studied the evidence and arrived at a just and fair verdict based on the truth or falsity of the charges? It was a political vote all the way, and matters of principle don't follow political lines.

The subject of the personal ethics of the men who practice politics is too vast except for sketchy mention here. My own experience leads me to conclude that the game cannot be played successfully except under its own special moral rules, which are entirely different from those in most other areas of men's work.

When the larger good of the party is involved, the rules permit a legislator to vote against his own beliefs. The penalty for those who do not go along is loss of party support, patronage, and almost everything else vital to their political careers. The rules permit deals, special arrangements, *quid pro quo*'s. A politician, for example, must raise money to get elected. To raise money, many politicians must often perform or promise favors. A politician incurs obligations that must be discharged. His objectivity, his freedom to think things out and act as his conscience and intelligence dictate, is thus circumscribed.

One new congressman, speaking at a panel discussion that sought to learn how members of the House feel about their jobs, said, "I came here thinking this was for real, that this was the only parliament where democratic processes were at work. That is a myth, I find. . . . If anybody thinks he is going to come down here to legislate he is crazy. When I first arrived and looked about the Capitol, the White House, and the Washington Monument, I had a lump in my throat and I felt pretty humble about being part of this great scene. But now all I see is skulduggery and shenanigans."*

It is not always skulduggery and shenanigans, of course. As another congressman stated, "Despite my criticism, by and large, it's amazing how good the system is." Certainly, men of honor and

* Charles L. Clapp, *The Congressman, His Work As He Sees It*. The Brookings Institution, 1964, pp. 22–23.

integrity have been in Washington and will continue to come to help make the laws of our land. But even they will have to operate under the rules of the game.

It was these rules that McCarthy broke. It was these rules that called for the censure of McCarthy. And censured he was.

Second, the legality of the censure proceedings is open to serious question.

At the very outset, Senator Watkins made it clear that the censure hearings would be conducted as "in a court of law." Courtroom rules of evidence would apply; only "material, relevant, and competent" testimony would be allowed. Moreover, Watkins emphasized that the inquiry "is of a special character which differentiates it from the usual legislative inquiry. It involves the internal affairs of the Senate itself in the exercise of a high constitutional function . . . It is by nature a judicial and semi-judicial function, and we shall attempt to conduct it as such."

The select committee, many have suggested, was sitting as a kind of ethics board in judgment upon one of its own, and therefore the rules of law did not apply. William White, for example, wrote in his study of the U.S. Senate: "They [the Senators] were not hearing an action at law; they were determining simply the degree that a member had transgressed the rules, written or not, and the spirit of the club to which he belonged."

But according to its own stated ground rules, as enunciated by its chairman, the select committee was sitting as a court of law, hearing a legal case, and was bound by the principles of law and justice as are all the courts of the land.

Then let us examine the proceedings as a "court of law."

The "judge" and "jury" were the members of the select committee. The chairman himself would probably have been disqualified in a court of law as having previously indicated bias and prejudice against the defendant, while the committee itself would probably have been challenged on the basis of its curious composition.

After Senator Watkins had been named to head the select committee, he received a message of "encouragement and support" from President Eisenhower. Sherman Adams himself has reported this interesting footnote. Then on December 4, following the censure vote, Eisenhower summoned Watkins to the White House for per-

sonal congratulations on having performed a "very splendid job."
The interview was supposed to be secret—Watkins' arrival, by the
President's own admission, was "off the record." His name was not
on the appointment book; he came to the Oval Room via the East
Wing, walking all the way through the White House basement "to
avoid notice," the President wrote in *Mandate for Change,* his
memoirs of his White House years. However, word of Watkins'
presence soon reached reporters, who clamored for an interview. He
told Press Secretary Hagerty: "Tell them I asked Senator Watkins to
come down here so that I could tell him how much we appreciate his
superb handling of a most difficult job."

The "jury" was unfairly balanced against McCarthy. Ray Tucker,
the Washington journalist, analyzed it this way: "It is significant that
no member of the investigating group was chosen from a state which
has a large cosmopolitan population. None represents the Northeast,
the Middle West, or the Coast. None hails from a state in which there
is a powerful element of voters of McCarthy's race or religion, who
have shown their sympathy for him in their letters to members of the
House and Senate."

If I were defending a lovely blonde charged with embezzling large
sums from her employer, I would be dismayed to find that the jury
consisted entirely of bosses. All trial lawyers know the importance of
selecting jurymen who can understand the defendant's position and
motives, and thus be in a position to render a fair judgment.

But much more important, if we accept the argument that this was
an action conducted under the law, we must then seriously consider
the possibility that the resolution of censure itself may have been
unconstitutional.

The argument of unconstitutionality was advanced on the floor of
the Senate by Senator Herman Welker, Republican from Idaho, who
delivered a masterly analysis that in my opinion all but demolished
the legal grounds upon which the censure charges were based.
Unfortunately, Senator Welker's cogent brief went largely unrecorded
in the press; sadder still, it was not listened to by many senators. On
the day he concluded his remarks in McCarthy's defense, there were
only ten senators in the chamber—plus the presiding officer.

Senator Welker stated that the Watkins Committee tried the Senator on charges "that are nowhere in the Constitution specified as
punishable when applied to a member of Congress." According to
Article 1, section 5, clause 2 of the Constitution: "Each house may

determine the rules of its proceedings, punish its members for disorderly behavior, and with the concurrence of two-thirds, expel a member." However, nowhere in the original censure resolution, nor in all the subsequent amendments, was it charged that the acts allegedly committed by Senator McCarthy constituted "disorderly behavior," the only basis on which action may be taken under the aforestated constitutional provision. The censure resolution confined itself to the statement that the alleged acts were "contrary to senatorial tradition."

Nor should it be inferred that this is a mere quibbling over words. "Disorderly" behavior involves a violation of public order and morality and is a much more serious matter than the acts charged against McCarthy.

Let me quote from Senator Welker's excellent summation of this critical point, made in the Senate on November 16, 1954.

> I am insisting that basic legal, constitutional procedure be followed by the Senate of the United States in its action. This great deliberative body, under the Constitution, participates in making laws which are binding on the entire country. Such laws are so worded that everyone has notice of the nature of any violations which may be contemplated. In criminal law the exact nature of a crime is expressed; the penalty, sometimes flexible, is provided, and upon conviction the court imposes the punishment it deems to be appropriate. I am insisting that in the pending case, which is in the nature of a criminal action, punishment of a member being involved, we, the Senate of the United States, apply the same principles of constitutional law that apply to all our land.
>
> I am insisting, Mr. President, that if we seek to punish a member for an offense as described by the Constitution—"disorderly behavior"—not for conduct contrary to senatorial traditions, or conduct unbecoming a member of the Senate. Such conduct—unbecoming a member of the Senate—we have witnessed many a time and have invoked no disciplinary action.

There is a precedent for this view. One of the most significant yet least-mentioned points in the entire debate concerned the censure of two senators more than half a century earlier. In 1902, the Senate censured Senators Benjamin R. Tillman and John L. McLaurin, both South Carolina Democrats, for engaging in a fist fight upon the floor. The Committee on Privileges and Elections considered the matter and then brought in a resolution of censure. *This resolution was based, not upon conduct unbecoming a senator, but on disorderly behavior, the offen ? defined in the constitution.*

Under the American system of justice, this fact is of overriding importance. In law—and we must continually bear in mind that this was to be a case "as in a court of law"—a defendant is tried upon a charge and is subsequently either acquitted or convicted. If he is found guilty, a judge determines his punishment, which the law generally prescribes within certain limits. In the censure trial, however, the wording of "charges" in the original Flanders resolution went as follows: "Resolved, that the conduct of the senator from Wisconsin, Mr. McCarthy, is unbecoming a member of the United States Senate, is contrary to senatorial traditions, and tends to bring the Senate into disrepute, and such conduct is hereby condemned." The final text of the censure resolution, following amendments, also states that the "conduct of the senator from Wisconsin . . . is contrary to senatorial traditions and is hereby condemned."

Thus the senators were not given any discretion in the choice of punishment, which was incorporated into the resolution as a kind of package deal. This predetermination of the penalty is not authorized in the Constitution, which permits punishment only if a member has been found guilty of disorderly conduct. Then, although the word is not mentioned, it can be presumed that censure may be invoked as one of the forms of punishment. However, as Senator Welker pointed out, the Constitution is silent on punishment of members for the charges under which McCarthy was on trial: conduct unbecoming a member, acting contrary to senatorial traditions, actions that tend to bring the Senate into disrepute.

According to some, the famous "Rule XIX" of the Standing Rules of the Senate authorizes condemnation for unbecoming conduct. Paragraph 2 of this rule states: "No senator in debate shall, directly or indirectly, by any form of words impute to another or to other senators any conduct or motive unworthy or unbecoming a senator." Well and good. But what shall be the punishment for transgression? The answer is given in Paragraph 4: if any senator, in speaking or otherwise, in the opinion of the Presiding Officer transgresses the rules of the Senate, the Presiding Officer shall, on his own motion or at the request of any senator, call him to order. An offending senator may be punished by being ordered to sit down, and may not resume the floor until the Senate grants him the right.

There is nothing in the standing rules or anywhere else that authorizes more severe punishment for unbecoming conduct. Senator Welker pointed out that if the Senate wanted the right to discipline members for this type of offense, a code should be set up for that procedure under the Senate's constitutional power to punish for disorderly behavior. "If we wish to punish for refusal to answer an invitation to testify before a Senate committee or for abusive cross-examination in committee hearings," he said, "the elements of such offenses should be described in such a code; and the punishment—whether it be censure, fine, imprisonment, or expulsion—should be stated. Until the time when such a code shall be adopted, the power to punish does not exist. . . ."

Thomas Jefferson warned Congress that it possessed no powers other than those expressly granted by the Constitution. "But if one branch may assume its own privileges without control, if it may do it on the spur of the occasion, conceal the law in its own breast, and after the fact committed, make its sentence both the law and the judgment on that fact; if the offense is to be kept undefined and to be declared only *ex re nata** and according to the passions of the moment, and there be no limitation either in the manner or measure of the punishment, the condition of the citizen will be perilous indeed." The quotation is from Jefferson's Manual, a basic set of rules he wrote to guide the Senate in its deliberations and which is still a part of the Standing Rules of the Senate. Every United States senator has a copy in his desk.

It seems clear to me that the Senators were writing the law and stipulating the penalty "according to the passions of the moment," a procedure that was not only undemocratic but precisely the sort of tactic they professed to deplore in Senator McCarthy.

I will mention briefly another point involving the legality of the case that has nagged at my mind through the years. The charges in the first of the two counts, concerning McCarthy's conduct toward the Hennings-Hayden-Hendrickson Subcommittee on Privileges and Elections, alleged actions that took place in 1951 and 1953 during the session of the preceding Congress.

In this count, Senator McCarthy stood accused of refusing repeated invitations to appear before the subcommittee to answer

* A Latin phrase: "Out of the thing born."

questions on whether money collected to fight Communism was diverted to his personal use, whether some of his activities were motivated by self-interest, whether he had violated the law in some of his activities during his senatorial campaigns, and, especially, to explain his denunciation of Senator Hendrickson as "a living miracle without brains or guts."

I remain unconvinced that the Senate has the right to take action against a member for conduct during a previous session. The Watkins Committee ruled it did, holding that no controlling authority or precedent has been cited for the opposite position. The committee stated that a person who is *not* a member of the Senate may not be punished for contempt for the Senate at a previous session. However, it added, this does not mean that the Senate may not censure one of its own members for conduct antedating that session.

The second count upon which McCarthy was censured concerned his so-called abuse of Chairman Watkins and the select committee. McCarthy used harsh terms. He charged "deliberate deception" and "fraud." He called the special Senate session to consider censure charges a "lynch party" and a "lynch bee." He inserted into the *Congressional Record* a speech he had released to the press in which he called the select committee the "unwitting handmaiden" of the Communist party. He said in that speech: "I shall demonstrate that the Watkins Committee has done the work of the Communist party, that it not only cooperated in the achievement of Communist goals, but that in writing its report it imitated Communist methods—that it distorted, misrepresented, and omitted in its efforts to manufacture a plausible rationalization for advising the Senate to accede to the clamor for my scalp."

Strong words? Yes, strong words indeed. Abusive words? Calling Senator Hendrickson a "living miracle without brains or guts" was indeed abusive.

But was the tempestuous junior senator from Wisconsin the only senator in the history of the country to have uttered strong, abusive words toward other senators and persons in high office?

The question leads to the third and final point of my conclusion about the censure proceedings, which is that:

Other senators had been guilty of the same kind of "abusive conduct" and had not been disciplined by censure.

A good place to begin is not in the far-off past, but on November 30, 1954, with an excerpt from a debate on the Senate floor between Senators Jenner and Flanders over a Thanksgiving Day broadcast the latter had made to the people of the Soviet Union through Voice of America facilities. Flanders had referred to the Russians as "my friends, my Soviet brothers," a phrase with which Jenner took issue. The *Congressional Record* quotes this exchange:

> JENNER: I ask the senator from Vermont just one question, Mr. President. What did he mean when he appealed to these Communist tyrants, who were jailing and shooting American fighting men, "as my friends, my Soviet brothers"? . . . By what reasoning, by what process of mind, by what course of twisted thinking, did the Senator refer to these tyrants, these murderers, as "my friends, my Soviet brothers"?
>
> FLANDERS: The senator from Indiana is beside himself.
>
> JENNER: I am not beside myself, but I want to know what goes on in the United States Senate.
>
> FLANDERS: The Senator has taken leave of his intelligence. If he had read the message, if he had understood it—
>
> JENNER: I have read it. Will the Senator answer my question?
>
> FLANDERS: Just a minute.
>
> JENNER: Answer my question . . .
>
> FLANDERS: The Senator gives me no time to do so. He constantly interrupts. Let me say that that message, as anyone who has not taken leave of his intelligence would see, was an appeal to the people of Russia over the government which rules them.
>
> JENNER: Mr. President, I rise to a point of personal privilege. The Senator says, "anyone who has not taken leave of his intelligence." My intelligence is my own.

This dialogue, with its lively insults, took place on the floor of the United States Senate in the midst of the hearings on the select committee's resolution. When it ended, the senators gravely resumed their debate on whether to censure Senator McCarthy for, among other things, ridiculing and abusing a fellow senator.

In 1957, Senator Wayne Morse of Oregon "abused" the President in a talk, repeated the abuse on the Senate floor, and challenged his opponents to bring censure charges against him. On May 22, Morse was severely criticized by Republicans in the Senate for remarks made several days earlier about President Eisenhower and Dave Beck, the Teamsters Union president whose troubles with the law for plundering union funds were just starting. In a Jackson-Jefferson Day speech in Detroit, Morse spoke against the development of water power in the Northwest by private companies, asserting: "The President is reaching into the pockets of working people for interest-free money to finance these private companies, just as Beck reached into the coffers of his union . . . This is the most politically immoral Administration in our history. Compared to it, Harding was a hero and Grant was a statesman." Morse also referred to Beck and Eisenhower as "two of the same kind of immoralists."

Styles Bridges called the speech "a most shocking thing." Senator Capehart, the Indiana Republican, said it was "an undeserved, unwarranted, almost unbelievable and unprecedented attack upon the President." One after another, Republican senators rose to express their profound shock, grief, and dismay. Said Senator Hickenlooper of Iowa: "I was one who felt that facts justifying the so-called censure of Senator McCarthy had not been established, to the point of warranting a vote of censure. I said at that time that I disagreed with and criticized certain things which Senator McCarthy had said, but I could not bring myself to vote for official censure. I submit . . . that the statement attributed to the senator from Oregon is far more odious, far less considerate of the President of the United States and all that his office connotes, than anything which Senator McCarthy ever said, regardless of the interpretation."

A century earlier, the Senate did not even vote censure against one member who drew a pistol upon another member on the Senate floor. On April 17, 1850, Senator Benton of Missouri, enraged during a debate with Foote of Mississippi, advanced threateningly upon the southerner. Foote pulled out a pistol, and aimed it. Members swarmed over the Mississippi senator, possibly preventing a murder in the Senate chamber. The Senate appointed a committee to investigate the matter. Its report did not recommend punitive action. The matter died.

In a preceding chapter, I referred to the elder La Follette's invitation to Federal employees to violate an order of the President and send him information on what was happening within the Executive branch. Senator Frank B. Kellogg called for the expulsion of La Follette from the Senate on charges of "sedition and disloyalty."

Rarely had the chamber heard obloquy such as La Follette then proceeded to heap upon his opponent on the other side of the aisle. Of Kellogg, he said, "He is by nature a subservient, cringing creature, God almighty has given him a hump on his back, crouching, cringing, un-American and unmanly."

Before the Civil War, Senator Judah P. Benjamin of Louisiana, a Jew, was ridiculed on the floor because of his religion. To the offending senator, whose forebears were German, Benjamin made reply: "The gentleman will please remember that when his half-civilized ancestors were hunting the wild boar in the forests of Silesia, mine were the princes of the earth."

In 1917, during a debate on America's entry into World War I, Missouri's Senator James Alexander Reed all but accused Senator George W. Norris, one of the Senate's most illustrious members, of treason. The Nebraska Republican, charging that "this war madness" had been instigated by the financial and political powers of the nation, closed upon this impassioned note: "I feel that we are about to put the dollar sign upon the American flag."

In reply, Reed said: "Ah, Mr. President, I am sorry from my heart that such a statement should have been made at this time by an American citizen in the highest body of the American Congress. If that be not giving aid and comfort to the enemy on the very eve of the opening of hostilities, then I do not know what would bring comfort to the heart of a Hapsburg or a Hohenzollern. If that be not treason, it takes on a character and guise that is so near to treason that the enemies of America will gain from it much consolation."

Senator Williams of Mississippi interjected: "If it be not treason it grazes the edge of treason."

Tom Connally of Texas once charged Senator Robert A. Taft of Ohio with "cravenly going around begging a few dirty filthy votes." Senator McCarthy could hardly hope to match in invective the phrase Connally applied to the hapless Senator Ferguson, who had incurred his anger. "Everything he touches," Connally roared, "is covered with the vomit of his spleen."

In the summer of 1958, Senator Margaret Chase Smith, Maine Republican, accused Lieutenant General Emmett ("Rosy") O'Donnell, Jr., of having deliberately lied under oath during an executive session of a Senate committee.

Once proceedings began Senator McCarthy knew that he was going to be censured and was prepared for it. He knew censure to be an intangible thing carrying intangible but nonetheless considerable punishment: he would be *persona non grata* within the organization of senators, which meant he would not be listened to and would no longer exercise influence. To his friends he insisted that censure wouldn't matter much to him, that he had never been especially accepted as a member of the club anyway, and that he could carry on his work outside the Senate and be just as effective. He pointed out that censure would not affect his right to vote or to stay on the committee.

But those of us close to him were not fooled. McCarthy was far more profoundly affected than he wanted others to think. He was especially puzzled and hurt by the attitude of many of his colleagues who assured him in private how sorry they were they had to vote against him.

McCarthy told me that Symington visited him in his home during the censure hearing, and said he felt terrible about it. So did other senators, but all had to vote strictly along party lines. "Symington told me he hoped I don't get sore at the individuals participating because there was nothing any one of them could do about it."

McCarthy told me that at least twelve others had said much the same thing to him while the hearings were in progress. Not one claimed to be moved by principle, or that he would vote censure because he believed McCarthy had brought the Senate into disrepute. "Each of them said, 'Look, Joe, this is the story. You know it as well as I do. This is a top-level decision.' "

McCarthy believed that Watkins had been recommended for the chairmanship of the committee by the White House because he was a perfect middle-of-the-road conservative Republican and would lend enough prestige to the job so that even the pro-McCarthy people could not accuse the Administration of partiality. He believed Watkins was given a mission, and that he dutifully accepted it. When he heard that Watkins was summoned in secret to the White House for congratulations, McCarthy exploded: "It's vicious, slimy, back-door politics," his voice high-pitched in his excitement, "and nobody—not a soul—is saying anything! Well, I'm going to speak out."

And he did. Five days after the censure vote, McCarthy resumed committee hearings on Communist infiltration into the country's defense plants. On December 7, McCarthy attacked the President sharply at the hearing.

He thus made his break with the President final and complete. Bitterly, he apologized for having supported Eisenhower in the 1952 campaign. He had thought, he said, that Eisenhower would wage a "vigorous, forceful" fight against Communists in Government, but he now realized he was mistaken.

Two years later, McCarthy said, the nation finds that "the President on the one hand congratulates the senators who hold up the work of our committee, and on the other hand urges that we be patient with the Communist hoodlums who at this very moment are torturing and brainwashing American uniformed men in Communist dungeons. . . . If any senator in the future can justify a vote to draft the sons of American mothers, then he must repudiate this shrinking show of weakness."

McCarthy, I believe, made a serious mistake when he took on an attorney, albeit an able one, Edward Bennett Williams, to speak for him at the censure proceedings. He did not need counsel. The legal issues were simple to knock down. Of the forty-six original specifications, only one finally stood up and a second was tacked on as a late starter. Secondly, since he was predestined to lose, he would have gained in spirit had he gone down fighting.

For the glory of McCarthy was in his courage, in his strong defense of the issues in which he had come to believe, in his strength to stand up and refuse to be cowed, even though it meant opposing the President of the United States and the Republican and Democratic party leaderships. He said to me: "They could have taken the vote before the hearings started and the totals would have been exactly the same. That being the case, why couldn't I have gone down the way I was, being myself, instead of coming in with a new face and having to sit there and have a lawyer trying to talk to people in a kind of pleading way, trying to talk them out of the lynching party they were determined to have no matter what?"

Doubtless it was this not being allowed to speak that prompted

McCarthy to place into the record the speech he gave to the press in which he called Chairman Watkins the "unwitting handmaiden" of the Communist party. The Senate promptly added the remarks to the censure charges.

What would the Senator have said had he been given his voice at the hearings? I know what he would have said because, several months later, I asked him and he told me.

"I would not have allowed myself to take the role of a defendant pleading guilty to a lesser charge," he said. "The strategy was to water down the charges, make them less severe, chip away at them. But what difference does it make whether or not I was censured for two charges or twenty-two or two hundred and twenty-two? How many people will remember in a month, a year, twenty years, that the censure was voted on only two counts? What consolation is that? It's censure, period.

"So I would have demanded all or nothing. I would have made it very clear that I knew the cards were stacked against me. I would have said:

" 'Senators, this committee was created for the purpose of recommending my censure. The Army-McCarthy hearings did not do the job of killing me off. I still have some blood of life left in me, so this is supposed to be the final step. Well, Senators, I do not intend to be slaughtered. If you are going to slaughter me, maybe you can do it privately, but not publicly. You, Senator Watkins, are here because the Administration gave you the assignment. You have carried out your assignment. Now let us forget about all these details about whether or not I did this or that, and let us come face to face with the broad principles involved . . .' "

The Senate would have proceeded to censure Joe McCarthy, but the American people would have read his words and would have had a clearer idea of why it all happened the way it did.

THE RESOLUTION OF CENSURE

Text of Senate Resolution 301, voted on December 2, 1954

Section 1. Resolved, that the senator from Wisconsin, Mr. McCarthy, failed to cooperate with the Subcommittee on Privileges and Elections of the Senate Committee on Rules and Administration in clearing up matters referred to that subcommittee which concerned his conduct as a senator and affected the honor of the Senate and, instead, repeatedly abused the subcommittee and its members who were trying to carry out assigned duties, thereby obstructing the constitutional processes of the Senate, and that this conduct of the senator from Wisconsin, Mr. McCarthy, is contrary to senatorial traditions and is hereby condemned.

Section 2. The senator from Wisconsin (Mr. McCarthy), in writing to the chairman of the Select Committee to Study Censure Charges (Mr. Watkins) after the select committee had issued its report and before the report was presented to the Senate charging three members of the select committee with "deliberate deception" and "fraud" for failure to disqualify themselves;

In stating to the press on Nov. 4, 1954, that the special Senate session that was to begin Nov. 8, 1954, was a "lynch party";

In repeatedly describing this special Senate session as a "lynch bee" in a nationwide television and radio show on Nov. 7, 1954;

In stating to the public press on Nov. 13, 1954, that the chairman of the select committee (Mr. Watkins) was guilty of "the most unusual, most cowardly thing I've ever heard of" and stating further: "I expected he would be afraid to answer the questions, but didn't think he'd be stupid enough to make a public statement"; and in characterizing the said committee as the "unwitting handmaiden," "involuntary agent" and "attorneys-in-fact" of the Communist party and in charging that the said committee in writing its report "imitated Communist methods—that it distorted, misrepresented, and omitted in its efforts to manufacture a plausible rationalization" in support of its recommendations to the Senate, which characterizations and charges were contained in a statement released to the press and inserted into the *Congressional Record* of Nov. 10, 1954, acted contrary to senatorial ethics and tended to bring the Senate into dishonor and disrepute, to obstruct the constitutional processes of the Senate, and to impair its dignity.

And such conduct is hereby condemned.

CHAPTER 18

WHY THEY HATED

As 1955 OPENED, the Senator was dispirited and bewildered. He would sit at home in the evenings and talk endlessly about the immediate past. Jean, always loyal, was bitter against the political forces that had combined to pull her husband down. She sought above all else to restore his confidence.

It was difficult, because that winter after the censure there was no fight left in Joe McCarthy. The fight went out of him not, as Rovere suggests, because he lacked powerful convictions and therefore could not draw strength from his beliefs, but because he had taken more punishment than a normal man could be expected to absorb. It is a fact that no man in this century was subjected to such a campaign of vilification as the junior senator from Wisconsin. Never have so much vituperation and defamation been directed toward a person in public life.

One reporter wrote: "Senator McCarthy has few friends in the Washington newspaper corps. They despise him almost to a man. They sit around thinking up ways to embarrass him, and if possible to kill him off politically. . . . It pains me to write this, because I like newspaper people. But the truth is that 'most anything, news stories or opinionated columns, written on McCarthy under a Washington dateline, is the effort of a man who dislikes him intensely and would pass up no opportunity to jab him."

The attacks in newspaper articles, speeches, tracts, books, and fantastically concocted overnight "biographies" were venomous. They do not stop. They continue to this writing. He was and still is called every contemptuous name. The cartoonist Herblock drew him as an ape. Arthur Eisenhower, the President's eldest brother, called him "a throwback to the Spanish Inquisition." *The Commonweal,* an ultraliberal Catholic publication, called him a "reckless, irresponsible bogey-man." Emmet John Hughes, former aide to Eisenhower, in references to McCarthy in his book of recollections, *The Ordeal of Power,* uses such words as "snarls," "rants," "ugly sounds," "pettiness and foolishness." McCarthy was "diagnosed" as having paranoid tendencies by psychiatrists who had never examined him, an example of medical *chutzpah* exceeded only by the irresponsibility of the journalists who considered the findings as evidence of McCarthy's mental state.

Another side to the personal gossip—one as vicious as it was untruthful—was actually voiced by the aged Senator Flanders of Vermont in a speech from the Senate floor. Rumor had it that the speech was written by the National Committee for an Effective Congress, an organization headed by a peculiar brand of stuffed-shirt leftists operating from the Waldorf Towers, and spoonfed to poor old Flanders. If Senator McCarthy had said or implied something like this without any basis in fact, he would have been pilloried by the same liberals who propped up Flanders to do their below-the-belt dirty work.

It had been whispered about that McCarthy was a homosexual, a charge widely accepted by many of his enemies who were undeterred by its patent falsity. A flamboyant individual named Hank Greenspun, publisher of the Las Vegas *Sun,* wrote a column in which he maligned McCarthy as a "disreputable pervert."

In the midst of the Army-McCarthy hearings, Senator Flanders rose in the Senate and gave voice to innuendos that were as shocking as they were unprecedented. "The committee," Senator Flanders said, "has not yet dug into the real heart of the mystery. That mystery concerns the personal relationships of the Army private [Schine], the staff assistant [Cohn], and the Senator."

Flanders emphasized the *personal* relationships and the emphasis was not lost on the millions who read his charges in the newspapers. Flanders elaborated: "There is the relationship of the staff assistant to the Army private. It is natural that he should wish to retain the services of an able collaborator, but he seems to have an almost passionate anxiety to retain him. Why?" His choice of the word "passionate" was as deliberate as the use of the phrase "effeminate screech" by Potter to describe McCarthy's anger.

"And then there is the Senator himself," Flanders went on. "At times he seems anxious to rid himself of the whole mess, and then again, at least in the presence of his assistant, he strongly supports the latter's efforts to keep the Army private's services available. Does the assistant have some hold on the Senator? Can it be that our Dennis [Flanders had previously referred to McCarthy as Dennis the Menace, a boy in the comic strips who cannot keep out of mischief], so effective in making trouble for his elders, has at last gotten into trouble himself? Does the committee plan to investigate the real issues at stake?"

McCarthy was aware of the homosexual stories and he laughed them off. "Why should I get sore?" he told me once. "They called Jefferson the bastard son of an Indian woman, Lincoln a lunatic and a drunk, Roosevelt a Jew-bastard, and Grover Cleveland a lecherous old man."

Nor was Flanders the only important person who used an influential forum to help spread these stories. Army counsel Welch, in a widely applauded bon mot, drew nationwide attention to the slanders about McCarthy, Dave Schine, and me. When he examined Jim Juliana about the so-called cropped picture, he referred to the original, which had hung on Dave Schine's office wall in New York.

When Juliana said he never knew what had hung on Schine's wall, Welch demanded: "Did you think this came from a pixie?" At this point, McCarthy broke in: "Will the counsel, for my benefit, define—I think he might be an expert on that—what a pixie is?"

Swiftly Welch retorted: "Yes, I should say, Mr. Senator, that a pixie is a close relative of a fairy. Shall I proceed, sir? Have I enlightened you?" Spectators roared.

The remark was deft, but it was not without malicious intent because Welch was completely aware of the rumors. McCarthy was not offended by the remark, despite journalists' assertions that from that point on he reserved a special hatred for Mr. Welch. He told me later he thought it was funny. To me, the most significant aspect of the incident was that no one criticized the wicked and, if I may use the word in referring to Mr. Welch, indecent jab. In newspaper and magazine reports, there was only lavish praise for the brilliant ad lib.

I could never work up much anger against Flanders for his innuendos—for which he later apologized. He was, in any event, an eccentric. Consider the manner in which he launched his attack. On the morning of June 11, Senator McCarthy was on the stand at the Army-McCarthy hearings, under questioning by Counsel Jenkins. They were interrupted by Flanders' sudden entry. While those present watched wonderingly, the senator from Vermont walked to the witness chair and handed McCarthy a letter. McCarthy opened it and read the message: "This is to inform you that I plan to make another speech concerning your activities in the Senate this afternoon as soon after the morning hour as I can get the floor."

McCarthy demanded that the chair ask Flanders to remain in the hearing room. "I think, Senator," McCarthy told the retreating Flanders, "if you have any information of value to this committee, what you should do is do what my three Republican colleagues have done, what I am doing now—take the oath, raise your right hand, let us cross-examine you. If you have nothing except the usual smear, gleaned from the smear sheets, then you should tell us that, Senator, and I think you should do it, do it here under oath, rather than on the Senate floor. I would be glad to step aside and let you testify under oath as to any information that you have."

Chairman Mundt, however, ruled the hearing should continue without Flanders' testimony. McCarthy remarked that Flanders' unfounded attacks were not the result of viciousness but "perhaps senility," later adding to reporters: "I think they should get a man with a net and take him to a good quiet place."

The Watkins Committee considering censure charges against McCarthy called these remarks "highly improper" but found that "they were induced by Senator Flanders' conduct in respect to Senator McCarthy in the Senate caucus room, and in delivering provocative speeches concerning Senator McCarthy on the Senate floor."

It would be instructive to consider in some depth why the critical barrage against McCarthy was so incessant, so amazingly shrill and so monstrously abusive.

I believe we can dismiss, after reflection, the man's manner and appearance. It is true that with his burliness, his impatience, his aggressiveness, and his refusal to compromise he was cast for the role of arch-villain, but these were superficial characteristics hardly calling for such violent abuse. Moreover, he was not the only public figure in history who possessed such physical attributes as a heavy beard that could easily be caricatured.

We cannot dismiss as easily the charges that he played rough politics, occasionally took unfair advantage of people, and said harsh things in public. McCarthy's heat-of-battle pronunciamentos were often unnecessarily strong. His "Alger—I mean Adlai" reference to Adlai Stevenson was regrettable, and his characterization of the Democrats as the "party of treason" was an inexcusably broad (and therefore inaccurate) accusation. These tactics generated understandable antagonism.

But can we ascribe the hate and venom he aroused in many quarters to his campaign conduct? Americans recognize that politics is often a merciless contest. Political abuse is an old American custom. Jefferson the "bastard son of an Indian woman," Lincoln the "drunkard," Grover Cleveland the "lecher," and Andrew Jackson who was given names not fit for the printed page even by today's libertarian standards are rated by American historians as among our greatest presidents. Two others highly regarded, Woodrow Wilson and Franklin Roosevelt, also came in for extraordinary abuse and nasty innuendos. McCarthy's case is almost unique in the history of political slander in that the victim was not a liberal but right of center.

We have already dealt with the claim that his conduct was unbecoming a legislator. In the previous chapter I have cited a few of the many other congressmen whose behavior left something to be desired and yet did not result in such an outpouring of hate.

Was he reviled because his enemies feared him as a fanatic, a would-be dictator who wanted to foist a kind of fascism upon the United States? I think here we come a little closer to an answer. There was indeed such a fear, that much the stronger because the nation had just emerged from a bloody struggle with two fascist dictators. But upon further analysis, this explanation doesn't entirely hold up either. Even Rovere, who calls McCarthy a demagogue, ultimately admits that he did not have the soul of a Hitler, was never consumed by dreams of power, and was not a man possessed by demons.

Senator McCarthy knew his influence, but it is far-fetched to accept the mystique that he was a man driven by the need for absolute power over the lives of men and the destinies of nations. He was too cavalier, too disorganized concerning the wisdom of his own political moves, for there to be any substance to this theory. He did not seek his powerful chairmanship; it just happened by operation of the rule of seniority when the Democrats were temporarily dislodged in 1952. Despite the controversy over his use of the power, power for its own sake was never McCarthy's goal. He was politically ambitious, but the same might be said of every seeker after public office.

Many journalists took a dual approach to this charge of fanaticism. Privately, they thought he was an uncommitted crusader who had found a "good thing" that commanded publicity; in print, they sought to discredit him with charges of fanaticism. The truth is that McCarthy was basically a simple man who lacked the burning zeal of the single-track cause-fighter. He was courageous though, and when he became convinced that Communism was an evil, he took up the battle against its inroads into American life and fought the tough way he had learned how to fight early in life.

Why then was McCarthy so feared and hated? I believe there were two basic reasons. The liberal intellectual element in government and the communications media regarded him as a mortal threat; and political leaders, including the conservative Establishment, saw in him and in his "issue" a force that if allowed to carry on would split the Republican party from top to bottom.

McCarthy was the first public figure in a position of practically unchallengeable power to threaten by his activity the freedom, the livelihood, and the social function of liberals, chiefly in the Government. Liberals were and still are in control of large sections of the press, radio, TV, and motion pictures. These people believed that the facts McCarthy was digging after could, if carried to their logical conclusion, directly threaten them. Their own transgressions, stupidities, or mere indiscretions magnified by exposure and publicity would hurt them badly; their protective mechanism resorted to hate and obstruction aimed at the investigator and his allies.

Perhaps the chief reason for the distrust and scorn of certain elements of the rank and file was their acceptance of the image of McCarthy as a bully who habitually indulged, from a safe and entrenched position, in no-quarter attacks on vulnerable persons he seemed to have accused and condemned almost before they had sat down to be questioned. Such was the impression emanating from many newspapers and from radio and TV sets. He appeared to be running amock, with no one on the horizon to stop him. American political history had no precedent for his kind of attack before such a huge watching and reading public.

The juggernaut progress of this Irish bull seemed to pose a special problem for the Jewish community. Jews are numerous in the various branches of the communications industry. They had a special memory, and a long one, of persecution. Many had been led politically leftward by the terrifying rise of Hitler and they had a feeling of gratitude toward the Soviet Union for its major role in toppling the Nazis.

These factors along with the ever-present Jewish concern for civil liberties account for the opposition (often unreasonable in my opinion) of many Jews and Jewish organizations to anti-Communism. In my opinion they rendered a disservice to the Jewish community because they fostered the impression that there was a mystic link between Judaism and Communism. Such an idea is, of course, ridiculous, since Judaism's great historical contribution is a moral God, while Communism's crusade is for atheism.

Instead of excusing leftist causes, certain Jewish organizations would have done better had they pointed out the inconsistencies between Judaism and Communism, and the mistreatment of Jews in the Soviet Union. Instead of defending morally indefensible people (some of whom happened to be Jews) involved in Communist activity, they should have praised the many Jews in the forefront of the fight against Communism. While it is true that the Rosenbergs were Jewish, so too were those who prosecuted them, such as Irving H. Saypol, the competent and vigorous United States attorney (now state supreme court justice). And so is Federal Judge Irving R. Kaufman (since elevated to the United States Court of Appeals), whose conduct of the trial was so fair that even the Rosenbergs' lawyer praised it. American boys of Jewish faith died fighting for freedom in Korea and in Vietnam. The staunch Americanism of such Jews as presidential adviser Bernard Baruch, Admiral Hyman Rickover, the distinguished lawyer Edwin L. Weisl, who while serving as chief counsel to the

Senate Preparedness Committee fashioned the space act, Rabbi Joshua Goldberg, militant foe of Communism and Jewish chaplain for the United States Navy—these are only a few of the names that spring to mind. The mishandling of this Communist issue by some Jewish organizations resulted in the creation of the American Jewish League against Communism by a group of prominent American Jews including George Sokolsky, Eugene Lyons, and Alfred Kohlberg. As J. Edgar Hoover pointed out in his book *Masters of Deceit,* this League was "the first American organization to expose and document the Communist anti-Jewish policies." Russia bans the teaching of Hebrew, forbids Jews to visit Israel, and has barred Jews from positions of importance in the country. No Jewish organization can exist inside the U.S.S.R., and no Jewish publication may be issued.

McCarthy was the first important public figure to touch an exquisitely sensitive nerve in the thought leaders of our society. This small but immensely powerful group of intellectuals is committed totally to the idea of an open society, in which there is no officially accepted truth, no dogma handed down by authority and believed without question. Their leaders believe with John Stuart Mill that in a political society "there ought to exist the fullest liberty of professing and discussing, as a matter of ethical conviction, any doctrine, however immoral it may be considered." Thus the way to get at a truth is to have an open market of ideas, and the successful contender in the marketplace could be identified as the political truth—for the time being. Of course, the truth can change if a new contender should arise and displace it.

For this thesis to be implemented, it must follow that society can place no obstructions in the path of a full exploration of any new candidate for truth that may come along. Thus contemporary liberalism holds that it is the worst of sins to punish anybody for the advocacy of a competing idea. One must be left free to thoroughly examine any idea that comes along.

Doctrinaire liberals were angered when legislation designed to combat subversive activities was debated and enacted. They did not favor a law that ordered all agents of foreign governments to register with the Department of Justice (the McCormack Act of 1938), or a law barring from Federal employment any member of an organization that advocates the overthrow of the United States Government by force or violence (the Hatch Act of 1939), or a law punishing those who would advocate the forceful overthrow of this Government (the Smith Act of 1940). They did not like these laws, but neither did they quiver with fear and hate. Theirs was at least controlled hostility.

Now along came Senator Joseph McCarthy. And he came, these liberal leaders believed, with another kind of idea. McCarthy, they convinced themselves, was telling the nation that it was not enough to pass laws protecting ourselves from these outside dangers. We must excommunicate not only the *individual* from our society but also the *ideas* he espouses. And it was here that the liberals became alarmed and then enraged. The notion that any idea whatever, no matter how bizarre, how revolutionary, how dangerous in political effect, can be ruled out of the forum jarred the deepest commitment of the liberal community.

Professor Willmoore Kendall, in his book *The Conservative Affirmation,* develops this thesis that McCarthy was hated because he was the spokesman for a large group that would enforce a public orthodoxy—set up a code of officially accepted beliefs in this country, expunging ideas they believed immoral or which threatened our society's survival. His theory is enormously interesting, but he did not really know McCarthy.

The truth is simply that McCarthy embraced no such philosophy, or in fact any world-view whatsoever. He was no political thinker, no innovator. He was the enemy not of free speech but of the abuse of the First Amendment. He would outlaw only the advocacy of force and violence to change our form of government. He did not believe as did Thomas Jefferson in a whimsical moment that a revolution now and then is good for a society. He was rather with Calvin Coolidge and the D.A.R.: "We have had our Revolution." He belonged to the respectable political school (however unorthodox his actions may have been) that Americans are not afraid of ideas or public persuasion but only of espionage, sabotage, and the appeal to a violent change. His test was: after all the talking and debate, put it to the vote and abide by the decision of the majority.

Those whose hatred of McCarthy stemmed from confusing him with the Far Righters, who actually did advocate a patriotic orthodoxy, have a point, a reason for their confusion. The Senator and those on his right were patriots who elevated pride in the Flag to a religion, and regarded antagonists to prayer in the public schools as sneaking atheists and dissent from the war in Korea (or now Vietnam) or the failure to save China from Communism as treason.

In seeing him as the Man on Horseback, the would-be dictator working toward the take-over, they paid Joe McCarthy a tribute he did not deserve. He was a man not consumed by an ideology; one who, like Theodore Roosevelt, "thought with his hips." He was a man of action, but without a comprehensive plan to be President, much less a dictator.

But believing that he threatened the American way of life itself, many citizens found in that an ample justification for a very special hatred.

CHAPTER 19

THE FINAL YEARS

A FEW DAYS AFTER the Senate censured him, Joe McCarthy tried to find out if he could become President of the United States. His power with the electorate had always been formidable. He was able to sway voters in states other than his own. He accomplished political upheavals which Presidents could not. McCarthy's intervention felled such giants as Tydings in Maryland and Benton in Connecticut. His refusal to intervene in Massachusetts on behalf of Henry Cabot Lodge was at least in part responsible for John F. Kennedy's election to the Senate. He played a powerful role in the Republican landslide of 1952.

But his inquiry in 1954 was for a new purpose.

The Christmas before, some Wisconsin supporters had presented him with a collection of doll-size statuettes of the thirty-three Presidents from Washington to Eisenhower. A thirty-fourth figure stood next to Eisenhower. Its face was McCarthy's.

The Senator was delighted with the gift. But he didn't take the suggestion seriously. Now, a year later, he had a mild flirtation with the idea—born, I am convinced, of the anger and frustration he felt after Congress had passed unfair judgment on him. He looked at the thirty-fourth figurine and wondered.

He asked Don Surine to conduct a private poll among leading Republican figures to determine his chances in the 1956 presidential primaries. He told William F. Buckley at the time: "Obviously, not for myself, but to find out what votes I could swing away from Ike in fifty-six. I'd throw all my support to Bill Knowland, and then we'd have a real anti-Communist President in the White House for a change."

Buckley said later: "It was quite evident that Joe nursed the hope he'd prove so popular that his plan to deliver his delegate strength to Knowland would prove impossible, and he would have to accept the mantle himself."

The results of the poll were embarrassing. He discovered that only about 3 percent of Republican leaders would openly support him.

This brief period was the only time to my knowledge that McCarthy thought of the Presidency for himself. It would be wrong to draw the conclusion that the incident revealed substantial presidential ambition, or anything more than a wild and momentary hope in a time of distress. But the findings of this small survey had a disastrous effect on his emotional state. His sense of futility grew, his despair deepened. Where once he had enormous reserves of energy, he was now overcome by a great apathy. He stayed away from his office and the Senate floor more and more often. He took to late rising and sometimes spent the day gazing into the fire in his living room and watching television soap operas. Often he would refuse telephone calls, even from close friends.

By cherry-blossom time in 1955, McCarthy seemed suddenly to regain much of his vitality and good spirits. But it was not to last. Thereafter, there were peaks and valleys—periods during which he would work hard, plan enthusiastically, and even perform brilliantly, followed by intervals of lassitude. He would accept invitations to make speeches and fail to show up. I recall an "I-Am-an-American" day in Bridgeport, where the program had been created around him. At three in the afternoon he sent word that he couldn't appear, pleading "urgent Senate business." When he accepted the engagement his spirits happened to be high, but when the day came, he was back in the doldrums and couldn't face the public.

Senators pointedly left the chamber when he rose to speak. He was the only member of Congress omitted from the White House guest list for dinners and receptions in the 1953–54 and 1955–56 seasons. In March of 1956, when the White House social season concluded with a gala reception for legislators and other officials, James Haggerty, Eisenhower's press secretary, was asked if McCarthy was the only one of the 529 senators and congressmen who had not received an invitation to one of the six social functions that season. "That's right," he replied. The snubs were unforgivable, the more so because these were not personal soirées to which only friends are asked, but formal, traditional events, paid for by taxes.

Press coverage of McCarthy's activities shrank from vast to almost nothing. At the height of his fame, the Washington *Post* in one issue had run fourteen articles, two editorials, and two editorial cartoons about him. In 1955 and 1956, he rated a few paragraphs now and then on a back page.

Yet McCarthy in his final years was not quite the dazed and lonely figure wandering ineffectually through life he was made to seem. For instance, in June of 1955 he had emerged from his depression sufficiently to begin to take an active interest in the Big Four summit conference that was to be held in Geneva that July. He studied the plans for the meeting, talked them over with aides and friends in the Senate, and became certain in his own mind that the conference was bound to benefit the Communist states rather than the free world. He called in L. Brent Bozell, his able young staff assistant, and asked him to prepare some material for a speech of dramatic warning. On June 16, he delivered the address. It received almost no attention from the senators and hardly more from the press.

In some ways I believe this foreign policy address, delivered while *Time* was alluding to him as a "virtual stranger on Capitol Hill," to be a high point of McCarthy's Senate career. The "complacency and visionary thinking the Administration is encouraging" about the meeting, he said, was "every bit as lethal to the free world's cause as an atomic fallout is to the tissues of the human body." McCarthy warned that this country was going to negotiate about areas the free world now controls ("We are going to talk about what we may give away instead of what we may get"); that even should we get reciprocal concessions from the Soviets, we know they will not keep their half of the bargain; and that in the event there are no concessions we will suffer a crushing propaganda defeat by appearing to be uncooperative.

McCarthy then introduced a resolution requesting the Senate to call upon President Eisenhower and Secretary of State Dulles to obtain the Soviet Union's agreement, in advance of the summit meeting, to place a discussion of the Red satellites upon the agenda. It would, he knew, prevent the conference from being held at all, because the Soviets would hardly agree to any such discussions. At the meeting of the Foreign Relations Committee, it was defeated 14 to 0. The next day the Senate itself voted it down 77 to 4.

These were stunning defeats—and they contributed to McCarthy's decline.

The summit talks went well. They were conducted in an atmosphere of good will and international fellowship. Out of them came the "spirit of Geneva." President Eisenhower returned home filled with hope because he thought that "agreements had been reached to study ways of increasing friendship between the peoples of the West and of the Soviet Union, and these contacts could, we thought, presage the beginning of a more open society in the U.S.S.R." It delighted him that the Soviet Union had agreed that "the settlement of the German question and the reunification of Germany by free elections shall be carried out in conformity with the national interests of the German people and the interests of European security."

But, alas, the spirit of Geneva had a short life. "Disillusionment" —the word is Eisenhower's—soon followed. He wrote in his memoirs: "At the October Foreign Ministers' conference, held in the same room as the Summit Conference, the Soviets had repudiated every measure to which they had agreed in July . . . to those of us responsible for the conduct of foreign relations, the Soviet duplicity was a grievous disappointment indeed."

McCarthy was right, but Eisenhower was President.

McCarthy knew now that while he still had powerful support throughout the country, his strength had all but collapsed in Washington. On my visits to the capital, I would find him at home, sunk deep in his armchair, staring into the fire. When he spoke about the fight we had waged together over the great issue of Communism in Government, he would shrug his massive shoulders and rub his hand over his forehead and down his face. Continuing the battle, he would say, using a leatherneck phrase, would be as futile as "shoveling shit against the tide."

Always the censure was on his mind. "I was fighting for my life," he told me, "and they didn't let me fight. You and I, we had our ups and downs but we were always able to bring things out, weren't we? We were always able to fight. We never said to each other that we had hid or that we had pulled back or that we were cowards. I felt like a coward at the censure hearings. I had to sit there and take it. They back you into a corner and you have to do one of two things. You jump off a roof or you try to stand up like a man to fight your way out. I lost without fighting."

But still McCarthy did not become a recluse in 1956 and 1957.

Ray Kiermas, his administrative assistant since 1947, found him at his office early and often. "He came and he worked damned hard," Ray told me. There were five thousand pieces of mail to go through weekly, bills to study, bills to prepare, telephone calls to make and take, constituents to see. He would summon Brent Bozell and discuss ideas for new legislation and for speeches. "To insist, as some have, that McCarthy was a shattered man after the censure is sheer nonsense," Bozell told me. "His intellect was as sharp as ever. When he addressed himself to a problem, he was perfectly capable of dealing with it."

In the fall of 1956, he and Jean went on a hunting trip to northeast Wisconsin and even there they could not have an uninterrupted, peaceful vacation. His car struck a fourteen-point buck near Oconto on October 19, damaging both car and deer, but leaving Senator and lady intact.

Despite his spells of depression, McCarthy did not give up on life. I was with him a number of times when he felt well, and on these occasions he planned actively to run for the Senate again in 1958.

I asked him, "What about issues?" He looked at me in surprise.

"My issue," he answered. "Communism in Government. There's nothing else as big."

The strange part was that when portions of the electorate were losing interest in the Communist threat, McCarthy's own moral commitment was stronger than it had ever been. He had a passionate conviction of having been right. He wanted to carry on his battle and win again.

"You'll win again," I told him.

"You're damned right I will!"

I think he would have run and I think he would have won, but for two factors which were ultimately to fuse and destroy him physically.

The first was liquor.

Joe McCarthy was a drinking man in a drinking town.

Liquor flows freely in Washington, which on the basis of statistical evidence has been called the booze capital of the United States. The average per capita consumption of distilled spirits in the District of Columbia, according to the most recent compilation, is 3,721.2 fifths of a gallon a year for every hundred persons, *five times the national average of* 759.6. In New York, it is 954.7, in Connecticut 1,137, in

New Jersey 1,061.5. Small wonder the *New York World-Journal-Tribune* stated: "The elephant may be the symbol of the Republican party, but the pink elephant is the fitting symbol for the bipartisan spirit of all those grand old parties in Washington."

Liquor prices are generally lower in Washington that elsewhere. Politics and Government work create extra tensions. Convivial social gatherings are the order of the day. Washington cocktail parties are famous—for the gossip that is bandied about and for the vast quantities of alcohol that are consumed. Whatever the cause, many people in Government drink and Joe McCarthy was no exception.

But many important people in Washington were and are impressive drinkers. Let me quote from *The Truman Merry-Go-Round* by Robert A. Allen and William V. Shannon: "Old-timers like Tom Connally, Millard Tydings, and Alben Barkley have a bottomless stock of stories and an almost bottomless liquor capacity. Acheson can both hold his whisky and tell funny anecdotes. For hour after hour he would sit in Connally's office drinking bourbon and trading quips and tales."

McCarthy's enemies overemphasized his intake. Since the subject has occasioned so much conjecture, let me explain his drinking habits and their effect on his work and life.

From the time I knew him until the beginning of 1955, McCarthy would drink hardly at all during working hours. He would have a drink at lunch, rarely a second. He was fond of what he jokingly called "Irish tea," unlike Irish coffee in that it was unspiked. It was simply brewed black and strong.

Despite reports to the contrary, McCarthy seldom drank during the Army-McCarthy hearings. Potter says in his book: "Sometimes I wonder if Joe's judgment doesn't go bad after his liquid luncheons at the Carroll Arms. He always seems to make his worst mistakes in the afternoon." Senator Potter never lunched with McCarthy at the Carroll Arms. I did, often, and I never saw him drink there. When I asked Frank Carr if he had ever seen the Senator drink, he told me: "Once he reached over to take a sip from somebody's cocktail. Jim Juliana just took it right out of his hand. Joe laughed and agreed it would be a poor idea to come into the Caucus Room with even a trace of liquor on his breath. He knew what his critics would say."

It was after the censure vote that McCarthy stepped up his drinking. Toward the end of 1955 some signs generally associated with problem drinkers became apparent.

He took to drinking in secret. When friends were visiting he would excuse himself, disappear into the kitchen, down a drink quickly and return to the company. Once a friend noticed that he opened a bottle of Coca-Cola, poured out a couple of ounces, poured some bourbon into the bottle, and replaced the cap. Later, announcing he wanted a soft drink, he helped himself to the spiked Coke. His friend Willard Edwards, the newspaperman, told me McCarthy would, on occasion, take along a bottle in his briefcase.

Even so, he did not drink constantly and did not qualify as an alcoholic. An alcoholic cannot control his drinking once he begins. The Senator drank, but he stayed in control. He was a sober husband and, later, a sober father to an adopted daughter. His drinking did not interfere with his friends, trips, vacations, or sports.

Joe McCarthy's drinking problem was, in fact, something quite different and had to do with his health. His physician warned that even a single social drink was one too many. But Joe couldn't follow orders that he did not take seriously. This was to be his undoing.

This brings us to the second factor—illness.

McCarthy had a powerful constitution, but in the last seven years of his life he suffered from a variety of ailments that slowly and inexorably sapped his strength and ultimately took his life.

In 1949, he underwent surgery to correct an infection and obstruction of his sinuses, a scraping operation that caused more distress than it relieved. Excruciating headaches hit him almost daily during the Army-McCarthy hearings, although few people knew it. His staff could tell, however, at the late afternoon and evening conferences. We would watch him sit for long minutes, one hand over his eyes and forehead. I recall a news photograph of him in that very position. The caption said he was showing the strain of an especially long afternoon. I happen to know that on this occasion, his headache was agonizing. In September of that year, he made daily visits to the Naval Hospital in Bethesda for sinus treatments.

In July of 1952, McCarthy had a major operation to repair a thoracic hernia, the rupture of the large muscle that separates the abdomen from the chest. The operation required the removal of a rib. Thereafter he would suffer bouts of intense chest pain. In the early part of 1954, he had an attack of acute viral laryngitis that put him to bed for a week. In the fall of 1955, after a speech in Wisconsin, surrounded by dozens of well-wishers, he stumbled on the steps leading from the platform and wrenched his left knee severely. A metal brace had to be applied to keep the strain off the joint as he walked. In the weeks that followed, the knobs on the brace, rubbing constantly against the inside of his right leg, caused an infection which McCarthy neglected to have treated. He was hospitalized at the Bethesda Naval Hospital for treatment.

Years earlier, he had suffered a severe leg injury in a shipboard accident during the war. He had to check into Bethesda several times for treatment of complications. In 1954, the debate on the censure resolution was held up for nine days while McCarthy underwent treatment for bursitis of the right elbow. In January of 1957, he had a fatty tumor removed from the lower part of his right leg.

Some of these ailments were merely nuisances, some viciously painful, but none actually life-threatening. McCarthy contracted another ailment, however, that, considering the man and his habits, was extremely dangerous.

In the early 1950's, large-scale outbreaks of infectious hepatitis struck several American communities, and the Senator was one of the many victims. It was not a "new" health menace, although many thought it was, but an old disease that doctors used to call catarrhal jaundice and laymen yellow jaundice. But there was no question that more people than ever before were being stricken. Some health experts estimated that there were nationally about one million cases, mild and severe, reported and unreported, every year.

McCarthy's was a mild case, one of the many that went unreported. He never spoke to me about it. He felt that it was "no big deal," but it turned out to be, for him.

Most persons recover, but they are cautioned that rest, proper diet, and total abstinence from alcohol are essential for many months to allow the liver cells to repair themselves.

McCarthy had strict instructions to rest, follow a rigid diet, and avoid even that one drink. For a while he obeyed, but because he had things to do and because he was McCarthy, he began to disregard orders. Feeling better, he decided the illness was behind him and resumed his old ways. Inevitably, though gradually, his damaged liver worsened.

In the beginning, there were only small signs. Jim Juliana noticed that during the Army-McCarthy hearings the Senator became unusually tired after the short walk from his home to the Senate Office Building. It was not until the fall of 1956 that his weakness was evident to the point that Jean became alarmed and insisted he see a doctor. He had lost forty-one pounds and was down to 179. He looked pale and haggard. When I visited him in Washington, I was shocked by his appearance. Jean told me the doctor's instructions were unchanged, but delivered with greater emphasis: rest, proper diet, absolutely no liquor.

McCarthy refused to rest, would not stay on his diet, and did not abstain from liquor. So blind was his confidence in his own strength it left no room for caution. He refused to accept the fact of his own vulnerability, a not uncommon reaction. He was a man of action, a man of great energy, of even greater impatience. Such men don't lie down just because doctors tell them to.

In January of 1957, a last ray of joy entered McCarthy's life. He and Jeannie adopted a five-week-old girl from the New York Foundling Home—I suspect through the kindness of that source of so many wonderful humanitarian deeds, Francis Cardinal Spellman. On my visits, I was amused to note that Joe was almost a comic-strip kind of father to Tierney Elizabeth McCarthy. He fussed over her endlessly, worried when she got the sniffles, bought enough toys to stock a nursery school, and picked her up so often that Jean had to explain to him, pointedly, that babies need sleep even more than adults. "I don't know very much about babies," he told me once, "but I'm crazy about this one."

In the spring of 1957 he felt worse and was ordered to bed. Nevertheless, he insisted on going through with a political tour in Wisconsin, even though, at this time, the doctor had forbidden him even to talk on the telephone.

One evening, Jean telephoned me in New York. "I'm terribly worried about Joe. He's traveling around the country to form committees and make speeches. Could you take over some of the Wisconsin talks in his place? He's got to rest and just doesn't . . ." and her voice broke off. "Joe, what are you doing out of bed? You know what the doctor told you . . ."

I heard Joe's voice coming closer. "Did you take a look at the doctor? He looks sicker than I do. He doesn't know what he's talking about. Anyway, I feel much better now."

His voice was clear. He sounded like his old self. He had taken the phone from her. "Thanks a lot for agreeing to make my speech," he said, adding with mock sarcasm: "What are you up to? You planning to run for the Senate from Wisconsin? I'm going to make those talks, doctor or no doctor. This rest stuff is a lot of nonsense. I rested a few days and I feel fine. They're not going to make an invalid out of me."

These were the last words the Senator was ever to say to me, and, in the summing up, perhaps they tell the whole story.

Joe McCarthy was defeated in his last years, but he was not crushed as a human being. He had descended into a depression from which he was showing signs of emerging, and the only way he could come out completely was by regaining his self-respect. He knew this. And his self-respect would return with renomination and reelection. Armed with a new mandate, he would have reopened the battle.

But Joe McCarthy did not want to live out his years as an invalid. Had he been told that he could prolong his life for ten years or more by following a strict regimen, not kicking up his heels, not working— he would have replied that that was not the kind of life he cared to live.

He made his Wisconsin tour. He looked thin and pale and had to be helped up the steps of platforms, but he went. In April, at the Milwaukee Press Club's gridiron dinner, newsmen were startled by his gaunt appearance.

On his return to Washington, McCarthy rested and gained some weight. On Easter Sunday, April 21, Mr. and Mrs. Alfred Kohlberg, old friends, paid a call at the McCarthys in the forenoon. The Senator was sitting in the spacious living room; Jean was in the kitchen. Mrs. Kohlberg does not remember the subject of their conversation, but she recalls vividly that at one point the Senator suddenly burst out: "They're murdering me, they're killing me!" He did not explain, but his cry was an obvious reference to his political enemies.

In a moment, the storm passed and the Senator was smiling and chatting amiably. At noon, he said he himself would drive the Kohlbergs to the home of Constantine Brown, where they were expected for lunch. He said he would enjoy the drive and fresh air. "I thought he looked well," Mrs. Kohlberg remembers, "except for some difficulty with his foot. He had trouble getting his shoe on."

Joe McCarthy may have looked well, but he wasn't. Exactly a week after the Kohlberg visit, he became violently ill. Jean called a doctor and at 5 P.M., the Senator was taken to the Bethesda Naval Hospital. Jean McCarthy went along and remained with him. He was placed in an oxygen tent.

It was early in May of 1957 that I heard on the phone the shocking news that signified the end of an era for me—in fact, for us all. But let me backtrack for a moment.

After I resigned from the subcommittee staff, I returned to the practice of law with Curran, Mahoney, Cohn, and Stim in New York. About the only quiet thing in my new life was the business end— cases did not come rolling my way. Many of the people who had pumped my hand enthusiastically during the hearings and told me what a bright young man I was and how wonderful it would be to have such a bright young man handle their legal work, either had no legal work to handle or had found other bright attorneys. But there was plenty of business from another source. Invitations for speaking engagements came from across the country. Lecture bureaus sought my services, offering lucrative fees. Had it all happened a generation earlier, no doubt someone in the Keith circuit would have offered to whip up a little act and send me on a vaudeville tour.

One of the few invitations I accepted was to address the Executives' Club in Chicago. I said in that talk what lay uppermost in my mind at the time, something still considered by me to be of grave importance:

> What I want to tell you here today is that we have a clear and present danger in this world concerning the Communist problem. Whittaker Chambers, when he left the Communist movement and came on our side, said that he felt in his heart that he was leaving the winning side and joining the losing side. I would be less than candid if I did not admit there is much logic to support the statement of Whittaker Chambers . . .
>
> At the same time I realize very well that the time has come to stop the petty bickering between people in this country who should be united in a common objective. I know that no human being is perfect, but I know, too, the effective work that has been done by congressional committees, the FBI, and others fighting Communism, and I know very clearly that with almost one-half of the world in Communist hands, with the Communists in possession of the A-bomb and the H-bomb, the time has come to stop investigating the investigators, and to allow the investigators to investigate our real enemies, the Communists.

Slowly, ever so slowly, some legal business came my way. I discovered that I liked virtually all fields of the law, particularly those cases which presented a challenge. I began to look into outside investments, finding that law business followed them.

I returned home from a trip on May 2. As I was getting off the plane at the New York International Airport, now Kennedy Airport, I was met by several airport security men, one of whom handed me a note. It was from George Sokolsky: "Telephone me before you talk to any newspapermen."

What could it mean? I went to the telephone and called George.

In a phone booth at the airport I heard the news.

Joe McCarthy's liver cells had been progressively destroyed until the organ could no longer carry on even a bare minimum of its vital functions. It became inflamed and he was taken to the hospital suffering from acute hepatitis.

At first, hospital spokesmen said that while his condition was considered serious, he had shown a slight improvement in the first twenty-four hours following his admission. Photographers were allowed into his hospital room and the oxygen tent was removed to allow him to be photographed. When they left, it was replaced.

Late on Monday, he became worse and from then he failed progressively. In late afternoon on Thursday, doctors knew there was no hope. Commander Gabriel J. Naughten, the hospital's Navy Catholic chaplain, was summoned, and at 5 P.M. Senator McCarthy was given the last rites of his Church.

He died on May 2, at two minutes past six, with Jean at his bedside.

At my home, newspapermen were waiting. I said some words expressing my shock, my distress, my deep sympathy for his wife and family. Soon they left and I was alone. I wept for the man.

They gave Joseph McCarthy a state funeral in the same chamber where sixty-seven senators had voted to condemn him for unsenatorial conduct less than three years before. Joe would have loved the irony.

Many of his sharpest critics were there: J. William Fulbright, Watkins, Flanders. In the front row sat Richard Nixon. President Eisenhower did not attend; he sent I. Jack Martin, the administrative aide he had once before dispatched on a different errand—to offer McCarthy a deal to stop the Army investigation.

The ceremony in the Capitol that Wednesday was moving and impressive. Not since William E. Borah's death seventeen years before had a memorial service for a member been conducted inside the Senate chamber.

The flag-draped mahogany casket bearing the body of Joseph McCarthy was borne up the steps of the Capitol by eight Marines and carried into the great room. Seventy United States senators and leaders of the House stood as the coffin was slowly brought down the aisle and placed directly below the Vice-President's rostrum. McCarthy's own Senate seat was covered with flowers.

Jean McCarthy by tradition could not see the Senate service. She came into the chamber to view the casket and the great banks of flowers, then, with the other members of the Senator's family, she retired to the private Senate foyer just outside the chamber.

At 11 A.M., the Senate's own chaplain, the Reverend Dr. Frederick Brown Harris, a Methodist, opened the ceremony and spoke of McCarthy's indomitable purpose and clearly defined objective—"to expose cunning foes who, under cowardly cover, plot the betrayal of our freedom." He said: "Now that his sun has gone down while it was yet day, those who praised and those who blamed agree that his ruling passion was to utterly destroy the subversion in high places and low which threatens the survival of our free life."

The Reverend William J. Awalt, assistant pastor of St. Matthew's Cathedral in Washington, who had married Jean and the Senator four years before, then told the assemblage that the Catholic Church had just given to Senator McCarthy the greatest honor she can bestow in the ceremonies and prayers of Christian burial. Only an hour earlier, at St. Matthew's, the Senator's parish church in the capital, the Archbishop of Washington, the Most Reverend Patrick A. O'Boyle, had offered a Solemn Pontifical Requiem Mass in the presence of one hundred priests and some two thousand persons, many of whom had come a long way to be present. Among the priests assisting in the Sanctuary was one who had been imprisoned by the Chinese Communists.

At the cathedral, the Right Reverend Monsignor John K. Cartwright, its rector, had delivered the eulogy: "Senator McCarthy filled in the last few years a role which will be more and more honored as history unfolds its record. . . . Of course everybody has become aware of the fact that Communism is the greatest enemy of our society, at least in its form of imperialism and aggression. Not everybody saw from the beginning, and many still do not see, that the threat of Communism is domestic as well as foreign, civil as well as military. But this man saw it clearly and knew that it is an evil with which there can be no compromise . . . Now he is where there is salvation for the faithful and honor for the brave."

The tribute to the Senator was one of the greatest in the memory of Washington officials. Prior to the services some thirty thousand persons visited Gawler's Funeral Parlors on Pennsylvania Avenue, not far from the White House, to pay their respects. Lines formed early and remained until late at night.

The Senator's body was placed aboard an Air Force Convair and flown to Green Bay, thirty-five miles north of Appleton. His widow, close friends, and members of a congressional delegation flew in a second plane. On the afternoon of May 7, on a hillside near Appleton, a squad of Marines and veterans fired a volley across the Fox River and Joseph R. McCarthy was buried between Timothy McCarthy, the rugged farmer, and Bridget McCarthy, who had always wanted her son to "get ahead" and to "be somebody."

Indeed, he had been somebody. He had become a national symbol for the war against Communists and their sympathizers. He had aroused the strongest of passions among his followers and his foes and these passions were not to lessen with the years. Even at the very end, as his body waited to be consigned to the earth, McCarthy aroused the extremes of devotion and bitterness.

In Appleton, schools were closed on the day of his funeral. The line of persons waiting to pay last respects at the church was four blocks long. More than seventy bags of mail containing condolences were received by Mrs. McCarthy in the first few days.

And in New York City a city councilman named Earl Brown blocked a resolution to eulogize and memorialize the late Senator. Under the rules of the council, a resolution may receive immediate attention only if nobody rises in opposition. Mr. Brown said no and the resolution was not passed.

And so an era had ended.

CHAPTER 20

THE MAN—PROS
AND CONS

T HIS WAS THE MAN McCarthy as I knew him.
He was rough-hewn, never managing to throw off his country-boy origins. He was warm and friendly. He took his job seriously but never himself. He would go to great lengths to help those he knew who were in trouble. He had more real personal courage than almost any man I ever knew.

To his enemies he was something else entirely. He was the "Prince of Nihilists," a man with a "total disregard for normal ethical standards" who got "an enormous pleasure out of kicking people" (Professor John P. Roche). He was bestial and fiendish (Tommy McIntyre, former press aide to Senator Charles Potter).

That I saw him differently is hardly surprising, because I knew him intimately and the others did not. Let me recount a few incidents recalled from my association with him over the years that may shed light on the kind of person Joe McCarthy really was. Let me also try to analyze his behavior and answer, as candidly as I can, some of the charges leveled against him, on the basis of my own knowledge of the facts.

This "ruthless" man was unable to hurt anyone's feelings by telling him he didn't want to speak to him on the telephone. Instead of instructing Mary Driscoll, his secretary, to tell an unwelcome caller he wasn't in or wouldn't be available for the call, McCarthy would fabricate a long explanation: "Tell him I just received a call from Senator Dirksen, who wants to discuss a very special matter that just came up, and after that say I have an appointment with Senator Symington in the Senate dining room, and I'll be there until two, then I've got to be on the floor and will probably stay there until four. Get that? Now repeat it to me to make sure you've got it." Even persons quite unimportant in the Washington hierarchy would receive this kind of special consideration. Often I thought it would have been easier for him to have taken the call.

McCarthy genuinely liked people. Once in New York several of us were walking up Park Avenue with him toward the Waldorf-Astoria. Passersby hailed him: "Good work, Joe," and "Keep at it, Joe." The Senator did more than smile and accept the good wishes—he stopped and got into earnest conversation with every greeter until Frank Carr had to take him firmly by the elbow and drag him away. It was also in New York that Carr became edgy one morning because the Senator, who was flying up from Washington, was late for the start of a hearing. Carr left the hearing room in the Federal Court House and went out into Foley Square to look for McCarthy. He was anxiously pacing the top of the Court House steps when finally a taxicab drew up and McCarthy stepped out. With him were a young man and a pretty girl, the three of them chatting animatedly. Carr ran down the steps to pull Joe inside. "Frank," the Senator said, "I want you to meet Bob and Ruth, wonderful young couple. I invited them to listen in at the hearings." On the way inside, Carr asked about Bob and Ruth. Who were they? Were they related to important constituents back home? "Gee, I don't know," McCarthy answered. "I just met them on the plane—they were going to lower Broadway and there was just this one cab so I gave them a ride. Awfully nice people."

McCarthy never protected himself from press critics. He should have known his enemies were scrutinizing every move and listening intently to every word, waiting for the exploitable opening. Joe talked freely to all journalists, friendly or not. During the Army-McCarthy hearings, Richard Harkness broadcast an especially lacerating criticism. Next day, Harkness approached the Senator with some trepidation. "Joe," he said, "I need a line for tonight. Have you got an angle?" McCarthy, who had heard the broadcast, willingly conferred with him while we seethed. I told Joe, "You know how far he would have gotten with me." He replied, "Oh well, it's his job. He's got a living to make and the easiest way to do it these days is to blast me."

Once a reporter for *Time* wrote an account in *Time*-style sarcasm at its worst. This man, too, came to McCarthy a few days later and asked for an interview. Joe was rushing to fly to Wisconsin and offered to take the reporter along in a private plane he was using. The Senator talked to him at length during the flight. The *Time* reporter wrote another vicious story.

Actions such as these have been misinterpreted by critics who postulate either that McCarthy was too thick-skinned to realize he was being insulted or that he couldn't understand how others felt about him. Richard Rovere, whose biographical hymn of hate about McCarthy is a classic example of frothing-at-the-mouth reportage, says "this ogrish creature" was unable to "comprehend true outrage, true indignation, true anything." Another interpretation is that he didn't care what was said about him so long as his name continued to appear before the public.

The actual explanation, in my view, could be found in McCarthy's simple friendliness. He was a hard, tough fighter, but he was not a devious man, not a plotter, not a shrewd calculator of the odds, not a manipulator. Everything he did was done openly. The question must be asked, If Joe McCarthy sought political power for himself, as many insist, would he have left himself so foolishly vulnerable? Wouldn't he have taken care to get the best possible press on every occasion?

I am not suggesting that McCarthy was unaware of his position and importance. Actually, he liked being Senator and he enjoyed importance. I cannot see that this sets him apart from fellow mortals. Someone told him a story he liked so much he repeated it many times. It is somewhat inelegant, but then, as I have indicated, McCarthy lacked Ciceronian polish. And it did make a point.

Acheson, the story goes, died and went to heaven to find St. Peter barring the gate. "You can't come in here. Go through the door at the end of the corridor." Acheson went, opened a door, and fell up to his neck into a ditch filled with excrement. In the distance, he spotted Owen Lattimore, another McCarthy target. "We're sure in trouble," Acheson called out to Lattimore. The latter replied, "This is nothing. Wait till Joe McCarthy comes through in his speedboat!"

McCarthy was never pompous; he had simple tastes and a horror of the fancy life. He was miserable in a salon and rarely went to the parties for which Washington is famous. In all the time I knew him, I can only recall two formal Washington functions he attended. He had a miserable time at each. He preferred to stay home and relax with a western story, or play gin rummy, at which he was expert. He knew little about art and music; his entertainment tastes ran to exciting movies. He hated cold weather and liked to swim and water-ski and would occasionally play golf. I don't think Joe ever ate a full-course meal in his life. In restaurants, while others in the party would begin at the top of the menu and work down, McCarthy ordered cheeseburgers and tea, occasionally roast beef or steak. He would never have made the list of best-dressed men: he paid little attention to clothes and before he was married, his ties and socks would match his suit only on a lucky day.

When he wasn't working, McCarthy could always be found at home. He was once described by a woman journalist as "homeloving, wife-loving, baby-loving," which may sound sticky but isn't far from the mark. One Christmas, a staff assistant brought four of his children to visit the McCarthys. The day before, Joe had gone out and bought toys—four dozen of them—and hidden them all over the house. Then, all through the day, he would suddenly "discover" toys and present them to the delighted children. Each kid went home at the day's end clutching a dozen packages. Overdoing it, perhaps? But that was Joe McCarthy.

Money did not concern him. He could have become wealthy by exploiting his name, but he never did. He bought no clothes beyond the basic necessities. He never owned an expensive watch, boat, or car, and altogether lived on a more modest scale than anyone I have ever known in a similar position.

While devoted to his wife, he never bought her any luxuries. I arranged for his engagement ring for Jean at wholesale. It was a very small diamond and cost about 10 percent of what he could afford. But she didn't care either. It would not have occurred to either of them that some people might measure his love by the size of the ring he bought her.

Anyone who tries to fault McCarthy on profit-seeking grounds comes up against a blank wall, yet it is surprising how many have tried it. Various biographers have accused him of trying to make big money through investments. The truth is he made little investments all the time, but he played around the way the average man would play gin rummy. He would come up with a "sensational" idea upon which he would proceed to place a small bet in the form of an investment. Then he'd forget about it. He dabbled in the stock and the commodities markets. He was in and out all the time I knew him;

it was a form of relaxation, without much common sense or judgment or even real interest.

But of course it is the public senator, not the private Joe McCarthy who is important. The fact that Joe McCarthy lived well within his means did not prevent his enemies from accusing him of trying to line his pockets out of hours. The chief harassment along these lines was led by former Senator William Benton, Democrat of Connecticut, who launched an investigation into his income-tax payments and occasional sources of outside income. This grew into a campaign that plagued McCarthy for years, even after the charges were dropped. Benton's opening gambit was a politically explosive resolution before the Senate on August 6, 1951, which called for McCarthy's impeachment and charged that the Wisconsin senator had accepted ten thousand dollars in "influence money" from the Lustron Corporation, manufacturers of prefabricated homes.

I am acquainted with the facts in this case and can say that they were disgracefully distorted. The Lustron case actually dated back to 1947, when the housing shortage was acute and returning veterans were unable to find homes for their new families. McCarthy proposed to the Joint Housing Committee that laws should be enacted making it possible for veterans to build or buy a house. He further suggested that the committee draw up a simple explanation free of legal jargon telling veterans how they could take advantage of these laws.

When the committee, while agreeing that the project was a worthy one, declined to act, McCarthy forgot he was a very junior senator and proceeded on his own. In 1948, with the help of a staff of researchers and writers, the Senator issued a pamphlet entitled *A Dollar's Worth of Housing for Every Dollar Spent.*

McCarthy told me some time later that he first approached the Henry Luce publications and offered them the book free, since *Time, Life,* and *Fortune* had published a good deal about deplorable housing conditions. The Senator said they rejected his offer on the ground that it would not sell.

Casting about for some way to finance publication of the pamphlet, McCarthy finally turned to Lustron, which agreed to distribute the booklet at ten cents a copy, paying the Senator a royalty on the understanding he keep the book up-to-date. Shortly after he sold the booklet to Lustron, McCarthy called a press conference and related the details of the transaction and the ten-thousand-dollar royalty, adding that "I have to split it with ten people who helped me."

The incident might have ended there had not Lustron gone into bankruptcy in 1950, offering McCarthy's critics an unexpected chance. The first rumbling of trouble was a statement by Clyde Foraker of Cleveland, receiver in bankruptcy for Lustron: "I'll bet he couldn't have gotten it [the ten thousand dollars] if he weren't a senator."

The Luce magazines chimed in, deploring McCarthy's "ethics" in giving the rights for his booklet to a company making prefabricated houses and accepting money for it. In 1951, Benton put in his impeachment resolution, and the lawmakers tossed it to a subcommittee of low-seniority senators headed by Guy Gillette, Democrat of Iowa.

Gillette wrote a letter to McCarthy asking him to come in and talk over Benton's charges. He got one of the swiftest replies in the history of the U.S. mail. "Frankly, Guy," McCarthy wrote, "I have not and do not intend to even read much less answer Benton's smear attack." But Benton's cries of indignation grew so loud that McCarthy was forced to answer. In 1952, the Gillette subcommittee suddenly clamped a lid on its investigations and its findings. Then one of its members informed the press that "I've had enough. I'm resigning from this smear committee as of this moment." He added that the subcommittee had conducted the investigation "to smear McCarthy and whitewash Benton."

Benton and his friends hoped to prove through the Lustron case that McCarthy had accepted money from a business firm in return for using his influence to get it contracts. But the argument had a flaw. The Republicans were out of power and had lost control of Congress. Add the fact that McCarthy was detested by the Truman Administration, and where is the influence? Actually, the subcommittee never uncovered evidence that McCarthy had tried to obtain favors for Lustron.

It is of course entirely customary for members of the Congress to take money on the outside from speeches, articles, pamphlets, books, and the like.

Some congressmen take salaries for heading up certain organizations. There is no law against this kind of thing, nor even any unwritten ethical code. They, for instance, can, and many do, maintain law practices as long as they do not appear in connection with Federal matters.

Need we go back to the deep-freeze scandals of President Truman's day, back to the Bernard Goldfine disclosures that swept Sherman Adams, vicuna coat and all, back to New Hampshire, to show that this is hardly a new subject?

There are public officeholders who are untouched by money scandals: the Kennedys, the Rockefellers, the Goldwaters. They don't need to worry like Senator Dodd about meeting three-hundred-dollar bills or paying debts or taxes. They need only to nudge the family trust fund. But consider the consistent violation of the spirit of Federal campaign laws by wealthy political families who plow untold amounts of money into campaigns. A fellow from the wrong side of the tracks is at a distinct disadvantage.

Opponents raking over McCarthy's career have asserted that he was not the very model of a Marine Corps captain and that he faked a part of his combat record. The charges were first made by Drew Pearson, the columnist-commentator, and persisted long after they were answered on the floor of the Senate on July 13, 1951. Senator Harry Cain, Republican of Washington, making it clear he was acting of his own volition and not at McCarthy's request, placed a long and thoroughly documented rebuttal on the record.

Senator Cain obtained permission from the U.S. Marine Corps to examine McCarthy's complete service file and make photostatic records which he inserted into the *Congressional Record*. Pearson abuptly abandoned his attacks on McCarthy's combat record after they were refuted in statements from Admiral Chester C. W. Nimitz, commander-in-chief of the Pacific Fleet, and Major General Field Harris of the Marine Corps.

Senator Cain concentrated on Pearson's main charge: that there was nothing in McCarthy's wartime Marine file, which he claimed to have seen, to indicate he had ever flown a single combat mission. Cain made it plain he doubted that the commentator had actually read the war record. How could he have missed an official citation from Admiral Nimitz himself, saluting McCarthy's record? As quoted below, it left no doubt that McCarthy had flown not one but many missions against the enemy:

The Commander in Chief, United States Pacific Fleet, takes pleasure in commending Capt. Joseph R. McCarthy, United

States Marine Corps Reserve, for service as set forth in the following citation:

"For meritorious and efficient performance of duty as an observer and rear gunner of a dive bomber attached to a Marine scout bombing squadron operating in the Solomon Islands area from September 1 to December 31, 1943. He participated in a large number of combat missions, and in addition to his regular duties, acted as aerial photographer. He obtained excellent photographs of enemy gun positions, despite intense anti-aircraft fire, thereby gaining valuable information which contributed materially to the success of subsequent strikes in the area. Although suffering from a severe leg injury, he refused to be hospitalized and continued to carry out his duties as Intelligence officer in a highly efficient manner. His courageous devotion to duty was in keeping with the highest traditions of the naval service. . . ."

This citation is signed by C. W. Nimitz, and comes from the flagship of the Commander in Chief, United States Pacific Fleet.

Senator Cain submitted a companion citation from General Harris, wartime commander of the Marine's air arm, in the form of a letter to McCarthy:

May 14, 1945:

Dear Judge McCarthy: I note with gratification your unusual accomplishments during 30 months of active duty, particularly in the combat area, and that you received a citation from Admiral Nimitz for meritorious performance of duty. Without exception, the commanding officers under whom you served spoke of the performance of your duties in the highest terms.

The Marine Corps will not forget the fine contribution you have made. It is largely through the devoted effort and sacrifice of patriotic Americans like yourself that the corps is able to maintain its unbroken tradition of defeating the enemy, wherever, whenever, and however encountered.

You have my warm appreciation of your services, and my wishes for your continued success and good luck in the years ahead.

Sincerely yours,
Field Harris,

Major General, United States Marine
Corps, Assistant Commandant (Air).

Finally, Cain concluded by quoting from a recommendation for a citation for McCarthy by his immediate superior in the field, Major E. E. Munn. This commendation not only stressed McCarthy's record as a volunteer tail-gunner, observer, and aerial photographer on combat missions, it named the air strikes he took part in, including such heavily defended areas as Kolombangara, Kara, Ballale, Kahili, Buka, and Bonis.

The cool bravery and high devotion to duty consistently displayed by Captain McCarthy are in keeping with the highest standards and traditions of the United States Marine Corps.

Such tributes are not usually accorded one who faked his combat record.

I was fully aware of McCarthy's faults, which were neither few nor minor. He was impatient, overly aggressive, overly dramatic. He acted on impulse. He tended to sensationalize the evidence he had—in order to draw attention to the rock-bottom seriousness of the situation. He would neglect to do important homework and consequently would, on occasion, make challengeable statements.

His impatience with detail sometimes caused minor explosions at executive sessions of the subcommittee. Much of a senatorial committee's work consists of tedious and often uninteresting detail, so that whenever McCarthy knew that a meeting was to be devoted to ratifications of appointments, promotions, and what he called "office manager stuff" he would deputize an assistant to act for him. Once, when he could not dodge such a session, I watched him grow more and more irritated. When two senators actually quarreled over the promotion of a girl on the staff, McCarthy banged with an ashtray—he never used a gavel—and shouted: "Look, I'm trying to get my appropriation for the year so that I can get Communists out of Government. I'm not going to sit here all afternoon listening to you two arguing over whether Mary is going up to grade eleven or not. I don't want to hear about it. Fight it out later."

Ultimately, this inattention to detail, this failure to check and recheck every point he made, enabled his enemies to divert attention from the main thrust of his attack to the details—which, in too many cases, did not bear close scrutiny.

But it must be understood that in an important sense McCarthy was a salesman. He was selling the story of America's peril. He knew that he could never hope to convince anybody by delivering a dry, general-accounting-office type of presentation. In consequence, he stepped up circumstances a notch or two.

Did the urgent need to get the story across excuse a broad-brush approach? I can understand why he did it, as I can realize that his dramatizations hurt him in many quarters. I quarreled with him frequently on this score and stressed that by using this technique he sometimes placed himself in an indefensible position. But I never disagreed with the substance of his thesis.

This controversial technique was evident in the very first speech that launched McCarthy upon the great issue of his career. He was planning a nationwide series of talks, beginning at Wheeling, on an explosive subject he hoped would arouse the country. Surely this called for careful advance preparation. The speech should have been written out beforehand and copies distributed. And surely, precise information on the number of individuals concerned was essential. But because the speech was not prepared in advance, and because he really wasn't certain exactly how many persons were Communists and how many security risks, he gave his enemies a perfect opportunity to throw up a smoke screen. Thus the so-called numbers game began.

A great controversy arose after McCarthy's Wheeling speech. McCarthy's critics claimed that whereas he said there that 205 Communists were working in the State Department, later in Reno he whittled the number down to 57. Still later he spoke of "81 cases." They demanded to know what he really meant. Didn't his confusion over the figures reveal that he didn't know what he was talking about?

Eleven days after the Wheeling talk, McCarthy was summoned to explain his charges before a quickly created special committee of the Senate Committee on Foreign Relations, headed by the venerable Maryland Democrat, Millard E. Tydings. The Tydings subcommittee, after taking 1,498 pages of testimony, issued a report calling McCarthy's charges against the State Department a "fraud and a hoax."

Buckley and Bozell, in their analysis of the Tydings episode, state that McCarthy showed himself to be "inexperienced, or, worse still, misinformed. Some of his specific charges were exaggerated; a few had no apparent foundation whatever." Let us accept the fact that McCarthy was unable to offer conclusive evidence that there were

"57 card-carrying Communists" in the State Department. Let us accept the fact that McCarthy's material was drawn from a four-year-old letter written by Secretary Byrnes. Let us accept the fact that McCarthy was forced to step nimbly in an effort to explain his figures. He insisted that at Wheeling he referred to 205 persons declared unfit for Government service who were still in the Department, that the 57 referred to Department employees who were either members of the Communist party or loyal to it, that the 81 included the 57, plus additional cases of less importance against whom the evidence was less conclusive.

But let us never forget that the substance of his charges was true. There *were* persons working in the State Department whose activities and associations indicated they had pro-Communist leanings. Could any American rest easily, knowing pro-Communists may have been helping to shape our foreign policy?

McCarthy's broad-brush technique was again illustrated by his charge that the Democratic party was guilty of "twenty years of treason." This is nonsense if taken literally. Frederick Woltman, the late Scripps-Howard journalist, pointed out that this statement pinned the label of traitor on the 26,898,281 Americans who voted the Democratic ticket in 1952.

Certainly McCarthy did not intend the statement to be accepted at face value. He meant to shock, to awaken. He singled out the New Deal era, during which Communism in Government flourished with impunity. This attack on the Democrats made McCarthy many powerful enemies and accounted for the solid Democratic vote for censure in 1954.

Let us examine McCarthy's attacks on Owen Lattimore, a Johns Hopkins professor, an authority on China's borderlands, and a leading figure in the Institute for Pacific Relations. He had been editor of I.P.R.'s publication, *Pacific Affairs*. The I.P.R. was, on the surface, a scholarly organization collecting and disseminating information about the Far East. In reality, it "was taken over by Communist design and made a vehicle for attempted control and conditioning of American thinking and American policy with regard to the Far East." This description is from a 1952 report of the Senate Internal Security Committee.

Lattimore had considerable influence over our Far Eastern policies. On President Roosevelt's recommendation Chiang Kai-shek appointed him his personal adviser during 1940. He was deputy director of the OWI overseas branch in 1942 and 1943, and served on the Pauley reparations mission in Japan and Manchuria.

Two years before, McCarthy had told the Tydings Committee at a closed session that Lattimore was "definitely an espionage agent . . . one of the top espionage agents . . . the key man in a Russian espionage ring." The remark was leaked to Drew Pearson, who published it, and an uproar resulted.

When challenged, McCarthy said on the Senate floor: "I fear that I may have perhaps placed too much stress on the question of whether or not he had been an espionage agent . . ." But he had said, as part of the charge against Lattimore, "I am willing to stand or fall on this one."

A unanimous Senate Internal Security Subcommittee of Democrats and Republicans, including Senator Arthur Watkins, found after hearings that Lattimore "was, from some time beginning in the 1930's, a conscious, articulate instrument of the Soviet conspiracy."

It was never proved that Lattimore was a Soviet espionage agent. Subsequently, an indictment charging perjury was brought against Lattimore, but the Government dropped the case after two key counts were dismissed on technical grounds.

It was in a 72,000-word speech on June 14, 1951, in the Senate (read into the record but not actually given) that Senator McCarthy reviewed the weaknesses he found in the career of General George C. Marshall. The Senator, without any doubt, severely damaged his own image with many Americans when he called Marshall "a man so steeped in falsehood who has recourse to the lie whenever it suits his convenience" and went so far as to suggest that Marshall was some kind of traitor to his country. This was dynamite in the context of Marshall's reputation as a beloved old soldier.

A calmer, more conservative presentation might have gotten across the valid and important point that despite his highly respected military career, Marshall's role in China directly after World War II was disastrous to the interests of the United States—which were to prevent a Communist take-over in that enormous country. Marshall's political naïveté let him fall victim to the then-prevalent line that the Chinese Communists were not a menace, but were merely agrarian reformers interested only in fighting local corruption. History has shown how we were taken in, and Marshall bears a heavy responsibility. But the violent characterization with which Joe emphasized the Marshall role in this disaster dwarfed the issue into comparative insignificance—and battle lines were drawn instead on Marshall's reputation.

Looking back with whatever objectivity I can muster, I believe that even after all the excesses and mistakes are counted up, Senator McCarthy used the best methods available to him to fight a battle that needed to be fought. The methods were far from perfect, but they were not nearly as imperfect as uninformed critics suggest. The use of Executive sessions to protect witnesses from publicity until they had an opportunity to explain adverse evidence; the respect of the constitutional privilege; the right given each witness to have counsel beside him at all times—these compare favorably not only with methods of other investigating committees but with methods of certain prosecutors. The "methods" attack on McCarthy suffers from a credibility gap because of the double standard of many critics, particularly the press, radio, and television. To them, anything McCarthy did was wrong, but the excesses and outrageous methods of those not investigating subversion are often overlooked or excused.

He may have been wrong in details, but he was right in essentials. Certainly few can deny that the Government of the United States had in it enough Communist sympathizers and pro-Soviet advisers to twist and pervert American foreign policy for close to two decades.

He was a man of a peculiar time: the Cold War. His particular "package" would not have been deliverable in the depressed but exhilarating thirties. But he came forward at the time of Communist aggression in Korea and the triumph of Mao's revolution. The job he felt he had to do could hardly have been done by a gentle, tolerant spirit who could see all around a problem.

What is indisputable is that he was a courageous man who fought a monumental evil. He did so against opposition as determined as was his own attack—an opposition that spent far more time, money, and print seeking to expose *him* than Communism.

Since his day, Cuba has fallen to the Communists. The free world was rocked in 1967 by the Harold Philby revelation of Communist infiltration in high Government security posts. Nuclear explosions echo over China and the Soviet Union. American men are defending the borders of South Vietnam against Communist aggressors. North Korea has laid down the gauntlet to us.

Has not history already begun his vindication?

APPENDIX

The complete text of the rules of procedure follows: 1. For all purposes of these hearings, Senator McCarthy will not participate in any of the deliberations of the subcommittee; in any of its votes; or in the writing of the report; and he will nominate some other Republican member of the Committee on Government Operations to replace him on the subcommittee during these hearings for such purposes. It is the understanding and the rule of this subcommittee that during these hearings Senator McCarthy or his counsel and counsel for Messrs. Stevens and Adams (or Messrs. Stevens and Adams themselves) or other principals involved in the controversy, shall have the same right to cross-examine as the members of the subcommittee. These same rights shall also prevail for the new Republican member of the subcommittee to be nominated by Senator McCarthy and confirmed by the Committee on Government Operations, and for Messrs. Cohn and Carr, or other principals, or any counsel selected by them.

2. During the course of these hearings, it is the rule of this subcommittee that counsel for the subcommittee will first complete his questioning of all witnesses without interruption or limitation as to time, then the chairman will proceed with questions for a maximum of ten minutes without interruption, then alternating from Democratic to Republican sides of the table and from senior members down the line, each senator shall proceed with questions without interruption for a maximum of ten minutes. At the conclusion of these questions, Senator McCarthy and Mr. Welch, or those associated with them, shall proceed with questions for a maximum of ten minutes to each side, after which, starting with counsel for the

subcommittee, the same procedure will be repeated until all those having questions to ask shall have concluded their interrogatories.

3. All examinations in the case shall proceed without interruption except for objections as to materiality and relevancy.

4. If in the course of the proceedings any motion is presented or any objection is raised by anyone competent to make an objection, and it is submitted to the committee for its determination and there is a tie vote as to whether the motion will be adopted or the objection sustained, such motion or objection will not prevail.

RULE ON PROXY VOTE

5. There shall be no votes by proxy except where the absent senator files with the chairman of the committee a wire or letter stating his position upon the specific issue before the committee and in which he asks that his vote be recorded and directing the chairman to record it accordingly.

6. Any matter or issue that may be presented during the course of these hearings not specifically covered by the special rules adopted for these hearings, or covered by the standing rules of the subcommittee, shall immediately be submitted to the subcommittee for its determination by a majority vote.

7. Any member of the committee may at any time move that the committee go into executive session for the purpose of discussing any issue.

8. Where these special rules of the subcommittee do not apply, the standing rules of the subcommittee, where applicable, shall control, provided, however, that where these special rules may conflict with the regular standing rules of the subcommittee these special rules shall prevail.

9. Because of the peculiar nature of the current controversy and the unusual problems created because of the positions of the individuals involved, these procedural rules are not in any way intended to establish a precedent.

INDEX

ABOUT THE AUTHOR

Roy Cohn is a native New Yorker, the son of accomplished
parents—State Supreme Court Justice Albert Cohn and Dora
Marcus Cohn. He was educated at Fieldston Lower School and
Horace Mann School for Boys, and, at the age of sixteen, entered
Columbia University, where he earned both a college degree and
a law school degree within three and a half years.

He began to work as a clerk in the United States District
Attorney's office, and later became a prosecutor. He was a key
figure in the courtroom prosecution of the Rosenberg spy
trial and the second-string Communist party leaders. He was
then called to Washington, where he served a brief stint as
special assistant to the Attorney General late in 1953. At the age
of twenty-six he was named chief counsel for the Senate
Investigating Committee under Senator Joseph McCarthy.

Within a year he had become a hero to millions, who regarded
him as a brilliant young Communist fighter, and a devil to
millions, who placed him alongside McCarthy as a destroyer
of civil liberties.

After the Army-McCarthy hearings described in this book,
Mr. Cohn returned to New York. He has been and is a key figure in
some of the most renowned legal cases of our time. He is now
counsel to one of New York's most active law firms, Saxe,
Bacon & Bolan, and also a very active business life. He
has taught law at New York Law School, is president of the
American Jewish League Against Communism, is a Regent of
St. Francis College, and is founder of the Roy M. Cohn
Charitable Foundation. 1968 marks a year of firsts for him—
his first magazine article (*Esquire,* February 1968), his first
Letter to the Editor (*The New York Times,* March 4, 1968),
and this, his first book.